BIRDS
OF THE RAINCOAST

BIRDS
OF THE RAINCOAST
HABITS AND HABITAT

BY HARVEY THOMMASEN AND KEVIN HUTCHINGS

WITH R. WAYNE CAMPBELL AND MARK HUME

PHOTOGRAPHY BY

MICHAEL WIGLE AND R. WAYNE CAMPBELL

Harbour Publishing

CONTENTS

PREFACE:
The Poetry and Science of Birds

Humans have long been attracted to what the poets have elegantly called "the feathered races": we love to consider the forms of birds, their various colours and physical attributes, the way they look when perched and in flight, their habits, preferences and modes of subsistence. But birds speak to something else in us as well, something difficult to quantify. Is it their remarkable ability to fly that strikes a chord in us, conjuring up childhood dreams of flight, the desire to attain something beyond the mundane realities defining much of our lives? Or do we owe some of our fascination to their music, tones warbled or chirped or screamed, and the wonder of non-human communication? As we contemplate these graceful creatures, science seems to mingle with art, physics with metaphysics, reality with what we have made of it.

Those of us who consider these things may be inclined toward one of two typical responses. On the one hand, we do well to focus on the ways our symbolic uses of birds inevitably distort their reality. With Sir Francis Bacon, one of the founders of modern science, we may exclaim against anthropomorphism (the human tendency to paint nature and natural phenomena in strictly human terms), advocating instead a rigorously objective approach to naturalistic study. What do artists and poets really know of birds, anyway? As John Burroughs complains in his elegantly and sympathetically written book *Birds and Poets* (1877), although many "birds have been game for the poetic muse, in most cases the poets have had some moral or pretty conceit in mind and have not loved the bird first."

On the other hand, it is possible to speculate that over the course of evolution our humanity has been subtly shaped by avian influence. After all, we have lived with birds, hunted them, contemplated them and told stories about them throughout the long course of our own natural history. Perhaps, by considering the various roles birds have played as cultural symbols, we may learn some valuable lessons—if not always about birds, then perhaps about ourselves. These lessons, among other things, will hopefully teach us to coexist with wild creatures more effectively than we do today.

Mary Austin once claimed that birds are "symbols for free roving, skyey thought." William Blake looked into the sky and asked "How do you know but ev'ry Bird that cuts the airy way, / Is an immense world of delight, clos'd by your senses five?" Gerard Manley Hopkins saw a kestrel pass overhead and perceived in its graceful flight the presence of a godly grandeur. Insights like these may have no scientific purpose, but that doesn't mean they are not worth pondering.

When the analysis of wildlife was first systematized in 18th-century Europe, the widespread scientific desire to categorize all birds, plants and animals according to their various species helped people to acquire a clearer understanding of the natural world, but taxonomic studies often treat wild creatures as discrete objects removed from their environment. In the 19th century, the English working-class poet John Clare, like many of his Romantic contemporaries, vehemently opposed this systematic approach to nature. In a poem entitled "Shadows of Taste," for example, Clare argued that when we abstract creatures like birds from their natural environments they become "withered thoughts," mere "shadows of the things they seem." In other words, we will never gain an adequate understanding of natural creatures unless we consider them in relation to "their homes." To study birds without reference to their habitats, Clare asserts, is "to examine their carcasses in glass cases."

In contemporary environmental philosophy, a sustained concern to understand and address the ecological aspects of and environmental issues facing one's own area of residence is called "bioregionalism." Bioregionalism aims to address environmental concerns locally, maintaining that activity carried out at the grassroots level affects the health of our entire planet. This book's bioregionalism is located in coastal British Columbia, and in the roles birds play in ensuring the ecological health and equilibrium of this beautiful and sublime place. We believe that a world devoid of healthy bird populations would be a dreary one indeed—not simply because birds have as much right to exist in this world as we do, but because, like the proverbial canary in the coal mine, their loss would indicate larger environmental and social problems. We want our children and grandchildren to have the opportunity to know birds as we have known them, to take delight in their song and marvel at their flight. It is our hope that this book, by encouraging or inspiring an interest in birds, will help in some small way to generate a wider concern for the integrity of their local populations and habitats.

—Kevin Hutchings

Following pages: In winter, flocks of Canada Geese feed and rest in estuaries along the coast. (Michael Wigle)

Male Rufous Hummingbird. Most of these birds return to the raincoast in early April. (Michael Wigle)

Introduction

Previous pages:
A Great Blue Heron
feeds on a blenny
eel, an important
part of its diet all
year round.
(R. Wayne Campbell)

Opposite:
Throughout the
year, wherever fish
are spawning, Bald
Eagles gather to
feast on the nutri-
tious carcasses.
(Michael Wigle)

The Cedar Waxwing
specializes in eating
fruit during summer
and autumn.
(Michael Wigle)

High waterfalls, steep granitic slopes and rugged snow-capped mountains dominate the landscape of British Columbia's mainland coast, which lies along the Pacific Ocean between the states of Alaska and Washington. In each coastal valley an intricate network of streams, ponds, lakes and rivers connects the highest alpine meadows to deep fjords that lead to the open ocean.

A temperate rain forest cloaks the coastal valleys of this region because of the mild climate, long growing season and generous rainfall. These valleys teem with plant and animal life that is woven together in a complex web of natural associations and interdependencies.

Plants with similar growing needs cohabit, functioning as integral parts of the region's larger dynamic ecosystem. Though people commonly refer to the "west coast" in the singular, this region comprises a multitude of botanical ecosystems, including grasslands, rivers, estuarine meadows, bogs, forests, subalpine meadows and alpine tundra. Birds have been living and co-evolving within these coastal plant associations for more than a hundred million years, each one having become a highly skilled specialist in feeding, nesting and breeding in the context of its preferred habitat.

Running through this fantastical array of ecosystems are the salmon streams of the Pacific Northwest. These rich, diverse corridors of life—special because of the way sunlight reflects from the moving surface of the river and the air is filled with the mesmerizing sound of water on stone—seem to us to be the focal point, the apogee of nature in this region. Nowhere else does so much seem to happen, or does such beauty exist.

This book has been written to help birdwatchers, naturalists and environmentalists understand and appreciate the diversity of coastal bird species and specialized habitats along the South and Central Coast of the province. In particular, it will help readers identify which birds are to be found in our coastal valleys, when and where to look for them and what activities each species is engaged in over the course of a year.

The book will tell you that when red flowering currant blossoms appear in April, the *whirrrr* of the Rufous Hummingbird will soon follow. You will learn that when the tiny yellow-green leaves of the black cottonwood erupt in early spring, an array of similarly coloured wood-warblers will appear in the forest, like some kind of wild avian blossoms. While hiking a game trail through an old-growth forest in the springtime, you will learn to listen for the haunting song of the Varied Thrush, the long trill of the Winter Wren and the wheezy call of the Townsend's Warbler. At the same time, in the pristine spaces of a coastal estuary, where the air is charged with salt mist and the senses can be overwhelmed with the cacophony of feeding gulls, you will learn to listen for the sweet, distinctive notes of the Song Sparrow and Common Yellowthroat. High above, where the stream is born in the alpine meadows, in late summer you can listen for the electric thrum of ptarmigans taking flight and to the clear lilt of Gray-crowned Rosy-Finches.

Birdwatching and feeding wild birds are among the western world's fastest growing outdoor

activities. Indeed, across North America they have become favourite pastimes enjoyed by more than 60 million people. Many people flock, like the birds, to key migration points. But few realize that when you follow a salmon stream from its estuary to its headwaters, you travel along nature's most beautiful pathways, passing through an array of spectacular, bird-haunted spaces. This is a route that will take you through constantly changing landscapes, where you can see the most remarkable sights—a flight of white swans against a black forest, a submerged water ouzel wearing a cape of silver bubbles, an eagle beating its wings on the water as it fights to lift a salmon. And surrounding you, always, the sound of birds, from the spirit-like call of the raven that echoes over the forest, to the sweet chirp of a Winter Wren, calling from within its nest of moss.

We believe the streams of the Pacific Northwest and the birds that live there can take you on an incredible journey.

The Pine Siskin, a true nomad in the bird world, appears whenever cone crops are plentiful along the coast. (Michael Wigle)

1
Birds of the Estuary

Previous pages:
Migrating flocks of
Canada Geese are
commonly seen in
autumn along the
North Coast, where
they stop to feed
and rest in
estuaries.
(Michael Wigle)

Stepping into the field in the quiet stillness of a fine April morning, it is a pleasure simply to breathe. Rain has fallen almost incessantly for weeks, but now the grey dullness of the sky has lifted, giving a sense of lightness to the world. Soon the rising sun will appear. The air is cool but as the cloak of night is pulled back, it has begun to warm. It is clear that the spring landscape is emerging from winter's sleep.

As you move toward the river, last year's withered grasses crunch underfoot and the dried blades rasp against each other. Somewhere ahead the voices of eagles rise, not in fierce cries but in what sounds like content, communicative laughter. It is near Easter, and until recently the river would have been full of eulachon, small, sardine-like fish that are so rich in oil that First Nations people used to burn them like candles or render them into a clear liquid that enriched their diet. Along the edge of the water the eagles would be feeding on the carcasses of spawned-out fish that have washed downstream and settled in the shallows. The eulachon rode the currents of the open Pacific to reach

Bald Eagles nest in large, mature trees at the edges of coastal estuaries. The population of Bald Eagles is growing, but the number of valuable nest sites is not. In order to maintain their nesting territories, some eagle pairs in southern regions now reside year-round near their nests.
(R. Wayne Campbell)

coastal rivers and the eagles dropped down from the winds that lifted them near the mountain peaks. For centuries, they met here on the edge of a salmon stream. However, over the past two decades, eulachon populations have been declining in many of our coastal rivers, and no one is sure why. Increased sediment, the use of trawls and higher ocean temperatures are among the theories scientists have developed in order to explain their disappearance.

The estuary is an incredibly complex ecosystem whose diverse parts function in concert as a complexly organized symphonic whole. All things in this place weave together. As William Blake once wrote, "...every thing that lives / Lives not alone, nor for itself." Here at the mouths of rivers, fast-moving currents slow to meet the ebbing and flowing tidewaters and the milky glacial silt settles out of the water onto tidal flats. This process has repeated over thousands of years to form river deltas. Sedges and other intertidal plants thrive upon their watery terrain, stabilizing the nutrient-rich mud that provides homes for the many animals that live here. Just offshore, in the shallow coastal waters, countless microscopic plant-like phytoplankton drift in clouds, ensuring a strong foundation for the complex food chain of the region by feeding a host of animal life, both above and below the water.

If one were to compile a list of the most productive ecosystems in the world, estuaries would be at the top. Indeed, in terms of their ecological importance, estuaries surpass even tropical rain forests and coral reefs. The typical coastal estuary generates over five times the amount of organic material produced by the average corn or rice field. It is this life-giving organic productivity that makes coastal estuaries such crucial habitats for so many different wildlife species. Studies have found that over 80 percent of the wildlife activity occurring along 2,700 kilometres of coastline in the Pacific Northwest is concentrated in estuaries and wetlands, which comprise just 3 percent of the land. Estuaries are packed with life—it literally oozes up from the mud.

In the estuarine waters, phytoplankton are eaten by the animal-like zooplankton, which in turn nourish small fish that become food for larger fish, birds, mammals and reptiles. Beneath the surface one finds the benthos consumers: clams, annelid worms, round worms and many tiny and large crustaceans. Finally, but no less important, are the decomposers, those myriad creatures that break down dead plants and animals into organic nutrients, thus completing the food chain. Crucial decomposers include bacteria, fungi, amphipods and other crustaceans as well as a host of insects.

Female Mallard feeding. Although Mallards are largely vegetarian, they frequently eat insects, soft shelled clams and even small fishes. (R. Wayne Campbell)

From about mid-April to mid-May, millions of shorebirds and waterbirds begin their spring migrations from southern wintering territories to northern coastal and interior breeding areas. Once en route, many migrating flocks depend on coastal estuaries as necessary staging and feeding areas where they may pause to feed and revitalize themselves.

If you visit coastal estuaries during the springtime, expect to see diverse flocks of small sandpipers running along the muddy shores, probing for a critical meal. Sandpipers, with their dark upper parts and streaked chests, look like ungainly sparrows with Pinocchio-sized bills and outlandishly long, stilt-like legs.

The most common sandpipers are the "peep" sandpipers, named for their alarm call. Most of these birds are either Western, Least or Semipalmated sandpipers. Even for the veteran birdwatcher it is no easy task to sort out the various members of this group.

The Western Sandpiper, whose folk-names include mud snipe, sand snipe and snippet, is the most abundant migrant shorebird in British Columbia. Because most of the global population of Western Sandpipers migrates along the Pacific coast during the spring and autumn, one can, with luck, witness some spectacular bird activity. Single flocks of a hundred thousand sandpipers have been reported in the Lower Mainland and along the outer coast, but such large flocks do not visit the more secluded shores of our deep inland estuaries. The Western Sandpiper's distinctive features include dark brown legs and a relatively long bill that droops at the end. (The Semipalmated species can be distinguished by its shorter and slimmer bill.) The Western Sandpiper winters on the Pacific coast between California and Peru.

The Least Sandpiper is one of the "peep" sandpipers, so named because of the *peep* sound of its alarm call. (R. Wayne Campbell)

Above: A female Northern Pintail tips for food. (R. Wayne Campbell)

Left: An adult Black Oystercatcher probes for limpets. (R. Wayne Campbell)

Also present in the estuaries are grazing dabbling ducks, swans and geese. These waterbirds feed on the nutritious green vegetation (clover, grasses and various other water plants) that emerges from the warming soil in early spring. In the estuary you may also see diving ducks, grebes, loons, gulls, murrelets, herons and kingfishers.

At least 15 kinds of shorebirds can regularly be spotted in estuaries throughout the year. Most simply pass through, but the large Black Oystercatcher can be found any time of the year. Its all-black body, long bright red bill and pink legs are unmistakable. It probes for small snails and worms in rock crevices, seeks a variety of invertebrates in estuaries and rests on offshore rocky islets and islands.

Mallards, Northern Pintails, Green-winged Teal, American Wigeon and Northern Shovelers are all dabbling ducks. These waterfowl feed by submerging their heads underwater (dabbling) while their hind ends stick up out of the water (tipping). Although dabbling ducks are largely vegetarian, they frequently snack on mollusks, insects, small fish and even rotting salmon. Their preferred foods include such plant species as sedges, pond weeds, grasses and smart-weed.

Dabbling ducks are particularly fast and agile flyers: when taking off, they explode directly from the water's surface nearly straight up into the air. In order to suit their respective roles, the male and female adults of each species display different plumage patterns. The amorously feathered males are more brightly and distinctively coloured in order to attract discriminating females. Females, less showy than their male counterparts, are normally dressed in mottled greys and browns—an adaptation serving to camouflage them while they are nesting and caring for their young.

Campbell Fact

Many shorebirds and other intertidal foragers often feed at night when low tides offer rich food supplies that may be unavailable during high daytime tides.

In general, ducks have several distinguishing characteristics: the relative sizes of the head and bill, the upper and lower body patterns and the colour of the speculum (a colourful rectangular patch located on the wing near the body). In all species, both males and females sport a speculum.

As you walk along a widening delta, you may hear the Mallard's unmistakable call: a boisterous

The bright-coloured male Mallard is the best-known dabbling duck on the raincoast. (R. Wayne Campbell)

quack quack-quack, quack, quack-quack. Look for Mallards on the mud flats, where they feed along the edges of the receding tide. The Mallard is our most common and widespread duck—so common, in fact, that in North America its very name is almost synonymous with duck. Indeed, the seemingly generic term "wild duck" is in fact a common folk-name used specifically to identify the Mallard. An estimated two million Mallards fly up and down the Pacific coast each year, breeding all the way from northern California to central Alaska. They can be seen year-round but are more common along the Central Coast in March and April and again in October and November, when flocks migrate to and from their customary breeding areas. Male Mallards are particularly handsome, displaying forest-green head and neck plumage, distinctive yellow-green bills and neatly mottled grey sides. Attired like this they seem "dressed to kill," their appearance perhaps helping to explain the Renaissance poet Michael Drayton's anthropomorphic reference to the "lecherous mallard." Both sexes have a dark blue speculum; female bodies are generally mottled in colour, but they have characteristic orange and black bills and a white edge along their tails.

The Northern Pintail is a slender and graceful duck. The male has a chestnut-brown head, white neck and breast and a greyish body with attractive black stripes running along its upper rear parts. The speculum is metallic brown in colour with a white rear border. The female's plumage is mottled, but her slender body and grey bill set her apart from other duck species. Silhouetted against the sky, the Northern Pintail's long neck and graceful pointed tail are unique, making it easy to distinguish this bird from other western ducks. In allusion to its prominent tail, the Northern Pintail has sometimes been called a "sprig" in vernacular usage.

The Mallard is the most common of all North American ducks, but the Northern Pintail is the most globally widespread, for it is found in Eurasia and across North America. In North America, the Northern Pintail may be seen from the far reaches of northern Alaska all the way across northern Canada to Labrador and from southern California across the central United States to the state of Maine. Northern Pintails are among the earliest migrating ducks. They arrive at their interior breeding areas in early spring, as soon as open water forms along the edges of frozen lakes and sloughs; thus they may sometimes be seen well in advance of the completed spring thaw, at which time they are a welcome sight indeed.

One can expect to see Northern Pintail flocks migrating northward anytime after February, with their migratory period reaching its peak in March. Unlike most ducks, the male Northern Pintail will follow the female to her choice of breeding grounds instead of going back to his own birthplace to breed. Northern Pintails are also among the first to commence their southward migrations. Beginning in Alaska, they migrate down the British Columbian coast by early August. These northernmost breeders will be followed by Northern Pintail flocks from more southerly breeding sites right through until December, with peak migratory movement occurring from September to October. Most coastal pintails winter in estuaries along the Pacific coast from southwestern British Columbia to Mexico and the northern regions of South America.

Another dabbling duck, the American Wigeon, often mingles with Mallards and Northern Pintails. Comparable in size to a Mallard, the male (or drake) American Wigeon has a distinctive white forehead and crown, a metallic green patch extending from the eyes to the back of the head and reddish

The male Northern Pintail (above) calls to his mate (top) prior to spring migration. Pintails are among the earliest migrating ducks on the coast. (R. Wayne Campbell)

25

brown sides, breast and throat. The top of his bill is light blue and the tip of the bill is black. In flight, a white belly and large white shoulder patch become visible. The Wigeon's speculum is metallic green, matching the green patch on the sides of its head.

Like the Mallard and the Northern Pintail, the American Wigeon is primarily a spring and autumn visitor to coastal estuaries and it begins its spring migration early. This bird is often spotted in coastal estuaries as early as mid-March, though the peak period of its spring migration occurs throughout April. Each and every year, like nature's clockwork, approximately 850,000 of these dabblers migrate up and down the Pacific coast as they travel to and from their wintering ranges.

When visiting coastal estuaries, be sure to look for Cinnamon Teal. These ducks are known for their apparent social aloofness; typically they appear as single pairs standing by themselves, keeping a noticeable distance from the gregariously mixed flocks of Mallards, American Wigeons and Northern Pintails. In size the male Cinnamon Teal is a little smaller than a Mallard. Its head, breast, belly and flanks are a deep cinnamon red (hence the bird's name) and its wings are a darker brown. The drake's female companion is entirely dressed in mottled brown plumage. The Cinnamon Teal's bill is darker and proportionately longer and wider than that of a Mallard. One of the rarest ducks in North America, the Cinnamon Teal has an estimated breeding population of approximately 6,000 to 10,000 birds.

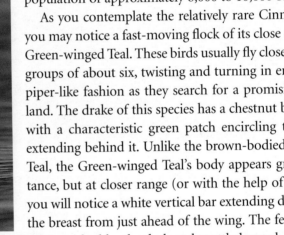

As you contemplate the relatively rare Cinnamon Teal, you may notice a fast-moving flock of its close cousins, the Green-winged Teal. These birds usually fly close together in groups of about six, twisting and turning in erratic, sandpiper-like fashion as they search for a promising place to land. The drake of this species has a chestnut brown head, with a characteristic green patch encircling the eye and extending behind it. Unlike the brown-bodied Cinnamon Teal, the Green-winged Teal's body appears grey at a distance, but at closer range (or with the help of binoculars) you will notice a white vertical bar extending down toward the breast from just ahead of the wing. The female can be distinguished by the dark and mottled grey-brown colour

Green-winged Teals, among our smallest ducks, often fly in small flocks that twist and turn in sandpiper fashion just before landing. (R. Wayne Campbell)

of her plumage. In some Canadian provinces the Green-winged Teal has been given the nickname "Butterball," because it can become rather plump in times of plentiful feeding. An estimated 280,000 Green-winged Teals migrate up and down the Pacific Flyway each year, moving to and from their preferred breeding areas.

You may also wish to scan the estuary for Northern Shovelers. These odd-looking ducks would be mistaken for Mallards if it were not for their unusually large spoon-shaped bills. The male has a Mallard-like bright green head, a white breast, a chestnut brown to rust-coloured belly and sides and a green speculum. Its wing coverts are an attractive greyish blue and the back is mottled in shades of black and white. The female, like other dabbler females, wears a relatively nondescript, light brown mottled plumage, which lends itself well to the function of camouflage. The Northern Shoveler's black bill is longer than its head, seemingly too large and heavy for such a slender little duck; therefore, some people think the bird rather comical in appearance. Equipped with prominent bristle-like plates that strain out food material, the Northern Shoveler's bill is more functional than attractive.

Animal matter makes up proportionately more of the Northern Shoveler's diet (about one-third) than that of other dabblers. The Northern Shoveler feeds in shallow water by thrusting its bill into the soft, muddy bottom and grabbing a "mouthful." The watery mud is rapidly pumped through the bird's sieve-like teeth, leaving an assortment of nutritious plant and animal matter for ingestion. Because of its prominent bill, the Shoveler has garnered such regional nicknames as "shovel-bill," "spoonbill" and even "spoony." Like the Northern Pintail, the Northern Shoveler is a widely distributed

Above: The male American Wigeon has a distinctive metallic green patch extending from the eyes to the back of the head.
(R. Wayne Campbell)

Left: The Northern Shoveler is readily identified by its distinctive bill, which is longer than its head and seemingly too large and heavy for such a slender little duck.
(R. Wayne Campbell)

The Trumpeter Swan is the largest North American waterfowl: an adult can weigh more than nine kilograms. The young are readily recognized by their plumage, which is all grey. (R. Wayne Campbell)

bird inhabiting many parts of the globe, including North America, Europe and Asia. Among the dabbling ducks, this bird is a relatively late migrant and is not seen until mid- to late April, with peak sightings occurring from mid- to late May of each year.

In the larger estuaries, look for the graceful silhouettes of elegant snow-feathered Trumpeter Swans. When you catch a glimpse of these ethereal creatures as they glide upon the water's surface, you will perhaps appreciate William Blake's poetic representation of swans as veritable emblems of the soul. Most often, Trumpeters will be found in flocks of 10 to 50 along the water's edge. Some will be sleeping, others busily preening their feathers. The bills of these swans are entirely black, contrasting sharply with their snow-white adult plumage. When startled, the flock takes to flight with a chorus of loud, sonorous bugles. Watch them as they fly away, getting smaller and smaller until all you can discern is a disappearing *V* in the distant sky.

The Trumpeter Swan is the largest of all North American waterfowl, measuring up to 1.8 metres (6 feet) in length and weighing over 9 kilograms (20 pounds). The younger swans, called cygnets, are easily recognized—but also comparatively well camouflaged—by their light grey plumage. Currently these youngsters comprise roughly 20 percent of their species' coastal population. This is a good sign for the overall Trumpeter Swan population, because when cygnets make up less than 20 percent of the total, nesting survival may be lower than optimum for the species' long-term survival. Many swans mate for life, lending some empirical support to their occasional anthropomorphic representation as models of faithfulness and fidelity (sometimes symbolized by the fanciful—if rather contorted—iconographic image of a loving pair of male and female swans "embracing" via a mutual intertwining

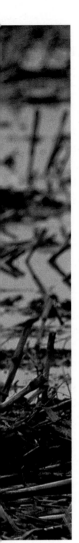

A Canada Goose feeds on shoreline animals. On land, this bird grazes on clover, grasses and other succulent plants.
(R. Wayne Campbell)

of long, slender necks). In the spring, the swans' white plumage appears strangely out of place against the backdrop of last year's dying brown and yellow vegetation. But on the breeding grounds in northern British Columbia, Yukon and Alaska, to which they will migrate during the first half of March, these birds will be effectively camouflaged against remaining patches of melting snow.

After Trumpeter Swans make their spring departure, smaller numbers of migrating Tundra Swans often appear upon the estuary, arriving from Oregon and Washington en route to their breeding areas in Alaska and the Canadian Arctic. The Tundra Swan is not easily distinguished from the Trumpeter, but it is much less common. The best way to tell these swan species apart is by listening to their calls. The Tundra Swan's call is a mellow, high-pitched *hoo-hoo, hoo-hoo-hoo*, and the Trumpeter Swan's call is much louder, lower pitched and more bugle-like.

When visiting grassy fields, you will almost certainly encounter one of Canada's avian icons, the ubiquitous Canada Goose. Among the most familiar of all wild birds (perhaps because of their common and sometimes controversial residency in so many of the nation's urban parks), these birds are especially common during the spring and autumn. Migrating flocks of Canada Geese fly high over the coastal valleys in long, undulating lines or in characteristic V-shaped formations, *ka-ronking* resonantly as they pass. Unlike many of its feathered counterparts, the Canada Goose migrates both by day and by night. Lift your eyes toward the evening sky, and if you are lucky you may see a flock of these birds silhouetted against the rising moon.

Like Trumpeter Swans, Canada Geese are monogamous creatures, remaining loyal to their chosen mates. Having distinct nesting populations, they also breed in the same place each year. Their north-

Campbell Fact

The most abundant goose in North America is the Canada Goose, whose population has been estimated at 5 million birds. It is very adaptable, and in some cities and towns it is considered a pest.

Male and female Canada geese have the same basic colours and markings. All 10 North American subspecies have the same general plumage markings, but some can be distinguished quickly by size. (R. Wayne Campbell)

ward movement, most noticeable outside the Lower Mainland, begins in late March, peaking during late April and lasting until mid-May.

At least 10 subspecies of the Canada Goose are recognized in North America. If you are lucky, you may easily identify at least three of these subspecies in British Columbian estuaries during the spring months. All three kinds share the recognizable Canadian Goose colouring: a black head and neck offset by bright, contrasting white patches on the cheeks and chin, a light pearly grey to dark chocolate brown body, and white tail coverts. (These markings are identical in males and females.) These three types of geese are distinguishable mainly by differences in size. In general, the smaller the type, the proportionately smaller the bill and head and the higher pitched the call.

The largest of these geese is the "Vancouver" Canada Goose, a dark brown bird weighing from 3.5 to 6.7 kilograms (8 to 15 pounds). This bird prefers coastal habitats, living and breeding along the Pacific coast from southeastern Alaska to Washington state. Unlike other Canada Goose species, the Vancouver Canada Goose is largely resident; that is, it tends to raise its young and winter in the same general areas. Less than five percent of the Vancouver's breeding population migrates from its various wintering areas along the coasts of Oregon, Washington and British Columbia.

A medium-sized member of the Canada Goose species, the "Dusky" Canada Goose, can also be seen passing through coastal estuaries during its annual migrations. In the warmer months of the year, this race breeds largely on the Copper River delta in Alaska, but during the winter season it is found primarily in the pleasant spaces of Oregon's Willamette Valley.

North America's smallest Canada Goose is the "Cackling" Canada Goose. The adult weighs only 1.8 kilograms (4 pounds) or less and is about the size of a Mallard. The body is dark brown and, compared to other species of Canada Goose, the neck is proportionately very short and the bill quite stubby. Its call may be described as a high-pitched, rather unmusical *unc-unc-unc.* The Cackling Goose winters in California's central valley and breeds mainly on the Yukon-Kuskokwim Delta in the far reaches of northwestern Alaska.

Another, rarer subspecies of Canada Goose is the endangered "Aleutian" Canada Goose. Formerly, thousands of these now rare birds would gather to breed on the outer Aleutian Islands, but non-indigenous Arctic foxes have wiped out most of the archipelago's breeding colonies. Today this bird frequents only a handful of breeding islands.

When springtime arrives on Canada's western shorelines, Pacific herring and eulachon return to spawn in the coastal channels. Both of these small fish species travel in schools whose populations can number well into the millions. Since they are remarkably nutritious, their annual arrival generally heralds a time of feasting for their various predators. Pacific herring average 19 to 23 centimetres (7 1/2 to 9 inches) in length, and 85 to 180 grams (3 to 6 ounces) in weight. You may identify these fish by the bluish green colour of their backs, which shades to a metallic silver on the sides and belly. Beginning around the first week of March and peaking by about the middle of the month, large schools of mature ocean-fed Pacific herring move back from the continental shelf to congregate in the coastal channels, inlets and bays. The Pacific herring come to spawn along the shores at depths ranging from the high tide mark to 11 metres (36 feet). In a typical year, 1.8 billion Pacific herring will return to spawn along the shores of the British Columbia coast. Of this number, an estimated 510 million will spawn in the Central Coast area of British Columbia and another 24 million will spawn in an area ranging from the North Bentinck Arm of the Burke Channel system all the way up to the Bella Coola River estuary. Each female Pacific herring will lay between 9,000 and 38,000 tiny, sticky eggs (each 1.2 to 1.5 millimetres (1/20 to 1/15 inch) in diameter). When these eggs are fertilized, the white milt or sperm released by millions of males literally clouds the water, producing a milky whiteness that is visible from airplanes flying high overhead. Eggs are usually deposited on kelp, but eelgrass, rock weed, boat hulls, pilings, branches or even trash make, suitable substitutes.

The eulachon is an important fish to coastal peoples as well as eagles, gulls and many other birds and mammals. (Michael Wigle)

The eulachon is a kind of slender smelt, slightly smaller on average than Pacific herring and reaching a length of 20 to 25 centimetres (8 to 10 inches) from the snout to the fork of the tail. These fish have light, silvery sides and the back and top of the head can vary in colour from dark bluish brown to black. Eulachon once returned to the coastal channels in dense schools containing hundreds of thousands of fish, their vast numbers darkening the rivers as they congregated and moved upstream to spawn. Streams with major runs of eulachon in coastal British Columbia include the Nass, Skeena, Kitimat, Kildala, Kemano, Kitlope, Kimsquit, Bella Coola, Wannock, Kingcome, Klinaklini and Fraser rivers. Some of those runs have disappeared entirely; others are experiencing a modest recovery. Fluctuations in eulachon populations have occurred in natural cycles of recovery and decline in recorded history, but scientists debate whether or not this present decline is more severe than others, and what impact it has on our complex estuary ecosystems.

A mixed flock of gulls feeds. Estuaries are critical seasonal foraging areas for gulls, as well as many other bird species. (R. Wayne Campbell)

There can be no mistaking the arrival of the Pacific herring or eulachon in a coastal estuary. As these nutritious fish make their way up the various coastal channels, they bring with them vast congregations of hungry waterbirds, as well as seals, sea lions and killer whales. At this time the sky becomes

Above: The Glaucous-winged Gull can live as long as 30 years. Over the past 50 years, the coastal population of these gulls has increased by a factor of three. (R. Wayne Campbell)

Right: The Herring Gull, an opportunistic feeder, frequently attempts to swallow food that looks far too big—including crabs. (R. Wayne Campbell)

clouded with bright flocks containing thousands of white gulls. Most of these seabirds fly back and forth above the fish's spawning beds, crying aloud in shrill, high-pitched voices, waiting for the right moment to plunge suddenly downward and pluck a scaly morsel from the tossing waves. Other gulls, having finished their meals, stand quietly on the shore, watching the ongoing feast. Observing these birds, you might notice how their grey, black and white colours enable them to blend beautifully with the granitic salt-and-pepper boulders strewn along the shoreline.

Campbell Fact
Many adult gulls have a coloured spot (often red) on the lower tip of the bottom beak. During the breeding season, chicks peck at this brightly coloured area to stimulate the parents to regurgitate food.

The gull flocks comprise a large family, whose members include Mew, Herring, Glaucous-winged, California and Bonaparte's gulls. The small black-headed gull that flies like a tern over the surface of the water is easily recognizable as the Bonaparte's Gull. Its call, a soft, rasping *keer*, is reminiscent of the sound a fishing reel makes when a salmon suddenly takes the lure and runs with the line. The other members of the family are harder to differentiate, for they all have white heads, necks, underparts and tails, and their backs and upper wing tips shade from black to a smoky grey. Because they are so similar looking, these gull species are generally identified according to differences in size, bill colour and markings, eye colour and wing-tip patterns.

The larger, goose-sized seagulls are either Herring or Glaucous-winged gulls. To tell these two types of gull apart, look at the wing tips: whereas those of the Herring Gull are black with white spots, those of the Glaucous-winged Gull are dark to light grey with white spots. Although their wing tips differ in appearance, these birds share other similarities, each species having pink feet and stout yellow bills with a noticeable reddish spot on the lower mandible. The Herring Gull, however, sports a yellowish, not solid dark brown, eye.

As for the remaining gulls, the California Gull is crow-sized; the Mew Gull has a somewhat smaller stature. Both species exhibit black wing tips with large white spots, and their legs and feet vary in colour from yellow to yellow-green. You may distinguish these two gull species by noting differences in the appearance of their yellow bills. The Mew Gull has a short bill without characteristic markings; the California Gull's bill has a red spot on the lower mandible.

Unfortunately for the avid taxonomist, even with this knowledge it can be difficult to distinguish the various gull species. When gulls are in their natural habitats and performing their daily tasks, their feet and bills are sometimes covered with mud. When they fly past, it is not easy to see whether the marking on the bill is red or black, or to determine whether it is a spot or a ring. Moreover, interbreeding commonly takes place between some species of gulls, resulting in intermediate plumage patterns and making identification all but impossible. Trying to identify immature gulls can be an even greater exercise in frustration. The darker juveniles take up to four years to acquire their adult plumage and, as if to complicate matters even further, the immature plumage pattern varies each year. In contrast to adult birds, young ones cannot be identified by leg and bill colouring. One must therefore embrace the challenge of distinguishing species on the basis of size and subtle differences in plumage patterning.

An adult and a juvenile Glaucous-winged Gull fight over a cracked cockle shell. This bird has learned to drop clams from the sky onto rocks and parking lots below in order to crack the hard outer shell and expose the meat.
(R. Wayne Campbell)

The various gull species form a fascinating and complex avian community, its members coexisting in the estuary with an assortment of other large birds as well. Perched upon beached logs, in the tangled branches of snags and in the foliage of coastal trees, there are dozens of eagles, not to mention

A Great Blue Heron waits for a fish or other aquatic animal to show itself in the shallow water. This bird is known as the patient predator. (R. Wayne Campbell)

innumerable ravens and crows. Furthermore, where the river meets the ocean there is an eye-catching assortment of fish-eating waterbirds: herons, goldeneyes, buffleheads, mergansers, loons, grebes, murrelets and kingfishers. All of these species may be easily sighted and accurately identified once you know a little bit about them.

Looking to the shallow waters you will see the unmistakable silhouette of the Great Blue Heron, who, to quote the Canadian poet Theodore Goodridge Roberts, seems to stand "Still ... as death; / Like a stone or shadow of stone"—until he lunges for his prey with a movement "sudden as death." Normally solitary birds, herons band together to form small flocks during the eulachon and Pacific herring runs. In flight, the Great Blue Heron may be recognized by its ungainly and almost primordial-looking form: large, slowly beating wings, a neck bent back contortively onto itself and long legs trailing behind. Its alarm call is a deep and croaking *frahnk, frahnk, frawnk*, which is loud enough to be heard from a substantial distance. These birds, which are sometimes miscalled cranes, are grey and white giants, standing almost 1.5 metres (5 feet) tall from head to toe.

With its long legs, extended neck and straight pointed bill, the Great Blue Heron is ideally equipped for hunting fish or the various crustaceans inhabiting shallow coastal waters. It hunts mainly by wading and stalking, often standing completely still for hours, head hunched on its shoulders, looking like an inanimate avian statue as it waits patiently to impale fish. When food comes within range, the heron's long, straight, pointed bill plunges lethally into the water, often emerging with a speared eulachon or Pacific herring that has been stranded by the receding tide. Sculpins, blennies and small flatfish are also among the heron's favourite foods.

Campbell Fact

At least 32 species of birds are known to eat snakes. Even our American Robin has been seen feeding young garter snakes to its babies.

Interestingly enough, during the winter months it will sometimes resort to grassy estuaries and fields in order to dine upon voles and the occasional late-hibernating frog or snake.

The Common and Barrow's Goldeneye, Bufflehead, Surf Scoter and scaups are collectively known as the diving ducks. Having wide-set legs and hind toe flaps, these heavy-bodied waterbirds feed on Pacific herring and eulachon eggs and on the fry that emerge from these eggs. They also catch some of the out-migrating salmon and sea-run trout smolts. Be on the lookout for flocks of crow-sized, chunky-looking Common Goldeneyes whistling past. Because of their rather portly and well-fed appearance, goldeneyes (and some of the other diving ducks) are occasionally referred to by the common name "whistler" (the unusually loud sound generated by the goldeneyes' wings in flight has also earned them the folk-name "whistle-wing duck"). The male Common Goldeneye has a glossy black head with a prominent round white patch between the eyes and the dark bill. The neck, breast, sides and underparts are white, the back is black, and large white areas are visible on the male's otherwise black wings. The females have brown heads and grey-coloured backs and sides. Looking through binoculars you may notice that the eyes of both male and female are a bright golden colour—hence the name goldeneye. Be sure to look for flocks of Common Goldeneyes swimming in the shallow water along the shores of streams. Some of the males may be practising their courtship displays: when attempting to attract the attention of females, they ostentatiously dip and bob their heads up and down and bend them over their backs with bills opened. Sometimes the goldeneyes' mating rituals become rather aggressive, as when the males make bold rushes at nearby females. The Common Goldeneye is the most common diving duck seen in coastal estuaries from around November until as late as early May. Generally, however, this bird is absent from coastal estuaries after the end of April, when it migrates inland to breed around interior lakes, ponds, sloughs and streams. The coloration

The Great Blue Heron strikes with lightning speed when food finally appears. (R. Wayne Campbell)

35

A prominent round white patch located between the bill and eyes is a distinctive feature of the male Common Goldeneye. (R. Wayne Campbell)

of the male Barrow's Goldeneye is virtually identical to that of the male Common Goldeneye, but instead of a round white patch near the base of the bill, the Barrow's Goldeneye displays a tear-shaped white mark in that spot. The Barrow's Goldeneye also has a distinctive short black spur extending down from the shoulders onto the breast. From a distance, the female Barrow's Goldeneye looks identical to its female Common Goldeneye cousin. Identification is possible only at close range: the female Barrow's Goldeneye has a steeper and shorter forehead and her bill exhibits a greater quantity of orange colouring at certain times of the year. Incidentally, the Common and Barrow's Goldeneye are among those waterbird species that prefer to nest in tree holes.

If you gaze beyond the mud and shallows toward the deeper waters of the estuary, you will likely see mixed flocks of diving goldeneyes, Buffleheads, Surf Scoters and White-winged Scoters. The Bufflehead is much smaller than both the goldeneye and the Surf Scoter. The male Bufflehead has a large, puffy black head and neck with a large white patch extending from behind the eye to the back of the head; the back is black and the sides, breast and flanks are a contrasting white. The female Bufflehead is coloured a comparatively drab greyish brown, but like the male she sports a white patch behind the eye (though her marking is much smaller and narrower than the male's). Being a little smaller than the Green-winged Teal, the Bufflehead is our most diminutive North American waterfowl. Like the Common and Barrow's Goldeneye, the Bufflehead nests in tree holes, preferring to appropriate abandoned woodpecker nests for the purpose.

Campbell Fact

The smallest of all waterfowl in North America is the female Bufflehead, which weighs only 325 grams (11.5 ounces).

The male Surf Scoter is entirely black except for a snowy white patch on the back of his neck and forehead. His thick-based, knobby bill is his most notable feature, for it is brightly painted with black, white and orange markings. The female has a less conspicuous bill and her plumage is shaded grey and brown. When taking flight, the Surf Scoter runs along the water surface for a short distance in order to achieve sufficient velocity to become fully airborne. As the bird takes off into the air, you will notice that the wings produce a high-pitched sound. Observe the bird carefully when it flies by.

If you see white patches on its flapping wings, you are most likely not looking at a Surf Scoter but at its White-winged relative. The White-winged Scoter, along with its Black Scoter cousin, is more commonly sighted farther out at sea. Remarkably, scoters can eat clam and snail shells whole, grinding them to fragments in their strong and sturdy gizzards.

When watching the various diving ducks, don't forget to look for the Greater Scaup. At a distance, a flock of these crow-sized birds looks rather like a collection of cork decoys, buoyantly bobbing up and down upon the choppy waves. The adult male has a pale blue bill (hence the popular name "bluebill"), an iridescent greenish black head, a black breast, a brownish black rump and tail, a greyish back and white flanks. The flight feathers are almost entirely white, so that when the male is airborne he looks black at both ends and white in the middle. The female is dark brown, having few distinguishing features other than a white patch encircling her face at the base of her pale blue bill.

In coastal stream estuaries you will also see three kinds of mergansers, which are fish-eating, fast-flying, diving ducks. These birds fly with their bodies outstretched, showing off white wing patches as they move through the air. In comparison to the Mallard, the merganser has a longer neck and a longer, thinner bill. The merganser's bill is equipped with prominent serrations on both sides and on the top and bottom; hence, among the bird's list of Canadian folk-names is the appellation "sawbill." In estuary environments, mergansers are particularly plentiful when the Pacific herring or eulachon arrive. In a single estuary on the Central Coast of British Columbia, for example, it is possible to tally as many as 200 Common Mergansers, 40 Red-breasted Mergansers and 20 Hooded Mergansers in an outing. Off the central east coast of Vancouver Island, mergansers may number in the thousands.

The Common Merganser is the largest of the group, reaching up to 63 centimetres (25 inches)

A male Common Merganser (right) and a pair of adult Hooded Mergansers (below). Long, toothy bills help these fish-eating ducks catch their slippery prey. (R. Wayne Campbell)

in length; the Hooded Merganser is the smallest, growing to a length of 45 centimetres (18 inches); and the Red-breasted Merganser is of middle stature, attaining a length as great as 58 centimetres (23 inches). At first glance, the male Red-breasted Merganser appears quite similar to the Common Merganser, both species having dark greenish black heads, white necks and white patches on their wings. But the Red-breasted Merganser is smaller and slimmer and, unlike the male Common Merganser, it has a crested head. The male Red-breasted Merganser may also be identified by its grey flanks and pinkish breast, which is streaked with black. (By comparison, the Common Merganser's breast and flanks are white.) The female Red-breasted Merganser is brownish in colour and looks virtually identical to the female Common Merganser.

Common and Red-breasted mergansers are usually seen in shallow waters close to the shoreline. In deeper waters, handsome Hooded Mergansers may be seen congregating in flocks. Male Hooded Mergansers have black heads with white patches behind the eyes, making them look somewhat similar to Buffleheads, but under close scrutiny these birds can be distinguished from Buffleheads because the male Hooded Mergansers' breasts are striped with black and their flanks and bellies are rust coloured. Female Hooded Mergansers are smaller in size and brownish overall.

Cast your gaze toward the deeper waters to look for the profile of the elegant diving birds known as loons. Often associated with romantic notions of solitude and loneliness, these creatures are among the favourite birds of Canadian nature poets, who often invoke them as symbols of a vast, untamed and mysterious northern wilderness. Loons have streamlined flat bodies with large, round heads. Sometimes these birds appear as dark shapes against the shimmering water, in which case their plumage patterns are not visible. However, the loon's profile is unique, making the bird easy to identify from a distance.

Common Loons are sometimes referred to as "divers" because they excel at diving and swimming rapidly underwater. (R. Wayne Campbell)

The loon's flight is unique as well: it navigates its way across the sky with its head held lower than its body. Sometimes it calls aloud, while on the wing, as if bidding farewell to its site of departure or announcing its imminent arrival elsewhere.

The loon's expertise in diving has inspired one of its common names: the "diver." The bird dives by first hopping into the air and then plunging headfirst into the water, leaving hardly a ripple on the water's surface when it submerges. After 20 seconds or so, it often resurfaces with a fish in its bill. As divers, loons are extraordinarily proficient: they can descend to depths of up to 40 metres (132 feet) and remain submerged for as long as two minutes. Such submarine prowess, combined with their impressive speed (they propel themselves via the force exerted by their large webbed feet, powerful legs and capable wings), enables them to chase down and capture small marine fish with ease. Although they are adept swimmers, loons move about rather awkwardly on land, lending credence to W. L. McAtee's proposition that the name "loon" might be traced to the Scandinavian word *lom*, meaning "lame." More likely is the possibility that the bird's name refers to its call, which can sound something like *ah-loo* repeated and which resembles the haunting laugh of a "lunatic." On warm, quiet summer evenings at lakes in the Interior of British Columbia, you may sometimes hear children imitating the loon's call and being rewarded by a querulous response from the loons themselves, whose "awful laughter" (to quote Archibald Lampman) rises to "pierce the lonely night." One rarely

An adult Common Loon incubates eggs. Important raincoast wintering areas for this bird include the Strait of Georgia, the Fraser River delta region and the Juan de Fuca Strait. (Michael I. Preston)

hears the loon's cry without experiencing awe and delight.

Four kinds of loons inhabit our coastal estuaries: the Common Loon, Pacific Loon, Red-throated Loon and Yellow-billed Loon. The Common Loon is the most familiar of the four. The Red-throated Loon migrates farther out along the coast, usually at moderate altitudes. The Pacific Loon, belying fanciful representations of loons as lonely and solitary creatures, is seen in large flocks, especially in the springtime in calmer waters or offshore. The rare Yellow-billed Loon, the largest species, is most likely to be seen in winter.

Loons have straight, tapered obsidian black bills. The Red-throated Loon swims with its bill tilted upward. The Pacific Loon's bill is smaller and proportionately thinner than those of the other loon species, but this subtle difference is difficult to appreciate from a distance.

Like most waterbirds, loons have two distinct plumages: one for winter and one for breeding. Males and females have identical colouring. The Common Loon's head and neck are velvet black, and the neck is marked by a striking white choker. The back is black spotted with white, and the breast and underparts are white. The Pacific Loon looks only slightly different: its head and the back of its neck are silvery grey; the sides of its neck are striped finely in black and white; its chin and throat are black. The bird's back is also black, but this colouring is offset by rows of bold white bars down the centre of the back; the breast and underparts are white. The Red-throated Loon has a more subtle look: its head and the sides of its neck are silvery grey, the back of its head and neck are finely striped in black and white, and its chin and throat are chestnut coloured. Finally, the Red-throated Loon's black back displays finer white spots than those adorning the back of the Common Loon, and its breast and underparts, like those of the Pacific Loon, are white.

If you look out to sea beyond the loons, farther out where the rougher wind-tossed waters roll toward the shoreline, you will see flocks of feeding grebes in the lee side of the swells. Specialized

Campbell Fact

Birds that spend a lot of their lives on the open ocean, or along marine shores, are able to drink seawater without any ill effects. This is because they have large salt glands nestled between their eyes that efficiently remove excess salt from the blood. The drips on a gull's beak are mostly salt.

swimmers, these aquatic birds propel themselves underwater by frog-kicking with their flattened and lobed toes. Small fish, aquatic insects and other aquatic animals such as snails make up the grebe's diet. Its pointed bill and streamlined body help it chase down its prey. The grebe's most astonishing trait is its ability to submerge itself vertically and sink beneath the water's surface with uncommon speed. Surely it is this trait that has helped earn grebes the folk-name "hell-diver" in some regions of Canada. Indeed, referring to the English grebe's uncanny diving abilities, the English Renaissance poet Michael Drayton once remarked that the bird submerges and resurfaces so often "that it is hard to prove, / Whether under water most it liveth, or above"—a remark that may be aptly applied to British Columbian grebes as well.

The most common members of the grebe species present near shore are the Red-necked Grebes, which may be identified by several characteristics: the forehead, crown, back and wings are dark brown, the cheeks and throat are white and the front and sides of the neck and upper breast are a rusty red.

In comparison to their Red-necked cousin, the Horned Grebe is smaller and the Western Grebe larger. Of the three kinds, the Western Grebe is the most serpentine, sporting a long, slender neck and piercing red eyes (devilish-looking eyes that have perhaps put the "hell" in the folk-name "hell-diver"). In summer, the Horned Grebe's head is black, but a golden yellow bar starting at the bill and running along the side of the face gives it some visual variety. The neck, upper breast and flanks are a rufous-brown colour; the upper half of the body is a dark greyish black and the lower half is a shimmery white.

The Western Grebe is less colourful than the Horned Grebe, being a two-toned black-and-white bird. Whereas the top of the Western's head and the back of its neck are black, the back and wings are coal grey and the rest of the body is white.

Scanning the tidal waters through binoculars, you may also see Marbled Murrelets. In contrast to the grebes, these timid-looking birds have almost no necks. Dressed as they are in modest summer

An adult Red-necked Grebe, in fresh breeding plumage, awaits spring migration in May. Male and female grebes of each species have the same colouring. (R. Wayne Campbell)

browns and whites, they are also rather more conservatively attired. Although the sharp *keer, keer, keer* of their cry is easy to recognize, it may be difficult to hear, for its sound is likely to be drowned out by the raucous calls of other more vociferous waterbirds.

Murrelets are members of the alcid family, a family of diving seabirds that feeds mainly on small fish. These birds move with ease through the air and water, but on land they are awkward and slow. Most alcids come ashore only during breeding season. On coastal islands other alcids, including the Pigeon Guillemot (nesting in rock crevices and burrows), the Common Murre (preferring rocky cliffs) and the Rhinoceros Auklet (which excavates dirt burrows) breed in large numbers.

The total breeding population of Marbled Murrelets in British Columbia is approximately 8,500 birds. Until recently, the nesting sites of these birds remained a mystery. Eggshells found at the base of old-growth conifer trees and abandoned nests found in the upper branches of logged trees provided researchers with some clues. None of the nests they found was actually in use at the time of their discovery, so there was no proof that the nests belonged to murrelets. Nevertheless, scientists found small, flightless murrelet young swimming in local coastal waters each year, evidence that these birds must indeed be breeding somewhere nearby. The mystery was finally solved when Marbled Murrelet nests were discovered in old-growth conifer forests along the California coast. The previous lack of nesting information could thus be attributed to the unexpected and obscure location of the nests. Unlike its ground-nesting cousin, the Ancient Murrelet, the Marbled Murrelet nests on thick pads of mosses found only on large branches of the tallest conifers. Here the female lays a single precious egg. Presumably the well-camouflaged nests give the young a greater chance of survival against predation, thereby ensuring the longevity of the species.

During the eulachon and smelt run, birdwatchers have a fine opportunity to encounter a variety of non-avian marine wildlife as well. Harbour Seals may often be seen close to shore. Poking their sleek,

The Western Grebe is the largest of five species of grebes found in British Columbia. In winter, rafts of thousands of Western Grebes can be found in protected bays and inlets along the coast. (R. Wayne Campbell)

whiskered noses above the water, they gaze at you for a moment before quietly sinking out of sight. As one looks into a seal's dark, sentient eyes, one can appreciate why some cultures regard the seal as a physical incarnation of a human soul.

Along with the occasional killer whale, Pacific White-sided Dolphins may be sighted off the estuary any time after mid-March. These playfully gregarious dolphins are commonly seen during the spring months, travelling the coastal channels in groups of up to 200. Like most members of the dolphin family, the Pacific White-sided Dolphin loves to show off, performing various tricks and acrobatics for almost anyone willing to watch and enjoy the show.

With the exception of the Harbour Seal, the above-mentioned marine mammals stay in the estuary only briefly. By the second or third week of April, the sea lions, dolphins and killer whales—and, indeed, most of the birds of the estuary—will have departed, leaving some of the more sensitive and romantic wildlife watchers to nurse a wistful sense of seasonal nostalgia.

Campbell Fact

The nest of a common North American species discovered most recently was that of the Marbled Murrelet. The nest was found in 1974 in California, sitting on a mossy branch of a Douglas-fir tree 39 metres (130 feet) from the ground. Since then, many more nests have been located along the Pacific coast.

Well fed and well rested, the birds continue their migratory journeys until they reach their summer breeding grounds. For the most part, their migrations take place at an astonishing rate. For example, a pair of Barrow's Goldeneyes was spotted near Vancouver on April 12, 1984, at 7:15 a.m.; before noon the next day, the same pair was sighted at its breeding territory 320 kilometres (192 miles) distant.

The Great Blue Heron migrates to small breeding colonies situated in various locations along the coast. Built in mature deciduous, coniferous or mixed forests, usually near tidal mud flats, on islands or in isolated mainland fjords, heronries can range in size from one to nearly 200 nests and occupy up to 2 hectares (5 acres) of forest. Remarkably, a single tree in one of these sites can contain up to 39 nests. Such sites and populations only occur on the South Coast.

When courting, the male makes a show of presenting sticks and nesting materials to a potential mate, in the course of which ritual he bows, spreads his wings and stamps his feet, all the while hissing and croaking to impress the object of his amorous desire. When mating is completed, each female

Marbled Murrelets in winter plumage. These diving seabirds nest in mossy depressions in the limbs of tall old-growth conifers. (Tim Zurowski)

The Great Blue Heron nests in colonies, often near estuaries and bays where the food supply is abundant. (R. Wayne Campbell)

lays three to five eggs in a thin, saucer-like nest; subsequently both heron parents incubate and care for the young. The incubation period lasts between 25 and 29 days, with the young generally hatching by June. The fledging period averages about 60 days; then the birds disperse and fly back to their wintering grounds.

As the spring migration period proceeds, flocks of crows also leave the estuary to form loose associations of nesting pairs. Among the gulls, the Glaucous-winged kind move out to nest on small, rocky islets off the Pacific coast. The other gulls fly north and east, nesting in similar habitats across British Columbia and as far north as the Arctic Circle. The Bonaparte's Gull and some Mew Gulls are unusual, preferring to nest in the branches of such coniferous trees as spruce, Douglas-fir and western hemlock.

As for the other waterbirds, some of the Common Mergansers, Green-winged Teals, Canada Geese and Mallards will stay to nest in wetland habitats along the coastal valleys, but most move away for the summer, nesting in the Interior of British Columbia and on the coast as far north as Alaska and the Yukon River Delta. Goldeneyes, scoters, Buffleheads, mergansers, loons and grebes will also move away to breed, some flying north to Alaska and the Yukon and some heading east to the British Columbia Interior. Until the autumn migration commences and the birds fly south once more, their calls and songs will echo along other shores.

Canada Geese nest almost anywhere, including in depressions in the tops of rotting stumps. Their nests have also been found on beaver lodges and apartment planters, and in the abandoned nests of Ospreys and Bald Eagles.
(R. Wayne Campbell)

2
River Birds

Upstream from estuaries the fresh, salty smell of the sea air gives way to more earthy odours rising from the soil, mosses and thick forest foliage. The crashing of waves is soon replaced by the soothing sound of meandering water or the louder rush of falling rapids. The expansive ocean view, with its far horizons and distant rising cloud banks, gives way to more sheltered prospects—the teeming nooks, crannies and glades of the streamside forest.

A day walking along the banks of a stream can teach one a lot about the nature of birds, the many ways they feed and how each species is perfectly adapted to its particular niche. Plan to visit a coastal river between late March and early April. At this time of year, the water is usually clear and cold and sweet to the taste. The birds you find here come in search of the abundant food the river supplies, including salmon fry, lampreys and a host of aquatic insect nymphs and larvae.

By far the most important and plentiful foods birds obtain at this time of year are the salmon fry, for spring is the season during which these tiny fish emerge from the gravel stream beds. Some salmon species, such as pinks, rapidly migrate out of fresh water, moving in clouds of tiny vibrating fish. Others, like coho, stay for a year, leaving as much larger smolts. The bigger a fish is when it migrates out of fresh water, the better its chances of survival, in large part because as it grows bigger, it becomes faster and is better at escaping predators. Of the billions of salmon fry that hatch from coastal riverbeds, less than half will survive the perilous journey to the estuary. In a study conducted along the Big Qualicum River on Vancouver Island, researchers discovered that Bonaparte's Gulls, loons, mergansers, dippers, scoters and gulls can consume more than 300,000 juvenile chinook in a single season of feasting.

Previous pages: The presence of the American Dipper is a sure sign that freshwater streams and rivers are healthy. (Michael Wigle)

Above: Chum salmon fry emerge in late winter and early spring. Salmon fry are an important food for many river birds. (Michael Wigle)

Many creeks, streams and rivers flow through the forests of the raincoast to reach the ocean. (Michael Wigle)

Often found fishing in rivers and streams, Common Mergansers congregate in groups of up to 100 birds. Stately and handsome, the male has a brilliant red bill, a dark greenish black head and a sharply contrasting white body with a black back. The female has a rusty brown head with a spiked crest, a white chin and breast, and greyish upper parts that are well separated by colour. With their streamlined bodies and crisply coloured feathers, these birds exude an air of elegance.

To obtain a fast but nutritious meal, Common Mergansers visit tidal areas to snap up fry that have been trapped in shallow tide pools. Proficient divers, mergansers can chase down and catch fish that are as long as 25 centimetres (10 inches). Occasionally they take larger fish. The merganser's bill is long, narrow and lined along the edges with backward-pointing serrations that help the bird grasp its slippery prey. When large numbers of fry are in the river, mergansers fish communally, forming lines and driving the panicked fish into the shallows for easy picking.

Breeding pairs of mergansers situate their nests in cavities and stumps of old-growth trees along the river, most commonly near the river mouth. It is known that Common Mergansers return each year to the same nesting area and that they sometimes use the same nest site year after year. Your best chance of discovering one of these well-hidden nests is if you are lucky enough to see an adult coming or leaving the site during nesting season.

Typically the Common Merganser nests in large coniferous or deciduous trees. Cavities such as those found in rock recesses or under tree roots will do, but where possible this bird prefers to nest in a natural crevice in a tree rather than one carved out by a large woodpecker. The female does all the

A nest of Common Merganser eggs located in a crevice. (R. Wayne Campbell)

A female Common Merganser and her brood of newly hatched chicks. (Michael Wigle)

incubating and rearing of the young. Indeed, the male generally leaves his mate before the eggs have even hatched, abdicating paternal responsibility in order to moult with other local males. At this time, however, the male and female mergansers' mutual association has merely been suspended; it will resume when the mated pair meet again in late autumn en route to their warmer winter getaway.

Among the ducks, the only males that assist with the raising of young are the Red-breasted Merganser, the Ruddy Duck and occasionally the Cinnamon Teal. The males of all other duck species leave their mates shortly before or after egg incubation begins. In contrast, the males of the various loon and grebe species display well-developed paternal instincts, making them handy "helpmates" when it comes to incubating eggs and rearing young.

After hatching, the young mergansers only spend a few days in the nest before going on their first outing. To lure her babies out of their comfortable tree house, the mother calls to them urgently from the ground below. One by one, like tiny speckled balls of fluff, they emerge from the cavernous nest, peeping wildly as they leap into the air. After a bounce on the forest floor, the ducklings follow their mother to the river, where they spend the next few weeks swimming, diving and feeding on fish eggs, fry, crustaceans and aquatic insects.

Naturalists have seen up to 23 fledging mergansers trailing a single adult female. Likely such a large brood was the product of more than one set of parents. Perhaps the motherly guardian was watching them, in an avian day-care arrangement, or she may have adopted them to rear among her own progeny.

When watching mergansers along the river, keep your eyes and ears open for Belted Kingfishers. They are garrulous birds that chatter vociferously in loud, staccato voices. Often you will see them perched upon dead snags hanging over the river. The Belted Kingfisher is a large, tuft-headed, pigeon-sized bird with a long sharp beak, cobalt head and shoulders and a white underside. The female sports a chestnut belt, in allusion to which the Belted Kingfisher gets its name.

In the spring, when salmon fry are about, keep a close watch on the Belted Kingfisher as it flies from perch to perch. Chances are you will see the bird leap off its perch, hover for a second, then plunge into the rushing current below. If the dive is successful, the kingfisher will emerge clutching a salmon fry in its bill. Then, dripping wet, it will hit its prey on a branch to stun it and settle back onto its perch to eat.

In early April, Belted Kingfishers are often observed flying in pairs. The average territory of a mated pair of kingfishers comprises about half a mile of river shoreline. Working co-operatively, the pair carves a burrow into the eroded, muddy or sandy banks of the river or into a cliffside, digging, as the poet–naturalist John Clare once remarked, "As well as ever did a mole." Typically kingfishers locate their nesting tunnels 1.5 metres (5 feet) or more above the base of the dirt bank. The entrance hole

Campbell Fact

Some birds get help in their nesting activities from siblings hatched from earlier broods. These juveniles may help build and clean the nest or even assist with incubation and brooding duties. Most, however, help feed the new nestlings. The Red-breasted Sapsucker, Bald Eagle, Northern Rough-winged Swallow, Red-tailed Hawk and Barn Swallow are some of the more than 125 species worldwide that are known as helpers. The role of helpers is being debated by ornithologists, but we know that the number of offspring produced in each nest is greater with family help.

generally measures between 9 and 13 centimetres (3 1/2 to 5 1/4 inches) across, with the burrow itself ranging in length from about 1 to almost 2.5 metres (3 to 9 feet).

Once the nest is completed, the female lays six to eight white eggs, requiring an incubation period of 23 to 24 days. Because kingfishers are born naked, blind and quite helpless, their nesting period is a rather lengthy one, taking up to 35 days to complete. The two kingfisher parents share parenting

The American Dipper is well adapted for feeding in the fast-flowing riffles of coastal streams. The bird's sooty grey coloration even matches the colour of the surrounding water and boulders. (Michael Wigle)

duties, participating equally in the incubation and care of their young.

Burrow nesting has a number of significant advantages. Most important, the burrow effectively shelters and insulates the nest, helping to maintain a constant temperature and to ensure the safety and survival of kingfisher babies. If you find a kingfisher burrow, you will be able to watch the parents fly back and forth, barely slowing each time they return to the nest to check on and care for their babies.

A common neighbour of the Belted Kingfisher is a small, sweet little bird that you will most likely see among the river stones. Because of its blue-grey or slate-coloured plumage, the American Dipper is extremely well camouflaged, blending in perfectly with the damp rocks where it alights. If you have trouble sighting the dipper, listen for its flute-like music. Rising from the river, its pleasant song will often reveal the place where the bird stands, effectively hidden from sight.

Looking awkwardly off balance, the dipper constantly dips up and down as it forages and feeds, demonstrating why it is sometimes called a "slate bobber." The American Dipper was named for this characteristic bobbing behaviour. At peak times, it may bob up to 60 times a minute. As it bobs, it searches for tiny fish and insect larvae hidden among the shadows cast by rocks scattered along the stream bed. In the fall it has been seen running along the stream bottom, picking up salmon eggs tumbling in the current. As it forages for food, the dipper hops on and off rocks and wades or swims in the water, all the while maintaining its bobbing gait. Sometimes when it plunges into the water, air bubbles cling to its feathers, giving it a silvery coat. A little smaller than a starling, the dipper is a stout and compact bird. When frightened, it will shout a buzzy warning before flying downstream to safety.

The dipper has adapted beautifully to its streamside habitat. Its well-oiled outer feathers repel water most effectively and a layer of soft inner down keeps it warm in the often frigid coastal streams. The oil gland in the American Dipper is 10 times larger than that found in any other songbird, an

adaptation for its aquatic way of life. Underwater, the bird's nostrils are closed by skin flaps and its eyes are protected by a third eyelid. With its strong legs and separated toes it can cling to the slippery rock bottoms without losing its footing. According to ornithologist W. L. McAtee, the dipper's seemingly "magical" ability to dive and manoeuvre under water has earned it the folk-name "water witch" in some Canadian communities.

In late autumn, snow and ice accumulations force dippers to seek refuge at lower elevations in the valley bottoms, where they remain until the spring thaw. In April and May they seek nesting sites. Constructed on rocky ledges or among tangled roots near streams, dipper nests take the form of bulky moss-covered domes. Following the rhythms of our changing seasons, these birds will return with their families to the lower valleys in the autumn, where they will begin their round of seasonal activities anew.

While exploring the coastal rivers, be on the lookout for two contrasting shorebirds: the ubiquitous Killdeer and the summering Spotted Sandpiper. Scruffy-looking robin-sized birds, Killdeer have huge, striking dark eyes rimmed with red. Male and female Killdeer are similarly coloured, being mottled brown on top and white underneath. The bird's most distinctive markings, a black collar and parallel chest-stripe, are easily spotted from a distance. Because of the Killdeer's vociferousness, some French-Canadian communities have given it the apt nickname *braillard*, meaning "bawler." Its loud call is often the first thing that draws your attention, with the sharp sound rising above the crash of rapids.

Although present year-round in the Lower Mainland, Killdeer come to our coastal rivers in early spring in order to rest and refresh themselves during the vernal migration. Subsequently, most migrate to rangelands, fields and ponds in the Interior, where they breed. When the autumn returns, this bird's migratory destinations will extend from nearby southern coastal British Columbia to the distant reaches of Mexico or even Peru.

The Killdeer is easily recognized by its black collar and breast band, and its striking red-rimmed dark eyes.
(R. Wayne Campbell)

The Spotted Sandpiper is most commonly sighted in summer, nesting along fresh-water streams, ponds and lakes. (Michael Wigle)

The Spotted Sandpiper is a common shorebird somewhat resembling a plover. Surveying the landscape, it teeters and bobs along the river's gravel shoreline. Its underside is white with black spots; its back is olive-brown and similarly spotted. Its bill, coloured orange but sporting a black tip, makes it look as if it had dipped into a bottle of India ink. When a Spotted Sandpiper becomes aware of your presence it utters a shrill *peet-weet!* and flies away. (Indeed, because of its distinctive cry it is sometimes known by the sonic names "peet-weet" or "pewit.") Unlike most sandpipers, which have deep wing beats, the Spotted Sandpiper's wing beats tend to be stiff and shallow, almost flutter-like in motion.

Spotted Sandpipers regularly breed in river valleys and around lakes along the west coast all the way to Alaska. Both parents feed and tend their precocial nestlings until the young birds are ready to fend for themselves, usually in July. At this time, adults and siblings gather in small flocks. With the return of cool weather in late August, they will leave the Pacific coast and migrate to wintering grounds in northern Chile. Adult females are the first to embark upon the autumn migration, followed by the adult males and then by the young ones.

By mid-April, look for the sprightly swallows and swifts, which may be seen feeding on black-flies, midges and other aquatic insects that rise up above the river's surface after hatching. As the season progresses, these birds also dine upon flies, flying ants and beetles, and small wasps and bees. Understandably, people living in buggier regions tend to develop a fondness for these voracious insect-eaters.

The swallow is easily recognized by its seemingly haphazard flying style, in which a rapid flurry of wing beats is followed by a brief glide. Characteristically, with each energetic flurry of wing beats, the

Each species of swallow has its own distinct nesting preferences. Tree Swallows (left) and Violet-green Swallows nest in sheltered cavities and crevices. (R. Wayne Campbell)

bird races off in an entirely different direction. But there is method to this aeronautical madness, for the swallow's frenetic airborne swerving and weaving helps to make it a deft and expert bug catcher.

Among the variety of swallows that visit our coastal valleys, one will find the Violet-green Swallow, Tree Swallow, Barn Swallow, Cliff Swallow, Bank Swallow and Northern Rough-winged Swallow. All of these birds are sparrow-sized, slender bodied, short necked and pretty, having small bills and mouths that open wide. Spending most of their time airborne on long, pointed wings, these birds have little need for feet. Thus their feet have evolved to become remarkably small, short and weak. In most swallow species, males and females are similar in appearance, but there are notable differences in plumage among the different kinds, just as there are differences in preferred nesting habitats.

Cliff Swallows plaster their bulbous mud homes under bridges and eaves, and in abandoned farm buildings and rock cliffs. For unknown reasons, nesting numbers of Cliff Swallows are decreasing along the raincoast. (Michael Wigle)

Of all the swallows, the Northern Rough-winged seem to be most fond of rivers and streams. These nondescript swallows have dusty grey-brown backs that nicely match the earthy tones of the muddy streambanks where they nest. They have grey throats and white undersides, and their tails are short and only partially notched. Look for them along riverbanks or steep dirt cliffs, where they excavate burrows in which to nest and raise their young.

Two truly aerial feeders, the Vaux's and Black swifts, come to our coastal valleys and lowlands each summer. Of the two birds, the Vaux's Swift is smaller and lighter in colour. Black Swifts have distinctive square tails and sooty grey plumage. In the air, swifts are like swallows, mimicking them in appearance and their tendency to be perpetually in flight. They may be distinguished from swallows, however, by their short rectangular tails and by their narrower wings. Flying with wings extended in a glide, the individual swift looks a bit like a strung bow, its narrow crescent wings curving backward and framing its cigar-shaped body. Instead of beating its wings simultaneously in the manner of a swallow, the swift beats its wings alternately. It is an impressive flyer, built for speed, agility and endurance on the wing. Among the fastest birds in the world, swifts can fly at speeds of over 160 km/h (100 mph)—hence their appropriate name. Amazingly, swifts do virtually everything in the air—feeding, drinking, bathing, mating and gathering nesting material—and land only to build a nest and feed and care for their young.

Although they forage over forests, marshes and lakes, both species build nests near rivers. The Vaux's Swift picks an old woodpecker cavity or a natural crack in a tall riverside snag in which to lay its four or five white eggs. The Black Swift lays a single white egg on a sheltered ledge of a steep rock cliff, often behind a waterfall.

Essential to the life of coastal rivers, and the birds and other creatures that need them, are salmon. Conjoining life and death, procreation and annihilation, the ancient spawning ritual has always defined the salmon's existence. Every year, runs of salmon gather in their home-river estuaries to begin their inland journeys. Some species, including coho and steelhead, may run far inland, braving whitewater rapids, crashing waterfalls and hungry predators in order to propagate and die upon their customary spawning grounds. Others, such as chum and pink salmon, may spawn closer to the estuary, making only a brief run upstream to reach their spawning grounds. Watching these fish thrash their way through the shallows, one can't help admiring their determination. Their imminent death (only steelhead survive spawning) isn't sad, because it in itself is an act of renewal. The rotting carcasses, which in late autumn give rivers a rich, pungent odour, supply vital nutrients to the river. If you don't mind the smell, this is an excellent time for birdwatching along the river.

Two immature Glaucous-winged Gulls feed on the spawned-out carcass of a coho salmon. (Michael Wigle)

During spawning season, look for salmon thrashing about in the shallow riffles. In the deeper waters, watch for female salmon digging out redds, as males wait nearby for their chance to deposit milt over the eggs. In the calmer waters, look for smaller dolly varden char waiting behind the spawning salmon, darting in and out every few minutes to gobble up stray eggs. At times when spawning salmon are particularly plentiful, their carcasses begin to litter every conceivable space, swirling in

stream eddies, flowing over rapids and covering gravel bars, the bottoms of deeper pools and dead-head logs lying in the riffles. You will even find dead salmon strewn upon the banks and in the forest, having been carried there by bears, otters and minks. This is the time when the various fish-eating birds come out in full force, gorging themselves like unabashed epicures of the wilderness. Prominent among these feathered banqueters are charcoal black crows and ravens and snow white gulls, for whom salmon eyes seem to be a particular delicacy—a preference that helps to explain why the salmon that have died most recently tend to be missing only their eyeballs. Birds also know instinctively that fish carry eggs, and if a salmon should die before it has spawned, gulls will quickly tear open its stomach to get at the eggs.

A Common Raven stands sentinel and calls a warning for others to heed. (Michael Wigle)

By the time the salmon are preparing to spawn, the crows and gulls will already have raised their families and will be gathering into flocks to explore the coastal streams where salmon congregate. As night approaches, watch the flocks of seagulls leave the salmon-choked streams, flying downstream to roost on the estuary, where they will spend the evening floating on the water. The crows, for their part, prefer to remain closer to the feeding sites, seeking out nearby trees for nighttime roosting. When daylight returns, everyone will head back to the side streams to resume their feasting.

Wherever there are salmon, one will almost certainly find Bald Eagles. Some of these birds will be flying overhead, slowly flapping their large wings; some will be wheeling through the air upstream and downstream, preparing to land; others will be soaring and circling high in the autumn sky. If you look in the tallest western redcedar, Sitka spruce and black cottonwood trees, you will probably encounter roosting Bald Eagles boldly returning your gaze and eyeing the river. In the largest coastal valleys, a single tree may have more than a dozen Bald Eagles perched in its branches, all showing their gorged throats filled with salmon. If you quietly approach one of these trees, you may find large eagle feathers, which occasionally fall to the ground when the birds are preening. If you are lucky, you may even discover a dozen or more such plumes, most of them dark brown in colour but a few of them variously flecked with browns and creamy whites (the former having belonged to mature birds, the latter to the youngsters).

Eagles are, of course, among the world's most popular avian icons. In literary writing, they are often invoked as symbols of

Campbell Fact

Ravens are not as sinister as poets have painted them. They are intelligent, resourceful, cunning and extremely adaptable animals. They lead complex and entertaining lives. They gather at evening roosts and communicate to others where they have found food during the day, they post sentries to warn others of impending dangers while feeding, they remember where food has been buried for months and they possess a vocal repertoire unparalleled in the bird world. That they are the most widely distributed species year-round in British Columbia attests to their success.

spirit or transcendence: thus Lord Byron's Manfred calls the eagle a "winged and cloud-cleaving minister, / Whose happy flight is highest into heaven"; and William Blake exuberantly exclaims: "when thou seest an Eagle, thou seest a portion of Genius. Lift up thy head!" Perhaps it is the eagle's transcendental symbolism, coupled with its common representation as the monarch of the skies, that has led such countries as Rome, Austria, France, Germany, Russia and the United States to adopt it as a national emblem of imperial power and glory.

In nature's realm, Bald Eagles are among the easiest birds to recognize. For one thing, they have a

distinctive, harsh, creaky *kleek-kik-ik-ik-ik-ik* call. Furthermore, the mature adult has a conspicuous white head and tail feathers offset against dark brown body plumage. In flight against the sun's light, the eagle's fanned tail feathers glow translucently. Lacking white plumage on their heads and tails, immature birds are sometimes mistaken for Golden Eagles; however, because Golden Eagles rarely visit coastal areas, one can safely assume that any mottled, dark brown eagle seen here is an immature Bald Eagle.

Bald Eagles sometimes kill living fish, ducks, seabirds and smaller mammals, but they are also expert scavengers, readily feeding upon dead fish, road-killed deer and smaller mammals, and food bits at the local garbage dump. During the tourist season it is not uncommon to hear American visitors to small coastal towns ask local shopkeepers where to go to view Bald Eagles; often, they are directed to the town dump. Some of them seem deflated by this unglamorous depiction of their national bird.

Coast-dwellers say that scavenging Bald Eagles prefer to eat salmon that have been dead and decomposing for four to six weeks—a preference that helps to explain why eagles sit above barely alive, spawned-out salmon for days, waiting vulture-like for the fish to die and the decomposition process to begin. An adult Bald Eagle's daily food requirement is estimated at 280 to 450 grams (10 to 16 ounces) (though the bird can store an additional half-kilo or so in its crop). Researchers have also found that an adult eagle can go without food for two weeks or more during periods of scarcity.

Bald Eagles mate for life and mated couples tend to nest in the same area year after year. Studies have shown that suitable nesting trees are essential for successful reproduction. On the coast, Bald

Above: The juvenile Bald Eagle can be mistaken for an adult or immature Golden Eagle because of its dark brown plumage. The Bald Eagle does not acquire its full adult plumage until it is seven years old. (R. Wayne Campbell)

Right: Two adults and one immature Bald Eagle congregate and battle each other for the slim winter pickings of a coho salmon spawner. (Michael Wigle)

Left: An adult Bald Eagle spies food and begins to dive in. It is said that eagles have a visual acuity eight times that of humans.
(Michael Wigle)

Below: During fish-spawning months, satiated Bald Eagles roost in trees, vulture fashion.
(Michael Wigle)

Eagles prefer to build their nests (also called eyries) in large coniferous and deciduous trees, particularly Sitka spruce, Douglas-fir and black cottonwood. Bald Eagle eyries are massive, conspicuous cup-shaped structures, usually built in high trunk–crotch intersections or on branches next to the tree trunk. Many of these nests are used again and again: each year, the eagle pair simply adds a new layer of sticks, branches and twigs to the old nest, refurbishing it for a new season. Because of this practice, a very old nest can measure up to 6 metres (20 feet) in depth and 3.5 metres (12 feet) across, weighing hundreds of kilograms.

The largest tree nest ever discovered for any North American bird was built by a Bald Eagle. It measured 2.9 metres (9.5 feet) across and 6.1 metres (20 feet) deep, and weighed nearly 2,772 kg (3 tons).

Each year the "new" nest is lined with sticks, marine debris or fragments of conifer boughs. When renovations are complete (usually in April, but sometimes as early as late March), the female lays one, two or three eggs requiring an incubation period of about 35 days. After hatching, Bald Eagle nestlings remain in the nest for 10 to 12 weeks, and fledging usually occurs sometime in July. A few weeks after fledging, the family unit disperses. In seasons when food is scarce, only the largest or strongest eaglet survives to leave the nest; the less hardy nestlings, unable to compete with their larger sibling for available food, die of starvation.

Although Bald Eagles prefer to use the same nest year after year, they do not tolerate harassment in their chosen nesting areas: if they are annoyed by disruptive or unwanted human presence, they simply desert their customary nests and move elsewhere. Naturalists therefore recommend that people keep their distance from eagle nesting sites.

Although its populations are showing some declines in many parts of North America, the Bald Eagle remains a common sight along the BC coast. Nevertheless, the enforcement of poaching laws and protection of Bald Eagle roosting, perching and nesting sites, as well as the preservation of healthy salmon, Pacific herring and eulachon runs, remain essential to the long-term survival of this magnificent species.

In the early winter, only a few short months after the last spawning salmon have died, all that remains to commemorate the great salmon feast are a few scattered bones, bits of flesh and indigestible stomach parts. This is an amazing testament to the efficiency of all the local scavengers. After the salmon are gone, some of the crows, Glaucous-winged Gulls and eagles will stay for the winter, but most will proceed to their winter homes in southerly harbours, estuaries, mud flats, tidal rivers, beaches, bays and garbage dumps.

Opposite: A pair of Bald Eagles perch over a river on their nest in a black cottonwood tree. (Michael Wigle)

Above: Newly hatched Bald Eagle chicks are covered with downy grey feathers. The largest known tree nest for any North American bird was built by a Bald Eagle, it weighed nearly three tons (2,772 kg). (R. Wayne Campbell)

3
Birds of
Open Fields
& Farmlands

Warming the frozen upper ground layer, the sun's strengthening rays begin to thaw and moisten the soil in March and April, awakening the worms, slugs, insects, snakes and other subterranean creatures from their long hibernating slumber. Spring signals its arrival in the rich, pleasant aroma of these revivifying soils, whose earthy fragrance mingles with the pungent odour of skunk cabbage, the sweet smell of black cottonwood nectar buds and the sharp ammonium smell of mountain ash. These signals attract the attention of migrating and resident Red-breasted Sapsuckers, Northern Flickers, Red-winged Blackbirds, Winter Wrens, American Robins, Varied Thrushes and Song Sparrows.

It is probably no coincidence that many of these birds are ground feeders. They eat earthworms, cutworms, beetles, caterpillars, grubs and other kinds of insects, as well as tender green shoots germinating from seeds in the warming soils. One need not look hard to find these early-season birds along forest edges and fields. Simply scan the open fields, lawns and plowed lands after a heavy spring rainstorm and you will see robins, blackbirds and crows hungrily feasting on creatures that have been forced to emerge from the soil in order to escape the flooding waters of spring.

Most of these early-migrating birds arrive from wintering grounds located between southwestern British Columbia and California. Birds that arrive and stay in a particular coastal valley are counted among the valley's summer visitants, and birds that simply pass through en route to other summering grounds are called migrants or transients. For summer visitants, pairing and mating will begin in the weeks following their spring arrival, after which commence the annual tasks of nest building and parenting. Early-migrating birds gain the advantage of a head start over later-arriving summer species such as warblers, vireos and swallows. Most of these latter birds arrive after the earliest migrators, because they must undertake long and arduous migratory journeys from southerly destinations as distant as Central and South America.

The last groups of early-season migrating birds follow circuitous northern migration routes taking them over coastal lowlands, then east up coastal valleys and shorelines, and later to the higher altitudes where they spend the summer months. The observant birdwatcher will notice that these birds arrive in distinct waves. Literally out of the blue, for example, hundreds of robins or juncos will suddenly appear in a valley that only the day before had been nearly bereft of avian activity. These birds will stay for a few days and then, as suddenly as they arrived, they will vanish. And yet, a week or so later, the same species will make another appearance. Why do migrations occur in such waves? The answer, from the bird's perspective, is quite logical: the first flocks passing through often consist of males intent on establishing breeding territories; the second wave of migrants, arriving a week or two later, is made up of females who will soon join their male counterparts to raise a family.

When these songbirds arrive, their territorial behaviour is stimulated by the growing number of daylight hours. The additional daylight in turn stimulates hormone production in the birds' brains, substantially increasing supplies of the male hormone testosterone. Scientists believe that this surge in blood testosterone levels causes male birds to become obsessed with singing and otherwise attracting females. Early naturalists, perhaps still enchanted by the charming anthropomorphic perspectives of

Previous pages: An American Robin perches on a branch, surrounded by a favourite late-summer food: mountain ash berries. (Michael Wigle)

Above: Open fields and farmlands, scattered along the rain-coast, are important habitats for a wide variety of animals. (Michael Wigle)

pre-Enlightenment science, sometimes represented this expanded courtship activity in the language of romantic love. Isaac Biberg, an 18th-century proto-ecologist, described mating male birds as virtual thralls of Cupid. Struck by "the stings of love," he declared, "Birds look more beautifull than ordinary and warble all day through lasciviousness."

For many people, the melodious sounds of these returning migrants are among the experiences most cherished during the first warm days of spring. The simple trill of the male Dark-eyed Junco, the cheerful *o-ka-lee-onk* bugle of the male Red-winged Blackbird, the harsh *ksh-eee* of the male Brewer's Blackbird and the familiar sweet carolling melody of the American Robin are among the natural sounds that seem to celebrate winter's end.

The American Robin is arguably one of North America's best known and most loved birds. It may be recognized by the unmarked orange colouring of its breast, undersides, flank and upper belly. The robin's bill is yellow; its chin and throat are streaked with white; its lower belly is white; its face sports a whitish eye-ring. Though male and female robins display the same basic colouring pattern, the keen observer will notice that the females tend to have somewhat paler and duller plumage. Compared to the female, the breeding male's head is darker, almost black; his bill is of a noticeably brighter yellow hue and his chest is brighter orange, shading almost to brick red. It is thought that the male robin's brightly coloured breast serves to intimidate other male birds aiming to intrude on his breeding territory.

The American Robin,
familiar through-
out North America.
(Michael Wigle)

The American Robin was named after the European Robin, a small Old World thrush with a red breast. British immigrants used the name "robin" wherever they travelled because it reminded them of the bird they knew in their homeland.

The ubiquitous robin is mainly a bird of lawns, farmlands, open fields and open forests. It is also surprisingly common in high-elevation subalpine regions. As a general rule, this bird avoids heavily forested lands, preferring to forage in open areas. Its hop-and-peck method of feeding is familiar: the bird takes a few bouncing steps across the turf, pauses, cocks its head looking for prey and then sticks its beak into the soil to pull up a worm or grab an insect.

The male robin's song consists of a loud, clear, seemingly endless medley of carols. Composed of short, rising and falling two- or three-syllable phrases, it sounds something like *cheery, cheery, cheer-up, cheerily.* According to some imaginative listeners, the singing robin often seems to exclaim *I have a theory, a theory it is going to rain!* Thus in his poem "Rain and the Robin," the Canadian poet Duncan Campbell Scott depicts our

Campbell Fact

Poets extol birds for singing "the music of heaven in this world" while scientists work diligently to understand the function of birdsong. We enjoy the emotional experience of hearing birds sing, but we need to bring together both perspectives to help protect birds and their habitats. We know birds sing for social, reproductive and individual reasons. Their songs and calls may be used to advertise for a mate, strengthen a pair bond, maintain a territory, drive away enemies, hold a flock together or serve as a release for nervous energy. The function of song in bird society and its subliminal impact on our lives are both profoundly significant. And some birds need different kinds of habitats to deliver their beautiful messages.

The male Red-winged Blackbird has distinctive jet-black plumage and a red shoulder patch. These blackbirds are among our earliest visitors in spring. The males arrive first, followed a few weeks later by flocks consisting mainly of females.
(Michael Wigle)

humble robin as a winged "prophet," a feathered seer heralding impending cloudbursts with "a song of warning."

Shortly after arriving at its summer residence, the female robin selects a mate and chooses a nesting site; then she and her partner set to work constructing a nest. The outer shell is a substantial bowl-shaped structure of small twigs, weed stems, straws and grasses. The nest is then mortared from the inside with a heavy layer of mud, forming a deep, round cup. Entering this structure, the female bird moulds it into shape by turning her body around and around. The nest's inner shell is then lined with fine grasses and sometimes animal hair, feathers and other soft materials.

Typically the robin locates its nest at a height of 1.5 to 4.5 metres (5 to 15 feet); favourite locations include forks in tree trunks or solid branches next to the trunk, the undersides of eaves and the flat surfaces of the ledges and beams on a building. In the fullness of time, the female lays three to five exquisitely painted greenish blue eggs requiring about two weeks for incubation. The male may assist with the domestic labour, but the female performs most of the incubation and brooding. As even the most casual birdwatcher knows, worms are among the robin's favourite foods. Indeed, studies have shown that the nestlings of one robin family consume an average of 68 earthworms daily. This voracious feeding keeps the worm-gathering parents extremely busy while helping the young robins to grow rapidly: only two weeks after hatching, they are ready to fly from the nest.

Turning your gaze to the foraging blackbirds, you will notice that this group includes at least three varieties: Red-winged Blackbird, Brewer's Blackbird and European Starling. The first two are true blackbirds belonging to the indigenous family Icteridae; starlings, by contrast, are recent European immigrants belonging to the Old World family Sturnidae.

The arrival of migrating Red-winged Blackbirds along upper coastal areas in early April is hard to miss. Small flocks composed mostly of male birds arrive first, exuberantly descending upon trees and flitting from branch to branch, loudly proclaiming their return. The adult male Red-winged Blackbird

The male Brewer's Blackbird has an iridescent purple-black head and body, with striking pale yellow eyes. (R. Wayne Campbell)

The Brewer's Blackbird nests in open, brushy habitats along roadsides and farmlands throughout much of British Columbia. Most nests are located on the ground or in low bushes. (R. Wayne Campbell)

is particularly conspicuous, being a robin-sized bird with dark black plumage and sharply contrasting bright red shoulder patches on the wings. Because these shoulder patches somewhat resemble formal military insignia or epaulettes, the Red-winged Blackbird has sometimes been dubbed "field officer" or "field officer bird" in common parlance. The conical bill is elongated, pointed and sharp. When the bird perches, its red shoulder patches are often concealed, with only their buffy white borders remaining visible. When agitated by an intruder, the male expresses alarm by spreading his wings and flashing his bright wing patches.

Similar displays mark the defensive territorial behaviour of various other bird species. For example, the Golden-crowned Sparrow, Golden-crowned Kinglet, Ruby-crowned Kinglet and Orange-crowned Warbler display their colourful head ruffs not only to ward off intruders, but also to attract partners during courtship.

The Red-winged Blackbird's call sounds like a scratchy *pot pour reeee* ending with a strong, trilling emphasis on the final syllable. Its other calls include a strangely metallic sounding *kink*, a high slurred *tee-rr* and a percussively emphatic *chack*. It should be noted that using human words to imitate the melodious sounds of bird calls is extremely difficult—but the calls, when identified, do come somewhat close to the sounds indicated.

The Red-winged Blackbird is present year-round in the Fraser River valley, but it is migratory at other locations along the mainland coast. When bachelor flocks of male redwings first arrive in early spring, some of the marshes north and east of deep coastal valleys are still icebound. At this time, cracks are just beginning to form in the ice covering the streams, and a few more weeks will have to pass before the still-frozen inland marshes will be ready for the birds' arrival. Since blackbirds usually remain in the coastal valleys for a week or two before moving on, it is likely that they are instinctively aware of this fact. During their short but noisy stay in coastal regions, the redwings compete keenly with robins and starlings for prey, seeking out worms, caterpillars, weevils, beetles and other agrarian insect "pests." To supplement their diets, blackbirds and starlings also consume the seeds of various wild and cultivated plants.

Flocks of female Red-winged Blackbirds arrive two to three weeks after their male counterparts. In appearance, adult females are very different from males, looking more like large sparrows than blackbirds. Their plumage, a dusky flecked brown colour above and paler underneath, is boldly streaked with dark browns and blacks.

A female Red-winged Blackbird on a cattail.
(R. Wayne Campbell)

The Brewer's Blackbird is another robin-sized, black-coloured bird that is frequently seen mixing with migrating flocks of Red-winged Blackbirds. In the spring sunshine you may easily recognize the males of this species by their black bills and legs, pale yellow eyes, shimmering iridescent purple heads and midnight blue-green bodies. The female Brewer's Blackbird resembles the male insofar as her brownish grey body is glossed with green and her head is dressed in iridescent purple tones, but her plumage is generally duller in hue. The main difference between the male and the female is that the female has dark eyes.

Another common black bird that feeds in the open fields and farmlands is the Northwestern Crow. Totally black in colour, this familiar bird casts its eyes to and fro while shuffling about upon well-developed walking feet. The Northwestern Crow is native to coastal British Columbia, but the American Crow has been introduced at various times on the South Coast and is difficult to distinguish from its kin. The American is the larger bird, having a stouter bill, proportionately larger legs and a different voice. The Northwestern's call is hoarser and more nasal than the American's, sounding a

The Northwestern Crow is native to coastal British Columbia. It is commonly seen feeding in intertidal zones and in open fields and farmlands on seeds, grains, shoots, insects, fruits and anything else that is at all edible. (R. Wayne Campbell)

bit more like *khaaa* than the classic *caw*. One should therefore bear in mind that these birds generally prefer different habitats: the ones encountered in the coastal rain forest are invariably of the Northwestern variety.

Crows typically build their nests in April and May, most often choosing to locate them between six and 15 metres (20 and 50 feet) above the ground in the branches of coniferous or deciduous trees. Occasionally, however, crows construct nests under bushes or windfalls, or on top of rocky ledges. The typical nest is a bulky mass of coarse twigs and sticks surrounding a central cup lined with soft grasses, mud, shredded bark fibres, hair and feathers. Both the male and female share in the labour of its construction. In this nest the female lays four to six eggs looking something like elliptical scoops of mint chocolate-chip ice cream. Forgoing the male's assistance at this point, the female incubates her precious eggs alone during a brooding period lasting from 17 to 20 days, but when hatching occurs—usually in late April or early May—both parents work cooperatively to feed their hungry youngsters. Baby crows can be surprisingly quiet and their parents are often highly secretive around their nests, trying to keep them hidden from predators. They are especially nervous around humans and will watch you closely when you pass anywhere near a nesting tree. If a crow dives at you, there's a good chance its nest is very close at hand.

The renowned author and 19th-century lieutenant governor of Upper Canada, Sir Francis Bond Head, once humorously remarked that the "crow is made up of a small lump of carrion and two or three handfuls of feathers," but the crow's common depiction as a carrion eater is only partially accurate. Crows are in fact omnivorous birds, eating virtually any plant or animal food they can find. Because they prefer foods rich in protein, it is not surprising that they are well-known nest robbers, often consuming the eggs and nestlings of various songbirds. Once their own young are fully grown, the families gather in hungry, raucous, roving flocks and roost together during late summer and early autumn.

Another bird common to open fields is the European Starling, which may be seen strutting stilt-legged among Red-winged Blackbirds, Brewer's Blackbirds and crows. Slightly smaller than these other birds, starlings have long, straight, pointed yellow bills, strong, stout legs and feet, and short, squarish tails. Their squarish tails and their bills, which are yellow in the summer, help to distinguish starlings from true blackbirds. Starlings may appear plain from a distance, but the careful observer knows otherwise. Like Brewer's Blackbirds, starlings display subtle but gorgeous plumage hues, which, to be fully appreciated, must be viewed from close range. The spring breeding plumage of male and female starlings is black, but this colouring in fact contains metallic purple and iridescent green highlights, and it is also marked by some light spotting on the back.

The (European) Starling, which means "little star," got its common name from the description of its seemingly star-speckled autumn plumage.

Aggressive and adaptable birds, starlings were introduced to North America in 1890 and 1891, when European-Americans released a few of them in Central Park in New York. These people are reported to have been members of a New York gentlemen's club whose whimsical aim was to fill North America with every species mentioned in the writings of their literary idol, William Shakespeare. Being successful colonizers, the starlings spread throughout North America and now number in the millions. It took more than 50 years for the descendants of the original Central Park starlings to reach British Columbia, where they arrived uninvited in the 1940s. In many of our coastal valleys, starlings have been present only since the 1960s.

As their success in North America attests, starlings have what it takes to be successful avian

Above: A European Starling pauses at its nest hole in a fruit tree before entering to feed its young. Although starlings are not native to North America, they can now be found in fields and farmlands, along shores and in other open habitats throughout coastal British Columbia. (Michael Wigle)

Left: In August and September, after the breeding season, European Starlings gather into large flocks to roost in trees at night. During the day they feed in fields, lawns and other open spaces. (R. Wayne Campbell)

colonizers. They are hardy and fearless, and to their great advantage they are comfortable living among people. Unfortunately, the starling's presence may affect some of our cavity-nesting native bird populations: starlings compete for the same foods as many indigenous species and they also have the nasty habit of usurping other birds' nests. Evidence suggests, among other things, that the upstart starling has contributed to the decline of bluebirds and woodpeckers throughout North America.

One recent spring day, a flock of starlings harassed and evicted a pair of nesting flickers from their home in a snag. Like flickers, starlings nest in holes, but they lack the drilling equipment necessary to excavate their own. Before commencing their assault, the starlings waited until the flickers had dug out an adequate cavity. Then, early in the morning, their attack began. Resisting valiantly, the male and female flickers attempted to defend their home, but against the starlings' ferocious onslaught their efforts came to naught. Indeed, one of the intruders managed to lock itself onto the back of one of the flickers, clutching and grabbing the bird's neck feathers with its beak. In this beak-to-feather combat the starling was determined to prevail, hanging on to the distressed flicker until it could resist no more. Before noon, the starling bullies had successfully evicted the flicker pair and, by the next day, all that remained of the flicker family was a scattered pile of broken eggshells at the base of the snag. Wasting no time whatsoever, a female starling had cleared out the flicker eggs to make room for her own.

When the autumn nights begin to chill, starlings migrate as far south as California, where they gather in flocks of up to a million birds. At the end of winter some return to British Columbia to share food resources with native robins, blackbirds, sparrows and juncos.

After feeding in the valley for a week or so, most migrating blackbirds and starlings depart for Interior nesting habitats. Red-winged Blackbirds generally nest around inland swamps, wet fields, meadows and marshes; Brewer's Blackbirds prefer to nest in drier, more open, brushy habitats;

The female Brown-headed Cowbird is a brownish grey, rather nondescript-looking blackbird. Cowbirds are named for their practice of feeding on the ground, on insects stirred up by grazing cattle. (R. Wayne Campbell)

European Starlings, for their part, tend to search out nooks and crannies located close to human settlements.

A few weeks after the blackbirds and starlings make their springtime appearance, look for the arrival of another kind of sparrow-sized "blackbird," the Brown-headed Cowbird. These birds are found in rural areas, sitting on the backs or scurrying about the feet of the cattle for which they are named. Somewhat gregarious creatures, they are sometimes seen mingling with flocks of starlings and other blackbirds. The male Brown-headed Cowbird's song is a bubbly *glug-glug-gleee*. The male bird's head is brown and the rest of his body is iridescent black; his tail and bill are short, stout and sparrow-like; his eyes, bill and legs are blackish brown. As in many songbird species, the female cowbird's plumage is duller than her male partner's: she is dressed in a uniform brownish grey and her head lacks the rich chocolate brown colouring characterizing the male.

Over the course of natural history, Brown-headed Cowbirds have taken advantage of changing North American ecosystems in almost unimaginable ways. The cowbird is indigenous to the continent and it has an ancient relationship to North American grazing animals. Hundreds of thousands of years ago, these birds probably followed herds of prehistoric elephants, horses, camels and giant pigs across the Great Plains. Much more recently, when the first European settlers made their way across this territory, they noticed large flocks of Brown-headed Cowbirds (which they called buffalo birds) following great waves of wandering buffalo, now called bison.

A male Brown-headed Cowbird. This species does not make a nest of its own. The female lays her eggs in the nests of other songbirds, which raise the juvenile cowbirds as their own. (Michael Wigle)

The birds profited greatly from their relationship with the migrating herds, regularly banqueting upon insects, grubs and other creatures stirred up by the massive animals' sharp hooves and feeding on undigested seeds and insect larvae found in their abundant dung. When nesting time arrived, however, cowbirds could not take time to build nests and rear their young unless they left the wandering herds that supported them. So, when it came time to lay eggs, Brown-headed Cowbirds simply used the nests of other birds, mostly those belonging to unlucky songbird species. By way of these seemingly crafty machinations, cowbirds were able to procreate without abandoning their wandering herds of bison.

When the great buffalo herds began to disappear, Brown-headed Cowbirds adapted to the situation by shifting alliances: instead of following herds of roaming bison, they accompanied cattle drives or simply hung around the cattle and horses that were grazing in the fields and feedlots. By adapting themselves to changing natural and historical circumstances, these birds have continued to thrive.

Over the years the enterprising little cowbird has managed to expand its range throughout the 48 contiguous United States as well as the southern regions of Canada. Following agricultural fields, cleared rangeland, transmission corridors and highways, cowbirds have also found their way into more remote areas of coastal British Columbia. Today there are an estimated 50 million Brown-headed Cowbirds living throughout North America.

Because of the vast expansion of its range and size of its population, the Brown-headed Cowbird has parasitized more than 200 bird species. However, less than half of these species are capable of raising the usurping cowbird chicks. Cowbird eggs laid in the nests of waterfowl, Killdeer, hawks, hummingbirds and woodpeckers do not survive; however, eggs deposited in the nests of sparrows,

Cedar Waxwings frequently nest in big, dense, shrubby hedgerows surrounding farmlands. (R. Wayne Campbell)

warblers, tanagers, vireos, finches, flycatchers and thrushes often do very well. The cowbird's favourite victims on the coast include the Song Sparrow, Chipping Sparrow, Common Yellowthroat and Black-throated Gray Warbler. Among these species, the young that survive hatching do not fare well in a shared nest, often starving while their parents work overtime to feed the larger and more quickly developing cowbird nestlings.

Campbell Fact

When incubating eggs, birds do not simply sit to keep them warm. They must frequently turn each egg so the temperature is evenly distributed to enhance even development of the chick. The American Redstart, for example, turns its eggs every eight minutes.

However, not all songbirds become passive victims of usurping cowbirds; indeed, some have developed effective strategies to deal with unwanted cowbird offspring. For example, the Gray Catbird, which nests in the Interior of British Columbia, will abandon a nest if a cowbird lays the first egg. Robins, for their part, simply eject unwanted eggs from their nests. Cedar Waxwings and Blue Jays, able to recognize eggs that look different from their own, may puncture and destroy them. Being resourceful builders, Yellow Warblers construct new nests on top of parasitized ones.

For the most part, however, insect- and seed-eating songbirds readily accept cowbird eggs as their own despite obvious differences in size and pattern and despite the fact that hatched cowbird nestlings are themselves different in size and appearance. Some songbirds are successful at raising their own offspring alongside nestling cowbird interlopers. But for most of the smaller songbird families, a young cowbird's presence in the nest spells disaster. Because the incubation period for cowbird eggs averages from 11 to 12 days, cowbird chicks often hatch a day or two ahead of their nest siblings. At

the very least, this circumstance gives the little intruders a head start on their nestmates. Being rather loud and aggressive, nestling cowbirds manage to obtain most of the food brought home by the parent birds, and sometimes they will go so far as to push their unfortunate foster siblings right out of the nest.

An average female cowbird can lay 40 eggs in a year, and under favourable conditions the species' local population can double every eight years. It is estimated that only three percent of cowbird eggs ultimately produce birds that survive into adulthood. Since there are an estimated 50 million cowbirds living in North America today, the population can thrive even when the survival rate of the young is so low.

Songbird populations, on the other hand, are vulnerable. Studies have shown that when cowbird parasitism is added to all other mortality factors, songbird numbers quickly decline. In a study conducted over five breeding seasons in eastern North America and involving more than 2,000 nests of 18 songbird species, researchers found that cowbirds parasitized 9 out of 10 woodthrush nests and 8 out of 10 nests belonging to arboreal birds like the Scarlet Tanager, Common Yellowthroat and Red-eyed Vireo. Appallingly—though perhaps not surprisingly—an estimated 60 percent of all nests monitored in this study contained cowbird eggs or young. Many songbird species were unable to produce enough fledglings to sustain their populations. In areas where cowbirds were trapped and killed, rates of cowbird nest parasitism dropped from over 90 percent to less than 30 percent.

Sparrow-like birds are another group of early-season, ground-feeding birds. The most common of these are the Dark-eyed Junco, Fox Sparrow, Song Sparrow, Spotted Towhee, Golden-crowned Sparrow, White-crowned Sparrow, Chipping Sparrow, Savannah Sparrow and Lincoln's Sparrow.

A male Dark-eyed Junco. This is a very common ground-feeding sparrow along the raincoast. (Michael Wigle)

Look for these birds in open fields and streamside openings as well as on brushy farmlands, lawns and meadows. In these habitats they compete with blackbirds, starlings, robins and thrushes to obtain insects, seeds and edible greenery. Although you will see them in open fields, sparrows generally prefer to forage noisily among dead, crispy leaves and naked salmonberry and thimbleberry canes, as well as in thickets of willow and red-osier dogwood located beneath the canopy of second-growth deciduous and coniferous trees. Birds like the Fox Sparrow and the Spotted Towhee will kick up leaves and dirt behind them as they scratch for insects, worms, grubs and other invertebrates. March and April are the best times to watch for sparrows: at this time of year the foliage that hides them in the summer months has not yet grown.

The Dark-eyed Junco is the most common ground-feeding sparrow. The race living along our coast is known as the Oregon Junco. A cute and bright-eyed little bird, the adult male has coal black colouring on the head, neck and upper breast; he also sports a rusty brown back, slate grey rump, white belly and pinkish brown sides. The junco's feet and bill are flesh-coloured and its eyes are dark. Before takeoff and during flight, it flashes its white outer tail feathers. The female is similar in appearance to the male, but she sports a dull grey hood rather than a dark black one. Although the junco is reputed to be a vegetarian, in the spring and summer months up to half of its diet actually consists of insects scooped up from the ground.

The most common coastal sparrow is the Song Sparrow, a small brown bird with a streaked breast and a short, cone-shaped bill. Its head, back, wings and tail are of a dark chocolate brown hue. In contrast, its underparts are pale white, though centred upon its breast is a prominent dark brown

A male Song Sparrow puffs out his chest in full, exuberant concert. More than 900 vocalizations have been reported for the Song Sparrow. (Michael Wigle)

(R. Wayne Campbell)

Campbell Fact
The nests of all birds must be kept dry and warm and clean of droppings to prevent fouling of the young and to keep nest parasites away. Most songbird chicks only defecate when the adult is near, usually just after feeding. The wastes are enveloped in a clean gelatinous sac that is taken away by the parent and dropped far from the nest. Some woodpeckers also use this fecal sac. Nestlings of larger birds such as hawks and eagles simply defecate over the edge of the nest; some pigeons have filthy nests.

area. Otherwise its neck and breast are heavily streaked with dark brown and it has a grey stripe above the eyes and grey on the cheeks. When you encounter this bird, you will likely see it alight on a branch, puff out its chest and begin performing the delightfully exuberant musical concert for which it is named.

Among its various field marks, the Song Sparrow's call is the most reliable. Generally beginning with three or four slowly and clearly uttered introductory notes sounding like *sweet, sweet, sweet, sweet*, then followed by four or five more rapid, higher-pitched notes, the bird's song concludes with a musical trill that drops in pitch. As a whole, the song is boldly delivered and rich in aural diversity. From the perspective of the female Song Sparrow, this musical range signifies the presence of a good prospective mate.

Of all animals, birds use song the most. Over 900 different vocalizations have been recorded for the Song Sparrow and as many as 20 different songs have been heard for a single individual.

In the Song Sparrow species, the sexes are coloured similarly, but it is the male bird that performs the singing. In flight, this bird has the curious habit of frequently pumping its long, rounded tail. The Song Sparrow is among the most familiar, versatile and widespread of our North American songbirds. At least 30 Song Sparrow subspecies have been recognized. Like most of the birds found in coastal valleys, our regional variety of Song Sparrow is characteristically darker than its Interior and eastern cousins, displaying a more heavily streaked breast.

Look for Song Sparrows wherever brush and dense thickets and brambles abound, whether these areas are in coastal estuaries or near streams, swamps, marshes and bogs. If you exercise patience, you will likely spot one of these diminutive birds close to the ground, busy plucking food from surface debris. Like most sparrows, the Song Sparrow spends most of its life on or near the ground, where it feeds, nests and finds shelter.

Margaret Nice, a pioneer in research on the life history of the Song Sparrow, determined that in a typical day in spring the bird spends nine hours singing, nine hours sleeping and six hours eating.

The Song Sparrow is one of the season's earliest breeders. Unlike some of the more gregarious coastal bird species, it is not very sociable: the male defends his few hundred metres with a display of aggressive determination seemingly at odds with his diminutive size. Because he is generally so preoccupied with singing and defending his territory, he leaves most of the nest building and child raising to his mate. Nests are usually located on or near the ground, carefully concealed under grass tussocks, shrubs or fallen branches. Because the Song Sparrow usually builds her nest before the trees burst into foliage, it makes little sense for her to locate it in a leafless tree where all sharp-eyed egg robbers may easily detect its presence. However, nests constructed later in the season are more likely to be built among the branches of a low bush or tree.

One of the Song Sparrow's feathered cousins, the Fox Sparrow, is a relatively large bird with a distinctive yellow lower mandible and a long, slightly notched tail. In this species, females and males share the same colouring. Our coastal Fox Sparrow is much darker than the sparrows residing east of the Coast Mountains. A dark brown bird, it has a light underside heavily streaked with chocolate-coloured upside-down *V*s, which come together to form a ragged central breast spot. Sometimes unseasoned birdwatchers confuse the Fox Sparrow with the smaller Song Sparrow. The Fox Sparrow's song is flute-like, consisting of a series of variable, clear and energetic notes sliding up and down in pitch. Occasionally the bird's musical phrase will end with one or two short trills or chirps.

The Spotted Towhee is a robin-sized sparrow that spends much of its time scratching the ground for insects and seeds. You are certain to appreciate the eye-catching plumage of this large, long-tailed bird. The male's head, bib, back, wings and tail are coal black; the black wings and back are dotted with white; the bird's reddish brown (or rufous) sides contrast nicely with its snow-white belly. A bright red colour lends distinction to the adult towhee's piercing eyes. The female's colour pattern resembles the male's, except she has brown shading instead of black. Like the Fox Sparrow, our coastal variety of Spotted Towhee is said to be noticeably darker than the race of towhees found east of the Coast Mountains. As a general rule, coastal birds also tend to have more white on their backs and wings. When moving in the air, the towhee usually remains close to the ground, pumping its tail and flashing a white tail patch as it flits among the branches and foliage of low bushes. Its song has been aptly described as a buzzy *teeeeee* or *chweeeeee*, making the towhee one of those rare birds that has been named sonically; that is, for the sound of its call. Some rather fanciful birdwatchers have suggested that the bird is saying *drink-your-tea*, trilling the last note.

The Fox Sparrow is larger than the similar-looking Song Sparrow, and it has a distinctive yellow lower mandible. (Michael Wigle)

The Spotted Towhee, formerly known as the Rufous-sided Towhee, is commonly seen foraging in brushy areas and thickets around the edges of fields and farmlands. (Michael Wigle)

By the end of April, some Dark-eyed Juncos and most Fox Sparrows will begin moving to the higher elevations of mountainous conifer forests to nest.

Golden- and White-crowned sparrows can sometimes be found together in mixed flocks containing hundreds of birds. In each species, male and female birds have identical markings. The adult Golden-crowned Sparrow's most striking feature is a broad yellow stripe running down the top of its head, a stripe that is bordered by an accompanying pair of broad black lateral crown stripes. The sides of the bird's face, as well as its throat, upper breast and the back of its neck, are a striking pearly grey. The other upper parts are brown with black streaking; the lower breast is a greyish brown, fading to a lighter shade on the abdomen; and two white wing bars are visible. The bird's bill and legs are a brownish colour.

In a delightful 19th-century treatise, *Birds and Poetry*, the American writer John Burroughs lavished praise upon the White-crowned Sparrow, calling it "the rarest and most beautiful of the sparrow kind" and fancying it "crowned as some hero or victor in the games." At first glance, Burroughs' favourite sparrow resembles its adult Golden-crowned cousin. But the careful observer will notice subtle distinctions: the White-crowned Sparrow's wide crown stripe is white; bordering the black lateral head stripe is a white one, accompanied by another black lateral stripe extending from the eyes to

White-crowned Sparrows commonly migrate north with Golden-crowned Sparrows, in large flocks consisting of hundreds of birds. (Michael Wigle)

the back of the head. The White-crowned Sparrow's bill and legs are paler than those of the Golden-crowned Sparrow, but the back, tail, wings and underparts have the same appearance in both birds.

In the spring, Golden- and White-crowned sparrows eat seeds, blossoms, buds, small developing leaves and insects. However, close observation often reveals that Golden-crowned Sparrows feed primarily on emerging greenery, and their White-crowned counterparts feed mainly on seeds. Sometimes you will catch mischievous Golden-crowned Sparrows shredding crocus flowers in someone's carefully tended garden or frequenting plum and cherry orchards to feed upon delicate fruit buds and flower petals. When frightened, a member of the flock will issue an alarm call, causing the entire flock to seek shelter in a patch of nearby bushes or small trees.

Some people dislike White-crowned and Golden-crowned sparrows, regarding them not as welcome springtime visitors but as troublesome pests. This aversion is perhaps understandable, for when these flocks descend upon our coastal valleys they sometimes destroy early garden plants, seed-growing operations and newly planted lawns. They can also clean out one's bird feeder in no time, frightening off chickadees, nuthatches and other resident birds in the process. Because of their aggressive behaviour at feeders, some people call White-crowned Sparrows "marauding banqueters." It is difficult to keep these birds out of your feeder, but you can minimize their domestic impact. If you wait until late May to seed your lawn or garden, for example, these birds will be forced to feed upon unwanted late-season weed seeds and seedlings, thereby helping you to tend your yard's domestic vegetation.

When crowned sparrows arrive in the springtime they are exceedingly vocal, uttering songs easy to recognize and pleasant to hear. The Golden-crowned Sparrow's song consists of a series of plaintive whistles, sounding something like *three blind mice*; the White-crowned Sparrow's song opens with two long introductory notes followed by a pair of different trills, which,

The Golden-crowned Sparrow is unpopular with some farmers because it feeds on newly sprouted grasses, vegetables, fruit tree buds and flower petals. (R. Wayne Campbell)

taken together, sound like a spirited *I say how a do ya do?* Once heard, the songs of these migrating sparrow flocks are easy to identify and distinguish.

After early May the crowned sparrows, particularly the Golden-crowned variety, are found in lowlands only rarely. The Golden-crowned Sparrow leaves the valleys to nest in the high-elevation subalpine regions of mountain slopes in Alaska and Yukon. For its part, the White-crowned Sparrow nests on the coast and as far north as the edge of the tundra regions of northern Alaska and Arctic Canada, though these birds will also nest in high alpine ranges extending from eastern British Columbia down to south-central California.

The Golden-crowned Sparrow is truly a western bird, for its preferred habitat lies mostly in British Columbia and Alaska. Other bird species belonging to this rather exclusive western North American group include the Varied Thrush, Townsend's Warbler, American Dipper, Chestnut-backed Chickadee, Northwestern Crow, Steller's Jay, Pacific-slope Flycatcher, Rufous Hummingbird, Black and Vaux's swifts, Band-tailed Pigeon and perhaps the Gray-crowned Rosy-Finch and the Violet-green Swallow.

When visiting the open fields and adjacent forest edges, look for small flocks of Chipping

Sparrows—small, slim birds somewhat resembling their Golden- and White-crowned cousins in behaviour. Chipping Sparrows have striped heads, unstreaked pearly grey breasts and cinnamon brown crowns. Below the crown you will notice a broad, bold white eyebrow, beneath which a black line passes through each eye and extends to the back of the head. The male Chipping Sparrow's back, wings and tail are a reddish brown colour variegated with numerous brown and black streaks. In appearance, adult females are duller and less boldly coloured than their male counterparts. The Chipping Sparrow is appropriately named, for its soft, trilling song consists of a rather long series of rapidly uttered monotone "chips."

Chipping Sparrows, like many other migrants, travel along the coast en route to inland nesting territories, pausing on our coastal fields and farmlands only briefly to feed on germinating seeds and grassland insects. Preferring dry, grassy plains and mixed forest edges, they tend to breed in those regions of the Interior.

Two relatively small and slender members of the sparrow clan, the Savannah and Lincoln's sparrows, also feed in grassy horse pastures, open fields or brushy areas during migratory journeys. The Savannah Sparrow is a brownish, somewhat nondescript bird. If you observe it through binoculars, you will notice dark brown streaking over its whitish breast, but unlike the Song and Fox sparrows, this bird's breast lacks a well-defined central dark spot. The Savannah Sparrow's distinctive field mark is a yellow stripe or eyebrow. It also has a pale central crown stripe bordered by darker stripes. As in most sparrows, the two sexes are similar in appearance. This bird is often seen perched on wire demarcating the edges of fields. While feeding on the ground, the Savannah Sparrow typically runs through newly emerging grass patches, stopping here and there to feed on seeds or insects. Its weak

Although the Chipping Sparrow eats mainly seeds, soft insects make up a significant part of the early diet of nestlings.
(R. Wayne Campbell)

The yellow stripe extending up from the beak and over the eyes is a distinctive feature of the Savannah Sparrow. (Donald E. Waite)

and trilling song sounds a bit like *tsip-tsip-tsip-se-e-es r-r-r.*

Some people refer to the Savannah Sparrow as a bird of the hayfield, but its customary environs extend far beyond any farming region. In fact, this bird is reputed to be one of the most widespread avian breeders, nesting from northern Alaska all the way to southern California and, indeed, across North America. Usually Savannah Sparrows are sighted during the last week of April, but migrating flocks can be seen throughout the warming days of May. Thereafter, Savannah Sparrows sighted in coastal valleys are likely to be summer visitants.

Like the Song Sparrow, the Savannah Sparrow is a ground nester. After choosing a well-concealed nesting location, the bird scratches a bowl-shaped hollow into the earth and lines it with fine grasses, mosses and soft plant stems. In the safety and comfort of this retreat, the female lays four to six eggs, usually in May or June. Ranging in colour from cloudy white to pale green or blue, these eggs are variously speckled, spotted and splashed with browns and reddish browns. The female incubates the eggs for approximately 12 days. The male may or may not contribute to the incubation process, but once the eggs are hatched he will help his mate to feed the young ones, who will be ready to leave the nest about 14 days after hatching. Occasionally a particularly amorous and energetic nesting pair will raise two broods of youngsters in a single year.

Another sparrow you will encounter in the open fields and farmlands along rivers is the Lincoln's Sparrow. This bird eats insects, seeds and sprouting grasses, searching for these delicacies among thickets and brush piles along the edges of fields. Lincoln's Sparrows resemble Song Sparrows in their overall shape and colour patterning: the dark brown back is heavily streaked in black, and the buff-white breast is streaked with dark brown. However, in comparison to the Song Sparrow, the Lincoln's Sparrow is slimmer and its tail is shorter, its buff-coloured breast has a much finer streaking pattern, and it also lacks a central breast spot. Gazing through binoculars, you will also notice that the Lincoln's Sparrow's face is noticeably grey and that its eyes are encircled by narrow white eye-rings.

If you are lucky enough to get close to a flock of Lincoln's Sparrows, listen for their sweet, gurgling song, which begins with low notes, rises abruptly and hurriedly and then falls again. A shy bird, the Lincoln's Sparrow dislikes human company, so you may find it difficult to get near one. More often than not, this small brown sparrow will greet even your quietest approach by making a furtive retreat into the underbrush.

In the springtime, migrating flocks of Lincoln's Sparrows visit our coastal valleys for a week or two, subsequently moving on to spend the summer months in northern and high-mountain thickets situated along bogs, streams and meadows. When migrating, this bird is quiet and secretive; thus, although it is relatively common, it is rarely seen.

Another important ground-feeding bird is the grouse. While walking through farmlands with mixed river-bottom woods in early spring, listen for this bird's percussive call, which sounds like a distant muffled engine starting up slowly, accelerating rapidly and then stalling abruptly: *bup ...bup ...bup ...bup—bup—bup-up r-rrrrrrr.* At first you may have difficulty locating the source of this peculiar drum-like sound, but if you proceed through the brush slowly and softly, you may encounter a

Left: The male Ruffed Grouse makes his courtship sounds by rotating his wings rapidly forward, then backward.
(Michael Kawerninski)

Below: The Ruffed Grouse frequently leaves his home in the second-growth deciduous forest to forage in open fields and farmlands.
(Michael Wigle)

greyish brown, chicken-like male perched upon a log. On each side of his neck you will see a patch of dark feathers raised into a ruff-like collar; on the crown of his head, you will notice another cluster of dark feathers rising to a ragged crest. For obvious reasons, this handsome male bird is sometimes called a "drummer," as he puffs up his chest and appears to drum his wings rapidly against it. Contrary to popular belief, the Ruffed Grouse produces his rhythmic noise by striking the air with his wings, not by striking his wings against his body. Hoping to find a mate, he "drums" to attract the attention of eligible local females. Should you slowly stand up and reveal your presence, the grouse will hop off his perch and skulk away through the undergrowth, peeping a high-pitched alarm call as he heads for the deeper woods. If you attempt to follow him, he will remain strategically silent, making it rather difficult to discern his well-camouflaged shape. But if you manage to get too close for the grouse's comfort, he will explode into flight, rapidly beating his short wings as he rises noisily into the air.

The Ruffed Grouse breeds mainly in mixed deciduous and coniferous woodlands (including mixed stands of alder, willow, trembling aspen, maple, birch and black cottonwood, as well as fir, pine and spruce). After mating occurs, the jobs of nest construction, incubation and nesting fall solely to the female bird, or hen. To build her nest, she scrapes out a shallow depression in the ground, lining it with such materials as dry leaves, mosses, grasses and sometimes soft feathers and down. The Ruffed Grouse's nest is usually located at the base of a tree or stump, beneath a fallen log or under a low canopy of bushes and shrubs. Here the female lays between 9 and 11 creamy eggs and incubates this

precious clutch for about three weeks. When the incubation period is complete, she will find her work and patience rewarded by the hatching of her downy, golden chicks. Within hours of hatching, this young brood will be running about in search of food, especially insects. They are subject to heavy predation by the Great Horned Owl and the Northern Goshawk.

One of our more surprising ground-feeding birds is the Northern Flicker. The flicker is to the woodpecker family what the robin is to the thrush family: a bird of open woodlands, forest perimeters, alpine meadow edges, logged areas, slash and second-growth plantations. Since it frequents human habitats, it is no surprise that the Northern Flicker is the best-known coastal woodpecker. It is well adapted to the open logged and farmed country found in most valley bottoms and is the only

A male Ruffed Grouse in full display. (R. Wayne Campbell)

native North American bird that nests in all states and provinces in North America. Because it feeds mostly on the ground rather than in trees, the flicker is unique among Canadian woodpeckers.

The coastal flicker—commonly referred to as the "Red-shafted" Flicker—wears a brown crown upon its greyish head, and its back and upper wing surface are greyish brown and spotted with black. The underparts are a light tan colour spotted with black, and the rump is white. This flicker is most commonly found in our coastal valleys and in the northeastern Interior, and the one most often seen to the east of the Coast Range Mountains is its "Yellow-shafted" cousin. Whereas males of the pure "Red-shafted" race characteristically have red moustaches and no red on the back of the neck, the "Yellow-shafted" male sports a black moustache and a red nape. But now and then, in the eastern part of the largest valleys, you will see a bird or two with a patch of red on the nape (such as the "Yellow-shafted" Flicker) as well as a red moustache (the "Red-shafted" Flicker). Sometimes you can even see male flickers with a moustache that is half black and half red. Studies have demonstrated that the

bird's moustache provides important visual stimuli during mating season. In one study, a biologist painted a temporary moustache on a mated female flicker; when she was reunited with her mate, he promptly attacked her and drove her away. When this mark of maleness was removed, however, the male flicker took her back.

Scientists believe that glaciation is responsible for the physical differences distinguishing "Red-shafted" from "Yellow-shafted" flickers. According to this theory, western flicker populations became separated from their eastern counterparts for thousands of years by advancing sheets of glacial ice. The birds living east of these vast ice sheets evolved to become the black-moustached "Yellow-shafted" Flickers, and the western population became members of the red-moustached "Red-shafted" Flicker race. Glacial-era separation is also thought to account for the two kinds of Yellow-rumped Warblers, namely the "Myrtle Warbler" (the more interior race) and the "Audubon's Warbler" (the more western race), as well as the two kinds of Dark-eyed Juncos (the "Slate-coloured" Junco of the more eastern and northern race and the "Oregon" Junco of the western race). As in the case of the Northern Flicker, the eastern and western populations of these newly evolved species readily mated after the glaciers withdrew. Nowadays, interesting mixes can be found wherever such interbreeding takes place.

When looking for flickers, watch and listen for pairs of duelling males. At the outset of a battle witnessed, one combatant was perched upon a dead branch high up in an old black cottonwood tree,

The "Myrtle" Warbler is the white-throated subspecies of the Yellow-rumped Warbler. This bird migrates in small numbers on the raincoast. (R. Wayne Campbell)

while his opponent waited in another tree nearby. When the fight began, however, the birds did not attack each other; rather, they vented their aggression on a nearby tree. Signalling the duel's formal commencement, one of the flickers began hammering away at head-blurring speed on a carefully selected hollow and resonating limb. During this impressive performance, his rival politely watched and listened. When the first flicker had finished hammering, the second one began as if on cue. After duelling thus for a few minutes, the weaker male surrendered and flew away, uttering the flicker's spring call *wick-a, wick-a, wick-a-wick*. Like all woodpeckers, he flew in an undulating wave-like pattern: after each series of wing beats he folded his wings against his body, rising each time he flapped his wings and falling each time he folded them.

The act of hammering or "drumming" upon resonant objects is not unique to flickers. Indeed, drumming is the means by which all male woodpeckers claim territory and attempt to attract mates. The longer and louder the drumming, the more powerful the woodpecker will appear to his competitors and the more attractive he will be to a potential mate.

Campbell Fact

Like the songs of many forest birds, the drumming of woodpeckers advertises for mates and defends territory. Some drumming can be heard half a mile away. Each woodpecker has its unique drumming sound. The beats per second, or cadence, may be slow (14 for a Pileated Woodpecker) or fast (26 for a Hairy Woodpecker). The tapping may speed up (Pileated Woodpecker), slow down (Downy Woodpecker), start with a roll (Red-breasted Sapsucker) or be fairly steady (Northern Flicker). With a lot of practice and patience you can differentiate the drumming patterns of the various species.

The "Audubon's" Warbler is a yellow-throated subspecies of the Yellow-rumped Warbler. This is the subspecies most likely to be seen nesting along the raincoast. (R. Wayne Campbell)

Instinctively, female woodpeckers seem to understand that a male energetic enough to hammer upon dead wood from dawn until dusk will likely be a good provider of food when her young ones are born. Sometimes birdwatchers confuse drumming with drilling, which is done to extract food and dig out cavities. If you listen carefully, however, you will discover that each woodpecker kind has its own recognizable drumming rhythm, which differs noticeably from rhythms associated with drill-

Widespread clearing of mature and old-growth forests contributes to local declines in Pileated Woodpecker populations. (R. Wayne Campbell)

ing. The Pileated Woodpecker's drumming is loud, but slower than that of smaller woodpecker species, often becoming softer toward the end. The Downy Woodpecker's drumming sounds like a long, unbroken, subdued roll; the Hairy Woodpecker's drumming is shorter in duration and louder in volume, with longer pauses between beats. The drumming of the Red-breasted Sapsucker is subtler, consisting of several rapid taps followed by a short pause and then by a series of slower and more rhythmic taps.

One year a pair of flickers moved into our neighbourhood, choosing for their home a nearby snag of rotting sun-bleached Douglas-fir. Announcing their arrival with a succession of *wick wick wick wick* and *flick-a flick-a flick-a* calls, the birds proceeded to conduct an elaborate and vociferous courtship. As the principal actor in this amorous affair, the male clung to a tree trunk, spread his tail feathers, pointed his bill skyward and began weaving his head in a curious circular fashion. He repeated this performance over and over, interrupting it occasionally with intervals of brief flight, which gave him an opportunity to show off his bright salmon-red underwings, boldly speckled undersides and bright white rump. His dance was obviously successful: a few days later, the mated flickers were taking turns excavating a nest cavity near the top of their snag. Eventually the birds produced a dark entrance hole approximately 8 centimetres (3 1/4 inches) in diameter. By early June, young flicker heads were eagerly poking out of the hole to gorge upon insects regurgitated by their hardworking parents, and by mid-June the youngsters had left the nest. No doubt they were out exploring the countryside, learning the art of insect hunting and snacking on wild fruits, berries and seeds. When September arrived, the flicker pair left for wintering grounds, probably in the Fraser Lowlands or more southerly climes.

The most colourful bird of prey is the American Kestrel, formerly known as the Sparrow Hawk. A local summer resident along British Columbia's coast, this falcon is the most recognizable of our migrating hawks: groups of 5 to 10 can sometimes be seen moving through coastal valleys as early as mid-April. By late July and August, these flocks will be replaced by smaller family units. Kestrels love to sit on power lines or fence posts overlooking open fields. If you see one of these birds while driving, pull well off the road and observe it closely for a few minutes. An attractive robin-sized falcon, the kestrel has two vertical black stripes on its white cheeks and a bright, rust-coloured back and tail. Its call consists of a shrill and rapid series of sharp *killy killy killy* notes; in some parts of eastern Canada, this call has earned the kestrel the sonic nickname "killy hawk."

If from its roadside perch the kestrel spots food, it swoops down onto the field, hovers momentarily and then drops suddenly into the tall grass. For the English poet Gerard Manley Hopkins, this kind of aerial prowess was a great source of delight and inspiration. In a poem entitled "The Windhover," Hopkins praised a kestrel for its ability to hover in place, to turn in the air "as a skate's heel sweeps smooth on a bow-bend," and to "rebuff the big wind." For Hopkins, the hawk's "mastery" of the sky symbolized nothing less than divine perfection itself. In the real world, of course, such aerial mastery serves the purposes of natural predation rather than spiritual striving. Although the kestrel frequently takes small birds or mammals, it specializes in hunting insects.

Typically the Kestrel situates its nest in old woodpecker holes or natural cavities occurring in living and dead trees; its favourite tree species include Douglas-fir, black cottonwood and trembling aspen. The female usually lays four or five eggs and performs most of the incubation herself; her young ones hatch after 29 or 30 days. The male helps to feed the hatchlings, which will be ready to leave the nest at about 30 days of age. Rarely seen in our coastal regions after mid-September, the American Kestrel migrates to wintering grounds ranging to Central America and Panama.

One can expect to see at least seven kinds of hawks along our coast: American Kestrel, Merlin (also known as Pigeon Hawk), Sharp-shinned Hawk, Northern Goshawk, Northern Harrier (also known as Marsh Hawk) Osprey and Red-tailed Hawk. Most male and female

More and more Sharp-shinned Hawks spend winters in and near residential areas.
(Mark Nyhof)

hawks look alike, though the female is usually the larger member of the pair. The American Kestrel is the smallest of our coastal hawks: when fully grown it is about the size of a robin, boasting an average body length of 10 inches. The Merlin and Sharp-shinned Hawk are larger birds, about the size of a domestic pigeon, with an average body length of 30 to 35 centimetres (12 to 14 inches). The Northern Goshawk, Northern Harrier and Red-tailed Hawk are all crow-sized birds, with average body lengths of 55 to 58 centimetres (22 to 23 inches).

An Osprey (above) flies over a field, carrying fish for its young (right). (R. Wayne Campbell)

Smaller hawks like the American Kestrel nest in cavities excavated by Pileated Woodpeckers; the Merlin uses abandoned crow, raven and Steller's Jay nests. Larger raptors like the Osprey, Red-tailed Hawk and Northern Goshawk build nests of twigs near the tops of snags, in the forks of tree trunks or in the forks of large branches next to the trunk.

All of these hawks are highly skilled predators. Their deeply curved beaks, powerful feet and razor-sharp talons enable them to grasp and rend their prey with deadly efficiency. Moreover, their vision and hearing—as sharp as their beaks and talons—are greatly superior to our own.

The various species of hawk differ not only in size but also in preferred habitat, prey and hunting methods. All are most easily spotted in fields and farmlands. Knowing these differences can facilitate hawk identification, and at the same time bring a greater appreciation of these fascinating animals. The Northern Goshawk prefers to hunt in mature coniferous forests, but other species are more likely to be seen searching for prey around or above open clearings and at the edges of forests.

The Northern Harrier's hunting style is ideally suited for meadows, tidal flats, grasslands and other open expanses situated around fresh- and salt-water wetlands. Hunting at low elevations, this hawk

The Northern Harrier is most commonly sighted during its autumn migration in October and November. (R. Wayne Campbell)

searches the ground for garter snakes, mice, voles and other small mammals. If you see a crow-sized, greyish brown hawk cruising over an open field, swaying slightly from side to side on long, narrow outspread wings, it will almost certainly be a male Northern Harrier. Gliding low over the earth, this bird frequently hunts only a couple of feet above the ground. When it sights food, it drops suddenly, stretches out its legs and grasps its prey in knife-like talons. The female Northern Harrier is some-what larger than the male and more brownish in coloration, and lacks the black wing tips seen in most males. In both males and females, distinctive features include long, narrow wings, a long tail, a white rump and an owl-like face. Its call is a weak nasal whistle sounding something like *pee, pee, pee.*

The best times to spot Northern Harriers along the coast are in October and April, when the birds visit estuaries on their way to and from wintering grounds in British Columbia's Fraser Valley and as far south as Mexico. They nest in the Fraser River valley around marshes and shrubby wetlands in dense grasses and sedges, or among willow, rose and hardhack. The nest is composed of grasses, small sticks and other marsh vegetation, and lined with finer grasses and weed stalks for comfort and safety. Here the female lays and incubates four to seven bluish eggs, usually in the month of May. Although the female does most of the incubation, the male assists later on by providing food for the youngsters. The incubation period for Northern Harrier eggs is 30 to 40 days; a month or so after hatching, the young hawks test their wings. When searching for a harrier's nest, be prepared to be attacked if you get too close, for these birds do not take kindly to intruders.

The other raven-sized hawk you might see above clearcuts, meadows and semi-open or open agricultural clearings is the Red-tailed Hawk, whose hunting grounds extend from the coastal waters of the estuary to the high country above the timberline. Often you will hear this hawk before seeing it: it is distinctive for its loud, harsh *keeeyerr* uttered from high above. If you should hear this call, scan the high reaches of the sky, looking for the bird's unmistakable broad-winged profile. The Red-tailed

Hawk uses its widely stretched wings, compact body and broadly fanned short tail to capture thermal updrafts, enabling it to glide gracefully and effortlessly in circles high above the land. From the ground it is sometimes difficult to identify the adult's characteristic rusty tail, but you should be able to make out the dark leading inner edge on its otherwise pale underwing. Seen in close proximity, our coastal Red-tailed Hawk displays a dark brown head and back, and the whitish colour of its chest and belly gains visual variety from its variable streaking.

Unlike the Northern Harrier, the Red-tailed Hawk likes to hunt from high elevations. From the loftiest heights, this soaring bird scans the ground with remarkably acute vision, looking for prey to feed itself and its voracious young. When it sights a snake, mouse, vole, squirrel or other prey, the Red-tailed Hawk plummets toward the earth in a steep dive, breaking only at ground level to seize its victim.

Another hawk found around coastal valley clearings is the Merlin, also known as the Pigeon Hawk. It is a dark, pigeon-sized falcon, notable for its prominently banded tail. Unlike the Red-tailed Hawk, however, the Merlin does not have vertical black stripes on its cheek, nor does it have a bright rust-coloured back and tail. The coastal race is very dark all over.

An impressive flyer, this small falcon specializes in high-speed aerial pursuit of its prey. It is indeed the cheetah of the aerial world: its head and body are streamlined, its tail is long and its wings are long, slim and swept back. In normal flight, on the one hand, the Merlin beats its wings rapidly to move directly through the air, often cruising close to the ground. If, on the other hand, it is in hot pursuit of a morsel sighted from on high, it will tuck in its wings, accelerating quickly toward the intended target. When the chase is successful, it generally culminates in a dramatic explosion of feathers. If unsuc-

The Red-tailed Hawk hunts by diving from the sky and pouncing on small mammals that run about in open fields and farmlands. (R. Wayne Campbell)

cessful, however, the Merlin will break off its assault and return to its aerial vantage point or perch to prepare for another attempt.

Each year Merlins return to our upper coastal valleys by late March. It is easy to tell when they have arrived, because they announce their presence with a staccato *ki-ki-ki-ki*, chattering almost incessantly until July. From about mid-July to mid-August, young Pigeon Hawks work to perfect their flying skills, while learning predatory strategies and hunting techniques from their parents. Usually by late August, these birds, sensing the impending demise of summer, will begin to make their way back to wintering homes located in southern Canada and beyond.

Swallows tend to nest in both dense and loose colonies, but each species has distinctive preferences with respect to where they will raise their families. Some prefer open fields and farmlands to feed and raise their families. Two species, the Cliff and Barn swallows, take over old buildings for nesting. Among the various swallow species, these two are perhaps the most difficult to tell apart, having similar blue-black iridescent capes and caps and nearly identical cinnamon-coloured cheeks. A few subtle distinguishing characteristics can enable the discerning observer to differentiate these feathered cousins fairly easily. The Barn Swallow can be recognized by its narrow, deeply forked tail and the butterfly choker that separates its chocolate-coloured face from its pale orange breast feathers.

The Cliff Swallow is chunkier in stature, having a square head and a short rectangular tail, and it is set apart most notably by its orange rump and buff-white forehead.

Cliff Swallows plaster their bulbous mud homes around bridges, overhangs and the cliffs for which they are named. For their part, Barn Swallows build cup-shaped nests upon high, sheltered branches and beams. Tree and Violet-green Swallows search out sheltered cavities and crevices.

In the dusky grey of evening, when the setting sun has slipped behind the ragged mountains, the Common Nighthawks emerge. Almost invisible in their mottled, down-feathered cloaks, these nocturnal birds fly in a bat-like manner in pursuit of their chosen food, the insects of the night. Like swifts and swallows, Common Nighthawks have short bills and gaping mouths, which are ideally adapted for capturing insects in mid-flight; their mouths are lined with bristles to help them to snag bugs even when their aim is off. Under the cover of darkness, nighthawks are not easy to see, but their call—a short, nasal *spee-ick*—can nevertheless be heard ringing out over the water. Every night the males embark upon their territorial flights, punctuating these excursions with sharp booms proclaiming their nocturnal lordship. In amazing aerial displays, they dive toward the earth at great velocity, pulling up sharply just before hitting the ground. During these manoeuvres the air passes swiftly over their shifting primary wing feathers, producing the impressive *boom*. For this reason, and because nighthawks are somewhat similar to swallows in shape and aerial expertise, they are occasionally called "booming swallows" in folk discourse; and their gaping, insect-seeking mouths have, in some French-Canadian regions, earned them the fanciful folk-name of *engoulevent* (meaning "wind-swallower").

Generally, Common Nighthawks make their spring arrival in British Columbia's coastal regions later than the swallows and swifts (usually in early June), and depart again in late August when cooling temperatures announce autumn's impending return.

Left: The female Tree Swallow hunts for flying insects during daylight hours.
(Donald E. Waite)

Above: The Common Nighthawk preys on flying insects mainly during the early evening hours. Nighthawks instinctively perch lengthwise on tree branches during daylight hours, a behaviour that helps with camouflage.
(R. Wayne Campbell)

4

Birds of
the Night

The owl is considered a creature of darkness, one of the avian lords of night. In characteristically colourful language, John Burroughs calls it the "Bird of silent wing and expansive eye, grimalkin in feathers ... mocking the midnight stillness with uncanny cry!" This "great bugaboo of the feathered tribes" has long graced our regions with its mysterious nocturnal presence. Following a tradition that has embraced the owl as a symbol of wisdom or thoughtful solitude, one can easily idealize these birds. However, their reality as violent predators also makes them apt representatives of what a dismayed Tennyson, poet laureate of the Victorian period, memorably referred to as "nature red in tooth and claw."

Along the coast, one can expect to see or hear at least six kinds of owls: the Western Screech-Owl, Great Horned Owl, Barred Owl, Northern Saw-whet Owl, Great Gray Owl and Northern Pygmy-Owl. As a group, they are large-headed, short-necked birds, gazing out at the world through uncommonly large forward-set eyes. Most are dressed in a discreet plumage of mottled browns and greys interspersed with white. Male and female owls look alike, though the latter are often larger.

The Great Horned Owl is the largest resident along the coast. The Barred Owl is slightly smaller than a raven, the Northern Saw-whet Owl is about the size of a robin and the Northern Pygmy-Owl is a bit larger than a sparrow.

Since most owls are nocturnal birds of prey, they possess sensory faculties designed to facilitate

Previous pages: The Barred Owl, a very rare bird along the raincoast two decades ago, is now a common year-round resident of coastal valleys and river bottoms with thick, mixed forests. (Michael Wigle)

Below: Juvenile Great Horned Owl, almost ready to hunt on its own. (R. Wayne Campbell)

night hunting. First of all, they have binocular vision, which helps them detect moving objects and catch food. Their eyes make full use of every glint and glimmer of light: in some species, night vision is so keen that owls can see their prey even when available light is equivalent only to that which is thrown by an ordinary candle burning 750 metres (2,500 feet) away. Second, an owl's hearing is so good that it can detect and capture mice on the darkest nights merely by listening to them rustling through the dry leaves. The owl's acute sense of hearing can be attributed in part to its characteristic facial disc, which functions like a parabolic reflector funnelling sound toward the eardrums. By triangulation, the owl can pinpoint its prey with remarkable accuracy.

Another anatomic feature contributing to the owl's predatory success is its oversized feathers.

Most owls hunt during twilight and nighttime hours, but the Short-eared Owl (below), Northern Pygmy-Owl and Snowy Owl hunt mainly during daylight hours. (R. Wayne Campbell)

Tipped with downy edges that muffle the sounds produced while flying, the owl's feathers enable it to move through the night sky with great stealth and silence. All owls are equipped with stout, strong feet, and their sharp, curved bills and claws are efficient and deadly predatory weapons.

People have long been fascinated by the call of the owl. In medieval times, an owl's call was sometimes thought to be an omen, a harbinger of bad luck or even death. Thus, in eastern Canada, a French folk name for the Great Horned Owl is *chaouin*, a word meaning roughly a "bird with the cry of an evil omen." At the beginning of his late 18th-century poem "Christabel," Samuel Taylor Coleridge invoked this ominous call to establish a romantic atmosphere of gothic gloom: "'Tis the middle of the night by the castle clock, / And the owl has awakened the crowing cock / Tu whit, tu woo and there again / How drowsily it crew." Perhaps primarily because of our cultural conditioning, owl calls often evoke in us a sense of fear and foreboding, but knowledge of owl calls can also be scientifically useful, for the best way to locate and identify owls is to listen to their calls.

In the coastal valleys, the best time to hear owls is during the late winter and early spring (February to April). The Great Horned Owl's familiar hoot is a resonant, low-pitched *who-who-who who who-whooo-whooo*. The Barred Owl is probably the noisiest member of its species; though it is relatively silent during its nesting period, its calls may be heard year-round. This owl's hooting call is an emphatic *hoohoo-hoohoo-hoohoo-hoohooaw*, and some imaginative listeners have suggested it sounds a bit like a culinary question: *who cooks for you, who cooks for you all?* The common hooting call of the small Northern Saw-whet Owl is a mellow whistled note sounding like *too, too, too* repeated over and over (up to a hundred or more times per minute). The Northern Pygmy-Owl can be heard throughout the night but seems to be most vociferous during dusk and dawn. Its call has been described as a penetrating repetition of dove-like whistled notes sounding like *too-too-too-too-too-too-too-too-took-too-took*.

Owls are among the first birds to begin mating and nesting each year. This early nesting seems to

Over the past decade, increasing numbers of Great Gray Owls have been sighted at the eastern ends of coastal inlets. (Michael I. Preston)

be part of nature's plan for the owl, for it ensures that owl nestlings will be out and yelling for food just as the migratory birds return to the valley to nest and small mammals begin to wander from their winter hideaways. Our owls, one might say, are born surrounded by a veritable smorgasbord of potential prey.

The Great Gray Owl lives mainly in the Interior of the province, but recently small numbers have been found nesting and hunting at the end of long coastal inlets. Among birdwatchers, this is one of the most sought-after North American owls. It is even larger than its Great Horned cousin, recognized not only by its grand size but also by its plumage: a brownish grey coat streaked with browns, whites and greys. The Great Gray Owl may also be distinguished by its egg-shaped head, which lacks the crown tufts or "horns" for which the Great Horned Owl is named, and by its large facial disc and bright yellow eyes. Other identifying features include the Great Gray Owl's yellow bill, below which may be seen a black area of plumage and a white throat. This impressive bird prefers to reside in dense coniferous and mixed deciduous forests, but it may also be found near open pastures and marsh edges.

After nearly 50 days in the nest, it is almost time for these young Great Horned Owls to leave their home.
(R. Wayne Campbell)

Opposite: The Barred Owl, a recent arrival from eastern Canada, has moved into areas occupied by the Spotted Owl in the southwestern mainland of British Columbia. There is growing concern that the Barred Owl will interbreed with the endangered Spotted Owl. (R. Wayne Campbell)

Contrary to popular perceptions of owl behaviour, Great Gray Owls frequently hunt in daylight, typically in the late afternoon. With a bit of luck, you may see one gliding from perch to perch at this time, occasionally swooping down to pick up unsuspecting prey. Their favourite foods include mice, voles, shrews, lemmings and the occasional bird. Great Gray Owls rarely take larger prey such as grouse and squirrels.

The Great Gray Owl typically raises its young in nests built and abandoned by such birds as the Northern Goshawk, Red-tailed Hawk, Common Raven and Northwestern Crow. These nests are located between 4.5 and 15 metres (15 to 50 feet) above the ground in broad-leafed or coniferous trees. Egg laying typically occurs in April, at which time the female produces between two and four dull white eggs. The incubation period varies from 30 to 50 days, depending on the size of the clutch and the intervals between the laying of each egg. Both parents contribute to the feeding of the young, which leave the nest when they reach 21 to 28 days of age.

The Great Horned Owl is a large and powerful predator. It is smaller than the Great Gray Owl, but stronger, heavier and more diversified in its habits. This owl has mottled brown plumage above and a barred brown and white breast and underside. The head features a large facial disk, prominent cat-like "ear" tufts, a black bill, white throat patch and large yellow eyes. The Great Horned Owl is a resident of coastal valleys, preferring wooded areas, rivers, lakeshores, marshes, estuaries and pastures.

Like its Great Gray cousin, the Great Horned Owl hunts mainly at dusk and dawn. By day it usually roosts in the branches of trees, but as soon as dusk begins to fall it ventures out to commence its pursuit of prey. Great Horned Owls kill and eat a wide variety of birds, mammals and snakes. Their favourite prey includes rabbits, rats, mice, grouse and waterfowl, but they also hunt domestic cats, minks, hawks, skunks, raccoons and other owls. These birds have voracious appetites: a single Great Horned Owl is reportedly capable of eating 2,500 mice in a year; during the same period, a family of such owls needs as many as 9,000 mice to survive.

In order to woo a mate, the male Great Horned Owl conducts an elaborate courtship, displaying both his aerial prowess and his ability to provide food. After mating, the Great Horned pair will often appropriate an open-stick nest previously abandoned by Red-tailed Hawks, Northern Goshawks, Copper's Hawks, Bald Eagles, Great Blue Herons or Common Ravens. These owls prefer nests built high in coniferous or deciduous trees, but occasionally nests are found on cliff ledges and in large tree cavities. Great Horned Owls may use the same nest for three or four years in a row, presumably because the birds have a rich food supply in the foraging area. Generally, between mid-February and mid-April, the female Great Horned Owl lays two or three white eggs, which require an incubation period of roughly 30 days. The males and females of this species work cooperatively to feed their young, which grow rapidly and usually leave the nest in 31 to 35 days. By about 10 weeks of age, these birds are already mastering the art of flight while beginning to hunt on their own.

Campbell Fact

All nests qualify as engineering feats, but most deteriorate rapidly after a season of use. For some birds, however, old nests are used as platforms for new structures. Rufous Hummingbirds are known to take advantage of such nests regularly. Another 23 species, including Varied Thrush, Song Sparrow, Winter Wren, Swainson's Thrush, Steller's Jay and American Robin simply repair old intact nests. The nests of larger birds may last for decades with minor alterations. Old nests should not be removed, as they provide refuge for many small animals during winter and a ready source of nesting materials for lazy birds in spring.

The Barred Owl, first observed on the coast in 1966, is a stocky, greyish brown, crow-sized bird with a round tuftless head, a yellowish bill and black eyes. In appearance it resembles the Great Gray Owl, but it is smaller in stature, having a barred chest and black eyes instead of yellow ones. Its head, back, tail and wings are greyish brown with buff-white spots. The underparts are of a buff-white colour barred with greyish brown. On the upper chest, the Barred Owl's stripes run horizontally; on the belly they run up and down.

The Barred Owl loves to prey upon songbirds, mice, shrews and other small mammals, as well as reptiles, amphibians and insects. According to some reports, it will also kill chickens, rabbits, squirrels

and smaller members of the owl family. Now a common year-round resident of coastal valleys, the Barred Owl's favourite habitat appears to be thick mixed coniferous and deciduous forests located along river bottoms. It usually nests in hollowed-out tops of dead trees situated 6 to 30 metres (20 to 100 feet) above the ground. On rare occasions it will also appropriate nests built and abandoned by hawks, eagles or ravens. Egg laying takes place from late March until mid-May. The female lays an average of two or three dull white eggs, which are then incubated for a period of 20 to 28 days. Four weeks after they are born, young Barred Owls are capable of flying; after six weeks they are out searching for their own meals.

The Northern Saw-whet Owl is much smaller than any of the owls described above. About the size of a robin, it has a wingspan of roughly 45 centimetres (18 inches). Its head is relatively large; its black-billed face is a buff-white colour; it observes the world through intense yellow eyes. Around the outer edge of the face appear numerous fine, short brown marks. The rest of the head and back is dark brown, and the whitish underparts are variegated by numerous brown streaks. As for preferred habitat, saw-whet owls reside in dense forests of both pure and mixed coniferous and deciduous trees, or in thick shrubbery growing along the banks and shores of creeks, ponds and rivers.

Like most owls, the Northern Saw-whet Owl is primarily a nocturnal bird, not likely to be seen during the day unless by chance it is discovered roosting in a dense thicket or deep in the forest. Deer mice, shrews, voles and insects make up most of this bird's diet, though it will sometimes eat bats and songbirds. A patient predator, the Northern Saw-whet Owl hunts by perching and waiting; when opportunity presents itself, the owl jumps from its perch, swoops down and pounces upon an unsuspecting victim.

Right: A female Great Horned Owl guards her nest. Use caution when approaching such owls, as they have been known to attack and injure people who ventured too close. (R. Wayne Campbell)

Although mice are the preferred food of the Northern Saw-whet Owl, this robin-sized owl will also eat squirrels, chipmunks, songbirds and even insects. (Glenn R. Ryder)

Occasionally the saw-whet owl kills diurnal animals such as chipmunks, young red squirrels, sparrows, juncos and warblers. Such predatory behaviour suggests that this owl engages in at least some daytime hunting, but it is likely that these animals are caught in dark, shady forests or thickets, or at dusk and dawn.

The Northern Saw-whet Owl typically nests in abandoned tree cavities originally excavated by flickers and other woodpeckers. In April or May, the female usually lays five or six pure white eggs and shares incubation duties with her mate. The incubation period averages 27 days. Like other owls, young saw-whet owls grow quickly, becoming fully feathered and capable of flying only a month after they are born. After mid-July, most young saw-whets have left their nest and are out hunting in family groups.

Saw-whet youngsters are quite distinctive in appearance. They have rich chocolate brown plumage above, rusty brown plumage below and a broad white *V* on the forehead. By the time young saw-whet owls come to experience the first chill of winter, this plumage is lost and they are dressed like the adults of their species.

The diminutive Northern Pygmy-Owl is even smaller than the saw-whet, being just bigger than a sparrow. An inhabitant of coniferous and deciduous woods, it is the smallest of our coastal owls. Its eyes and bill are yellow; its head is small, round and tuftless; and its barred tail is unusually long for an owl. Most of the head, back, chest and wings are a lightly spotted reddish brown colour. The spots are small on the head and larger on the back and upper sides. The central breast area and belly are white with brown stripes. On the back of its head and neck, the Northern Pygmy-Owl displays a distinctive black and white pattern looking remarkably like an owl's face, giving its owner the appearance of a

The Short-eared Owl and other owls are most commonly sighted hunting in open spaces along the raincoast during their autumn migration. (R. Wayne Campbell)

The Northern Pygmy-Owl is the smallest owl in British Columbia—just larger than a sparrow. (R. Wayne Campbell)

feathered Janus. But it would be an exercise in pathetic fallacy to suggest that this "second face" is a sign of owlish duplicity. Indeed, because few animals are willing to confront an owl face to face, one might assume that the patterning on the back of the pygmy-owl's head serves a protective function, enabling it to survive and thrive more effectively in its forest habitat.

The pygmy-owl is a rare and local resident of coastal valleys. Its call can be heard during every month of the year, though it is most commonly heard in November, December and January. The pygmy-owl's easy-to-imitate call is worth learning, for it will attract other pygmy-owls and mobs of scolding songbirds. But these songbirds, far from appreciating the owl's call, will be highly offended by it. Indeed, they will come to gang up on the intrusive pygmy-owl in order to drive it away from their nesting and feeding territories.

The Northern Pygmy-Owl is living proof that nature's general rules are never entirely hard and fast. Unlike most of its owlish cousins, which are nocturnal (or at least partially so), the pygmy-owl sleeps during the night and regularly hunts during the day. It has a varied diet, exhibiting different predatory preferences throughout the course of the year. During the breeding period, pygmy-owls prey largely upon songbirds. These sparrow-sized owls can kill birds the size of a robin or starling, proving that in the realm of nature, small stature need not imply weakness. In late summer, they feed mainly on large insects such as grasshoppers, but they also take snakes, mice and other small rodents. In the autumn and winter, mice and voles take on an increasingly important role in their diet.

When Northern Pygmy-Owls hunt, they can cause quite a stir. Recently, for example, a friend heard a European Starling screaming loudly in his backyard. Stepping out the door to investigate, he saw that a sparrow-sized bird had attached itself to the starling's back and was holding on tenaciously. Greatly distressed, the starling attempted to fly away, but its tiny assailant had other plans. By working to create aerodynamic drag, it was trying to bring its larger victim to the ground. Our friend's presence distracted the attacker, enabling the starling to break free. Only then did he realize that the attacker was a Northern Pygmy-Owl looking for a big meal.

Look for the pygmy-owl along the edges of mixed coniferous woodlands, on steep hillsides, near precipitous talus slopes and in steep ravines not far from water. Pygmy-owls nest almost exclusively in abandoned woodpecker cavities. During the months of April and May, the female lays a clutch of three or four white eggs. The incubation process requires roughly 28 days and the fledging period 29 to 32 days. The young are therefore present in the nest until late June or early July. Typically the female incubates the eggs, but when the new hatchlings arrive, her male partner contributes to their feeding by helping her to bring prey for the young.

Every year, like clockwork, a long-winged, light brown owl flops its way south in November and December from its northern Interior breeding grounds. The Short-eared Owl is a dusk, daylight and dawn hunter in any open habitats. It feeds almost exclusively on field mice, and when prey is abundant it will pass the winter in some coastal spot. Usually birdwatchers have a very narrow period during which to spot this bird. Look for it perched on a post in an open field or farmland, or hunting in a dry, grassy area of an estuary.

The impressive-looking Snowy Owl sometimes visits the open fields, estuaries and lighthouses along the coast in autumn and winter, arriving from its traditional hunting grounds in the High Arctic and along the north Alaskan coast. Every few years a few of these birds appear, driven by hunger and a scarcity of food. Heavily built and white of plumage, this crow-sized owl has a rounded head and large yellow eyes. Like the Great Gray and Northern Pygmy-owls, it defies owlish stereotypes by hunting during daylight hours. In winter you may see Snowy Owls hunting over the tidal flats, gliding just above the ground in search of such prey as small mice, voles and other rodents, hares and weasels, grebes and gulls, small wintering ducks and seabirds and even crows. When night falls, the Snowy Owl retreats from the hunting grounds and the Great Horned Owl takes its place in the darkness.

The Snowy Owl is an irregular winter visitor to the raincoast from its usual home in the High Arctic. When present, it is most commonly seen in the Fraser River delta. Elsewhere, this daytime-hunting owl commonly perches on fence posts and utility poles. (R. Wayne Campbell)

5
Birds of the Old-Growth Coniferous Forest

I n coastal old-growth forests—which are becoming increasingly rare and therefore difficult to experience—ancient mossy conifer trunks stand like massive architectural pillars, rising skyward to support a high canopy of green foliage. Here and there golden shafts of sunlight penetrate the forest's lush ceiling,

dispersing accumulated mists and brightening the shady corners of the forest floor. Gazing up from among the lowly ferns, you may experience a momentary feeling of vertigo, but the sight of a tiny wren probing the ground about your feet will help to restore your sense of perspective and equilibrium.

Although unspoiled patches of valley-bottom old-growth forest are scarce, most coastal valleys still have a few places where one may look for birds among giant western hemlock, Sitka spruce, western redcedar and Douglas-fir—trees that have grown for a thousand years or more. If you follow a river up from the ocean, you will likely find pockets of old growth

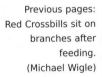

Patches of valley-bottom old-growth forest are becoming increasingly scarce. (Michael Wigle)

that have been overlooked by loggers or spared for some other reason. On British Columbia's Central Coast there are still some untouched old-growth watersheds and the Megin River, on Vancouver Island, is protected from its headwaters to the sea. These rivers are difficult to reach because they are in the wilderness, but they are worth seeking out. Failing that, you will be rewarded by searching along other more accessible rivers for the pockets of old growth that remain. Structural features defining old-growth forests include massive trees and large snags, giant logs decaying on the forest

Previous pages: Red Crossbills sit on branches after feeding. (Michael Wigle)

Right: The beautiful male Western Tanager is surprisingly common in mature mixed coniferous forests. (Edgar T. Jones)

floor, clear and clean streams and a ground cover of mosses and patchy thick shrubs.

During most of the year, old-growth forests harbour such forest birds as the Pileated and Hairy woodpeckers, Golden-crowned Kinglet, Varied Thrush, Brown Creeper, Red-breasted Nuthatch, Winter Wren and Chestnut-backed Chickadee. From late April until September, these year-round residents are joined by a diverse but select array of summer visitants like the Pacific-slope Flycatcher, Olive-sided Flycatcher, Hammond's Flycatcher, Townsend's Warbler and Western Tanager. All of these summer birds specialize in foraging for insects, which may be hunted up in the dizzying heights of the forest canopy, among the dense vegetation of avalanche chutes and all the way down to the green stream edges.

In order to exploit the rich insect populations found in old-growth coastal forests with maximum efficiency, birds have developed various feeding preferences. The Varied Thrush and the much smaller Winter Wren feed on insects inhabiting the forest floor. The Pacific-slope Flycatcher captures insects in flight. Chickadees search the upper and lower surfaces of twigs and smaller branches for dormant insects, eggs and larvae, hanging at all

The haunting flute-like song of the male Varied Thrush can be heard in mature coniferous forests in early spring throughout the raincoast. (Michael Wigle)

angles to obtain these delectable morsels. In the high forest canopy the Golden-crowned Kinglet and Townsend's Warbler compete with the Chestnut-backed Chickadee for insects, spiders and other food. As for the Pileated Woodpecker, Hairy Woodpecker, Brown Creeper and Red-breasted Nuthatch, all of these birds prey upon insects associated with tree trunks and branches, and fallen woody debris. Each species feeds in a slightly different manner. The woodpeckers feed while travelling straight up tree trunks, the Red-breasted Nuthatch searches for its food by moving headfirst down tree trunks and the Brown Creeper feeds while moving in a spiral from the bottom of the tree trunk to the top. Presumably each foraging method offers a unique perspective, revealing food sources that remain undetected by birds exhibiting different hunting techniques and feeding preferences.

Because forest birds, especially high-canopy foragers, can be difficult to see, it is a good idea to visit old-growth areas in May. At this time, bird songs will provide helpful aural clues, enabling visitors to locate male singers otherwise hidden among the high branches overhead.

When visiting coastal old-growth forests in the early spring, listen for the Varied Thrush's haunting call, which is especially

Campbell Fact

Over the years authors and naturalists have developed a wonderful collection of words to describe assemblages of birds. Some terms still in use include: gaggle of geese, murder of crows, raft of ducks, parliament of owls, commotion of coots, kettle of hawks, covey of quails and siege of herons.

common during the early morning hours. This plaintive call sounds like someone humming and whistling simultaneously; it consists of a long, quavering note that rises and then slowly fades away. Following a brief pause, the bird utters another note in a slightly higher pitch. Although the call of the Varied Thrush is flute-like in tone, its quavering vibrato lends it something of a mechanical and other-worldly quality. Seen from a distance, the Varied Thrush is sometimes mistaken for an American Robin. Perhaps this is why it has sometimes been called a "swamp robin" or "marsh robin" in folk discourse. The Varied Thrush and the American Robin are about the same size, boasting colourful orange-brown breasts and dark heads, backs, wings and tails. But on close inspection one notices obvious differences between these birds. Across its breast the Varied Thrush has a dark band (which in males is black and in females grey); it also sports orange stripes above its eye and an orange-brown wing bar. Unlike the robin, moreover, the Varied Thrush is a shy bird, preferring to forage on the ground among dense vegetation and in the shade of mature forests.

Issuing from the tops of the trees, the hurried, high-pitched, lisping *tsee-tsee-tsee* of the Golden-crowned Kinglet rings out across the forest. Some of our more imaginative birders have suggested that this bird's call sounds like a questioning *zee, zee, zee, zee, zee, why do you shilly-shally?* The Golden-crowned Kinglet is among the most common of our coastal birds, but it is so small and soft-voiced that it can be easily missed. Once you learn to recognize this bird's thin, lisping, high-pitched song you will be surprised how common it is. The Golden-crowned Kinglet has the distinction of being Canada's smallest songbird and, except for the Rufous Hummingbird, the smallest bird in North America, weighing under 4 grams (.14 ounces) and measuring less than 10 centimetres (4 inches) from bill tip to tail tip. Occasionally you will have the good fortune to spot one of these diminutive birds high up in a coniferous tree, flitting quickly from branch to branch. No doubt it will be searching for spiders and adult insects, as well as tiny insect eggs, larvae and pupae located on the tree's bark, twigs and conifer needles. When flying insects attempt to evade capture, the Kinglet snatches

A female Varied Thrush at nest with her young. These birds usually nest in conifers, sometimes quite high off the ground. (Donald E. Waite)

them out of the air as quickly and deftly as the most skilled fly-catcher. On rare occasions, this bird may be seen drinking from a sapsucker tap hole or feeding on seeds or fruit. By late April, the kinglet's breeding season is well underway, at which time the males attempt to attract females by singing and showing off their golden crowns (the yellow to orange-yellow patches on the tops of their heads). The bird's nest resembles a delicate deep basket or cup of mosses and it is usually located 40 or more feet (12 metres) above the forest floor. Typically the kinglet suspends its nest beneath the surrounding foliage in a cradle-like fashion, where it will be effectively hidden among the needles. It uses spider webbing and fine plant fibres not only to attach its nest to the tree, but also to bind together the mosses, lichens, plant twigs, animal hair, feathers, fine rootlets and strips of bark that make up the nest itself.

The tiny Golden-crowned Kinglet is more often heard than seen as it feeds in the crown of the old-growth forest. (Donald E. Waite)

Here, high above the forest floor, the female lays eight or nine creamy white eggs, whose shells are subtly speckled with numerous pale brown dots. The incubation period is about 12 days in duration. After the eggs hatch, both parents help to feed their young, which thrive on a diet consisting mainly of insects, insect eggs, larvae, pupae and spiders that have been gleaned from surrounding twigs and conifer needles.

Often seen foraging throughout the forest with Golden-crowned Kinglets are the Chestnut-backed Chickadees. Their loud *zhee che che zzee zee* call sounds a bit like the noise produced by a small child's squeaky toy. As you walk through the forest, don't be surprised if a small flock of these friendly little birds comes down to investigate your presence. Curious and fearless, they will flit from branch to branch, gazing intently at you and calling out frequently.

The Chestnut-backed Chickadee is easily recognized: the crown, back of the neck and throat are a dark black-brown, the cheeks and upper breast are white, the lower belly is greyish and the back, rump, sides and flanks display the rich chestnut brown colour for which the bird is named. As with

The Chestnut-backed Chickadee is named for the coloration on its back, rump, sides and flanks. (R. Wayne Campbell)

The highest densities of Chestnut-backed Chickadee (above) and Townsend's Warbler (right) are found in coastal old-growth forests. (Top: Michael Wigle; bottom: Edgar T. Jones)

all chickadees, the males and females of this species look alike. The Chestnut-backed Chickadee is most commonly found in temperate Pacific coastal valleys, preferring most particularly to reside in valley-bottom coniferous forests.

After the first week of May, be sure to listen for the songs of our summer visitant birds. Drifting down from the sun-streaked shadows of giant conifers, the drowsy *wee wee wee fun fun* of the Townsend's Warbler is pleasant to hear, even though the bird itself is rarely seen. This warbler's notable features include black cheeks, a black crown and a black throat; two white wing bars and a whitish underbelly; and an olive green back. Highlighted against these relatively dull hues, the yellow breast and upper belly and a pair of bright yellow stripes above and below its cheeks, give this warbler a strikingly colourful appearance. The female appears duller overall.

Be certain to look for the old-growth forest's most common flycatcher, the Pacific-slope Flycatcher. This nervous little sparrow-sized bird may be seen flying from branch to branch, frequently flicking its wings and tail in unison. It has a relatively large head, a conspicuous white eye-ring and a long, flat, wide bill with a slight hook at the tip. Its upper plumage is plain and olive green, and the undersides appear lighter and mostly yellow in coloration. On each shoulder the bird sports two distinct white wing bars. The Pacific-slope Flycatcher, formerly known as the Western Flycatcher, is one of the easier *Empidonax* flycatchers to identify. Among our coastal flycatchers, it is the only one that possesses a yellow throat, and a distinctive teardrop-shaped eye-ring that may be discerned with the aid of binoculars.

Like its Pacific-slope cousin, the Hammond's Flycatcher may also be seen in coastal valley bottoms where old-growth coniferous forests continue to thrive. It forages mainly in or just beneath the forest canopy. In contrast, the Pacific-slope Flycatcher forages in the lower and middle forest canopy, preferring especially riparian growth occurring along the edges of openings near creeks and ponds. In appearance, the Hammond's Flycatcher resembles the Pacific-slope Flycatcher, but its eye-ring is less pronounced and its plumage is less colourful, particularly in the throat area. The Hammond's Flycatcher and the Pacific-slope Flycatcher also have markedly different voices. On the one hand, the Pacific-slope Flycatcher's three-part song sounds like *pseet-trip-seet* (the last note of which is higher than the preceding ones), and its call note sounds like an exclamatory *peewhitt!* The three-part song of the Hammond's Flycatcher, on the other hand, sounds more like *sweep, tsurp, seep*; its call note sounds like a *peep* or *pirp*.

The Hammond's Flycatcher sings and forages for insects among the highest branches of old-growth trees. (Edgar T. Jones)

Both species return to our coastal valleys in late April and early May. The Pacific-slope Flycatcher's wintering grounds extend from Baja, California, south to the Yucatan Peninsula. The Hammond's Flycatcher spends its winters slightly farther south in a range extending from Mexico's western mountains and central plateau to the highlands of Honduras and Nicaragua. Pacific-slope Flycatchers begin their autumn migration as early as August; most have left by mid-September. The Hammond's Flycatcher begins to fly south roughly a week or so later and most are gone by the third week of September.

While enjoying a stroll in an old-growth forest, you are sure to hear the Red-breasted Nuthatch's distinctive call, a nasal and monotone *yank-yank-yank*. One of the nuthatch's most distinctive traits

The Red-breasted
Nuthatch searches
for insects in the
nooks and crannies
of bark by creeping
head first down large
tree trunks.
(R. Wayne Campbell)

is its habit of creeping headfirst down large tree trunks. Like the chickadee, which the American poet Ralph Waldo Emerson called a "defier of both frost and heat," the nuthatch spends both its summers and winters in British Columbia. Often seen during the winter months in the company of chickadees, nuthatches are bold but furtive birds. When food is scarce in winter, both chickadees and nuthatches will sometimes land on your fingertips to take seeds from your outstretched hand, but the nuthatch does so more hesitantly, landing just long enough to snatch a single seed before darting off.

The Red-breasted Nuthatch is a subtly beautiful bird, having slate blue upper parts and under-parts of a bright rust colour. It has a distinctive narrow black line running through its eye, with a corresponding white line above. Its bill is thin, straight and pointed, its legs are strong and its feet are sharply clawed. The tail is short, round and stubby: unlike the woodpecker or creeper, this bird does not use its tail for balance or support when foraging upon tree trunks.

The Red-breasted Nuthatch usually locates its nest in a cavity or crevice in an old tree or snag. Sometimes it excavates its own nest site, but more commonly it takes up residence in a hole dug out by a woodpecker or by Mother Nature. Presumably to defend its home from potential intruders and nest robbers, the nuthatch smears the entrance of its hole with pine, spruce or fir pitch.

Nuthatch nests are cup-shaped structures composed of leaves, mosses, rootlets, grasses, feathers and animal fur. Here the female lays five or six eggs, which must be incubated for 12 days or so. The female carries out incubation duties, and the male helps her feed and care for her brood once it has hatched. The age of first flight generally ranges from 18 to 21 days. By June, one can expect to see a new generation of nuthatches flying about and foraging in the forest.

Though rarely seen, the Brown Creeper is more common than most people realize. Its apparent scarcity is a consequence of its preferred habitat and its cryptic coloration, which makes it difficult to spot. Normally a solitary and secretive bird, the Brown Creeper tends to haunt the oldest, deepest and darkest corners of old-growth conifer forests. Its thin, sibilant song can only be heard when the bird is nearby. Although this song sounds like *see-see-see-sisi-see*, some listeners suggest that the Brown Creeper is exclaiming *trees, trees, trees, see the trees*. Its high-pitched call notes are not unlike those of the more common Golden-crowned Kinglet.

A well-camouflaged, sparrow-sized bird, the Brown Creeper moves up tree trunks in a creeping spiral fashion. Unlike the Nuthatch, which takes short, quick steps as it moves about the tree, the Creeper moves more methodically, using both its feet simultaneously and travelling in quick hops. The Creeper uses its short legs and powerful toenails to hold itself in place; all the while its stiff, pointed tail acts as a brace, enabling the bird to move its head back and forth as it forages. Hopping about in this manner, the Brown Creeper probes nooks and crannies with its slender, inverted crescent-shaped bill, searching for concealed insect eggs, larvae and adult insects—especially bark beetles. After progressing halfway up a chosen tree, the Creeper flies to the bottom of another tree to begin a new ascent.

When braced against a tree trunk, the creeper's deep brown and greyish white upper plumage provides excellent camouflage, allowing it to blend with its background to the point of near invisibility. In contrast, its underparts, hidden from view against the tree trunk, are white. From the Creeper's perspective, however, light reflecting off its bright white belly likely helps to illuminate shadowy cracks and holes in the tree trunk, enabling it to spot insects that might otherwise remain hidden.

April and May are the Brown Creeper's courting months. During this period the male sings his song in the hope of attracting a mate. When a female shows interest, he proceeds to demonstrate how quickly he can spiral up a tree trunk; if she is sufficiently impressed by his skill and bravado, she becomes his mate. At this point the amorous pair begins to build a nest. Generally the birds make their nest behind a slab of loose bark situated between one and 5 metres (3 to 16 feet) up the trunk of an old tree or snag. The typical Brown Creeper nest is a loose cup of twigs, roots, mosses and grasses, comfortably lined with feathers, fine bark, spider webs and animal hair. The female lays between four and eight very finely speckled white eggs, which she incubates for 14 to 15 days. Born naked and helpless, Creeper chicks are tended by both parents until they are ready to leave the nest, usually 14 to 16 days after hatching. Creepers are considered year-round residents of our coastal valleys, but members of this species residing in more northerly valleys usually disperse southward to milder coastal locations.

The Brown Creeper (top) and its nest (above). (Top: Mark Nyhof; bottom: R. Wayne Campbell)

115

If you see a tiny brown bird flitting around a log or root wad, you are probably looking at a Winter Wren. These birds are very small, brownish, stubby-looking creatures having short, thin, slightly curved bills. Their wings are short and rounded, their tails short and squarish. The Winter Wren's underside is a paler shade of the brown colour found upon its back and its entire plumage is beautifully barred. A rather inconspicuous feature is its buff-white eye stripe. In flight, the Winter Wren resembles a large bumblebee. In demeanour it is lively, energetic and inquisitive. Should you encounter one of these birds in its own territory, it will bob up and down incessantly, shouting *kip-kip*, then pause to observe your response. After determining that you are not a source of immediate danger, it will often begin its long-winded warble. Given the bird's diminutive size, its song is surprisingly loud, lasting up to eight or nine seconds; repeated four to six times a minute, it consists of a rapid succession of varied high and clear notes interspersed with short trills.

The Winter Wren is most at home in humid, temperate coastal rain forests containing mature and old-growth trees. It loves to forage on the ground and among thickets, shrubs, tangled roots and fallen trees, feeding mainly on insects and spiders. Soon after fledging, Winter Wren young return to the safety of their moss nest each night to sleep.

Like many of our year-round coastal residents, the Winter Wren's breeding season can begin as early as March in lowland forests. At this time one may expect to hear this bird's remarkable call for the first time. Although the Winter Wren is one of our smallest coastal birds, its assertive voice belies its tiny size, being among the loudest you will hear. Exercising a combination of shyness and

The Winter Wren resembles a large brown bumblebee. It has an amazingly loud and prolonged song for such a little bird. (Michael Wigle)

old showmanship, it sometimes sings from within the cover of dense foliage and it sometimes seeks out a high visible perch from which to project its song. When not singing, the male works to build a number of different nests for his potential mate to choose from. These nests are elaborate feather-lined structures constructed of twigs, leaves, mosses and grasses, each organized into the shape of a ball and having a small entrance hole in the side. Winter Wrens generally locate their nests among the roots of upturned trees, under old stumps or brush piles, or beneath mossy streambanks. Some are even built on outer branches.

The female Winter Wren lays five or six eggs. Although males do not participate in the incubation process, they do help to rear the young. Incubation requires between 14 and 17 days. After hatching, the young remain in the nest for another 15 to 20 days.

When winters are mild, the Winter Wren can be found in coastal valleys throughout the year. During colder winters, however, these birds retreat to more temperate coastal environs. When the weather is particularly cold, Winter Wrens roost together in order to share and conserve body heat.

In some mature to old-growth mixed stands of coniferous forest or in dense mixed woodlands, you may encounter the versatile Northern Goshawk and much smaller Sharp-shinned Hawk. Unlike the Red-tailed Hawk, which hunts by diving and pouncing on its prey, these forest hawks snatch their chosen victims, which may include squirrels, grouse and small birds, from the air. Although these two hawks are known to nest in most of our coastal valleys, few of their nests have been discovered to date.

A Northern Goshawk in its nest. This hawk frequently hunts in the old-growth forest for squirrels, small mammals, grouse and medium-sized birds.
(R. Wayne Campbell)

Near Burnt Bridge in Tweedsmuir Park, in the waning light of an early October afternoon, one of the authors spotted a Northern Goshawk hunting in an old-growth forest of Douglas-fir. The hawk moved from branch to branch with its characteristic flying style: three flaps and a glide, three flaps and a glide. In silence and stealth, it made its way toward a small red squirrel perched perilously near the end of a spruce branch. The unwitting squirrel was chattering loudly, scolding the human trespassing under its tree, perhaps fearing a raid on its cache of spruce cones. Preoccupied by the intruder, the little fellow didn't notice the goshawk gliding up from behind. Flapping its powerful wings to generate a final burst of speed, the large hawk suddenly struck its hapless prey. It disabled the poor squirrel with its sharply hooked bill and long pointed claws, then quickly flew off with its prize. In its hunting strategy the goshawk was reminiscent of a cougar, slowly but stealthily sneaking up on a deer, accelerating quickly and pouncing for the kill.

One of the goshawk's folk-names, "blue darter," is thought to allude to the bird's pouncing method of attack. W.L. McAtee suggests that the word "goshawk" derives from the Old English "goshafoc," meaning "goosehawk." The bird's name harks back to an era when European aristocrats flew goshawks at geese in the sport of falconry.

The adult Northern Goshawk is a little larger than a crow. Its upper surface is a dark slate grey; the under surface is a paler bluish grey and finely barred. The eyes of adults are red, topped by a prominent broad, white eyebrow. The goshawk's call sounds something like *kuk, kuk, kuk*. Goshawks appear to undertake a spring migration in March and an autumn migration in October, but these elusive birds are so rarely seen that the precise details of their migration remain a mystery.

Like the Northern Goshawk, the Sharp-shinned Hawk prefers to hunt in the edges and deep interiors of dense coniferous forests rather than in open fields or on the tidal flats in summer. Though it is robin-sized and thus much smaller than its closely related goshawk cousin, it is similarly shaped (having relatively long legs and short, rounded wings) and it uses basically the same stealthy hunting techniques to catch small birds and mammals. Adult birds have slate grey upper plumage, which shades to a rusty-barred coloration below. Although the adult Sharp-shinned Hawk has red eyes, it lacks the goshawk's prominent white eyebrow. The bird's call has been characterized as a series of higher *kik, kik, kik* notes.

Snags are standing dead trees that serve as important perching sites for birds of prey, and nesting sites for woodpeckers and a variety of cavity-nesting birds. (R. Wayne Campbell)

Small numbers of Sharp-shinned Hawks migrate along our coast in April, September and October. Sometimes they soar high overhead, circling the sky to take advantage of thermal updrafts. Because these birds are excellent flyers, French Canadians in eastern Canada have been known to call them by the nickname *bon volée* (meaning, roughly, "well-flown"). Occasionally, an individual Sharp-shinned Hawk will winter in the coastal valleys, where it hunts small birds on estuaries, at bird feeders and along the edges of forests. For the most part, however, coastal Sharp-shinned Hawks spend the cold months in wintering areas extending from southern Vancouver Island and the lower Fraser Valley to the tropical reaches of Mexico and Panama.

The woodpecker is another bird you can regularly expect to see and hear in old-growth valley-bottom coniferous forests. Two of the species encountered most often are the Pileated Woodpecker and the Hairy Woodpecker. The Pileated Woodpecker is a crow-sized bird often seen gliding downward from one large tree trunk to the base of another sizable tree or large rotten fir snag. Some of us recognize this bird as the one caricatured by Woody the Woodpecker of television cartoon fame. Woody's image is in fact a fairly accurate representation, but his boisterous call is a rather fanciful and embellished imitation of the real thing. Typically, before the Pileated Woodpecker begins to hammer upon tree trunks or deadfalls, it loudly cries *kik-kik-kik-kik-kik-kik*. This call is reminiscent of a flicker's call but it is louder, slower, lower-pitched and more irregular. The first barrage of wood banging enables the woodpecker first to test the quality of the wood and later to get access to food. Subsequently it stops, cocks its head as if listening for insect activity, then begins to hammer away again. In the process, wood chips fly and bark is pried off; periodically the bird pauses to nab a snack.

Sometimes these birds will hammer upon log homes and other human-made structures such as old barns and log retaining walls built to shore up a steep embankment. The damage that the woodpecker can inflict is most impressive. One of the authors will be forced to replace a log retaining wall in the not-too-distant future. In the meantime, however, he enjoys the pleasure of a large woodpecker's occasional close company—a fair compromise.

The Pileated Woodpecker has a distinctive appearance: its pointed crest, crown, forehead and moustache are bright red; the rest of its body is predominantly black, except where a pair of white stripes extend from each side of the face, below the eye and down the side of the neck. When the

The Pileated Woodpecker is North America's largest woodpecker. (Michael Wigle)

woodpecker is in flight, large white patches on the undersides of the wings flash in a highly noticeable fashion. The male of the species may be distinguished by the presence of a red moustache, which is lacking in the female. The Pileated Woodpecker is North America's largest woodpecker and, indeed, one of the largest woodpeckers in the world.

Campbell Fact

Pileated Woodpeckers mate for life and share the same territory all year. Each pair needs on average 500 hectares (1,250 acres) of mixed contiguous mature and old-growth forest with large dead trees for roosting and nesting. The oldest known Pileated Woodpecker reached the age of 9 years, 11 months.

Carpenter ants or wood-boring beetles are among the Pileated Woodpecker's favourite foods. A single adult bird can consume up to 2,500 ants at a single feeding. Of all coastal valley creatures, the Pileated Woodpecker is the best equipped to search out wood-destroying insects and their larvae hiding under tree bark. As it prepares for the hunt, the woodpecker first braces itself securely on the tree trunk using its short, sturdy legs and stiff tail. The bird's toes, equipped with sharp, recurved nails designed to dig deeply into the bark, allow it to climb straight up the tree. Two of its toes point forward and two backward; thus, as it hammers away with its powerful beak, the bird can rock back and forth, providing additional force. Like other woodpeckers, the Pileated has a thick skull, chisel-like beak and powerful head and neck muscles, enabling it to hammer holes into tree bark quickly and efficiently. In the bird's skull cavity, fluid-filled cushions help protect the brain from trauma-related injury. The bird also has a most impressive tongue, which can be extended to three to five times the length of its bill; it uses this appendage, which is covered with sticky saliva and armed with sharp barbs at the tip, to retrieve insects found in holes created during the hammering process.

Due to indiscriminate shooting by careless hunters, the Pileated Woodpecker was once a threatened species, but in recent years it has made a comeback. It is present year-round in most lowland coastal valleys, in very large collections of old trees.

Establishing a territory and courting take place in late March and April. A nest cavity is then excavated in a punky cored tree or dead snag, the male woodpecker providing most of the labour. Nest building is an arduous chore requiring up to 28 days. Ultimately the tree hole provides a fine nesting site: situated well above the ground, it is protected from the elements as well as incursions by most predators. Typically the Pileated Woodpecker locates its nest hole six to 10 metres (20 to 33 feet) up the main trunk of a large deciduous tree. The nest is generally spacious and sheltered: extending as far as 66 centimetres (26 inches) into the trunk, it is lined on the bottom with wood chips for comfort. Beginning around the end of April, the female Pileated Woodpecker lays an average of two to four eggs. The incubation period averages 18 days; fledging takes another 22 to 30 days.

In a practice common to all woodpecker species, adult Pileated Woodpeckers share the tasks of incubating and raising the young. Generally the male incubates at night and relieves his mate periodically during the daytime, enabling her to forage and feed.

The Hairy Woodpecker is elusive. If you catch a glimpse of it, consider yourself lucky, for this bird is one of the least-sighted members of the woodpecker family. It is challenging to spot partly because it is uncommon and partly because it prefers to live in the deep forest. Here, beyond the reach of prying human eyes, it feeds on the larvae of wood-boring insects and occasionally on small wild berries. The Hairy Woodpecker's call is similar to the Belted Kingfisher's, a strident and rattling *kweek kweek kweek kweek kweek*. Look for Hairy Woodpeckers searching for food upon the trunks and large branches of partly dead trees and snags. These birds locate food by tapping sharply on the wood and, presumably, listening for resonances indicating the presence of hollow insect tunnels just under the surface.

The Hairy Woodpecker's alarm call is a sharp, high-pitched *peek* sound. As it flies by, it noisily beats its wings, producing a *whuck-whuck-whuck* sound. In appearance this robin-sized bird has a yellowish bill and a black-and-white-striped head, its upper parts are black except for a white stripe in the centre of the back and some white spots on the wings, and its underparts are greyish white. The male

can be distinguished from the female by the red patch adorning the back of his head (a patch absent on the female).

The Hairy Woodpecker typically nests in cavities excavated high in the trunks of deciduous or coniferous trees. The female lays four or five round white eggs, typically between mid-April and mid-May. The incubation period averages 11 to 12 days and the fledging period lasts 24 to 27 days. Young Hairy Woodpeckers usually leave the nest by mid-June. The male helps the female with all aspects of nesting.

The association between woodpeckers and snags is an important one, for its helps to sustain the biological richness and diversity of coastal valley ecosystems. After a tree dies, it becomes a snag. In the process of deterioration, snag trees undergo a recognizable sequence of changes. First the needles, branches and bark slough off. Next the treetop falls off, after which the snag becomes progressively shorter and softer. Decomposition can take 20 to 200 years depending upon the age, size and condition of the original standing tree. An 80-year-old Douglas-fir having a breast-height diameter of 18 centimetres (7.2 inches) can take as long as 20 years to decompose and fall to the ground. A 200-year-old snag having a 47-centimetre (18.8-inch) diameter at breast height will take more than a century to do the same.

The Hairy Woodpecker is a challenge to find because it prefers to live deep within the mature rainforest. (Michael Wigle)

121

Woodpeckers utilize snags for many purposes, including foraging, roosting, courting, preening and nesting. During the spring months, woodpeckers can be heard "drumming." They search out particularly resonant snags or dead-topped trees and proceed to tap away. Researchers believe this "drumming" is an important aspect of woodpecker courtship and territorial claim, similar to the role played by the song of a warbler or sparrow. When drumming, a woodpecker will peck pieces of wood up to 10,000 times in a single day. This behaviour helps males to attract mates, facilitates the discovery and retrieval of food and enables woodpeckers to excavate cavities for spring nesting and winter roosting. Most woodpeckers carve out two or three extra cavities every year, presumably to keep predators unsure of their exact nesting location.

Snag cavities have many desirable attributes. Compared to the outside air, they are cool in summer and warm in winter. They also provide refuge from some predators. Not surprisingly, woodpeckers' snag cavities are also of great use to many other animals, making convenient overnight resting areas, fine winter homes, places of refuge from stormy weather and summer heat and, of course, safe locations for breeding. Chickadees, swallows, Brown Creepers, Red-breasted Nuthatches, Mountain Bluebirds, Vaux's Swifts, some diving ducks, mergansers, American Kestrels, owls, squirrels, chipmunks, martens, mice and salamanders all use snag holes for living and nesting. Some small mammals and birds also use these cavities as caches for the storage of prey and other kinds of food. It is no coincidence that the majority of our coastal winter birds also use snag cavities. The smaller birds (and mammals) tend to use cavities excavated by smaller woodpecker species, and animals of all sizes use snag cavities excavated by the larger woodpeckers.

Although woodpeckers are among the most important and versatile birds found in coastal valley forests, their numbers are showing local declines throughout the Pacific Northwest. This decline has been attributed to urbanization, agricultural development, clearcutting and removal of snags from forests, and other human activities. In recent years, an estimated 972,330 old-growth trees (measuring 1,264,029 cubic metres/1,643,238 cubic yards) have been harvested in the mid-coast areas of

Chickadees, swallows, creepers, nuthatches, bluebirds, swifts, diving ducks, mergansers, kestrels and owls all use woodpecker-excavated snag cavities for living and nesting. (R. Wayne Campbell)

The Red-breasted Sapsucker is sometimes referred to as a "Red-headed" woodpecker, which is a species found east of the Rocky Mountains. (Michael Wigle)

The home range for a pair of Pileated Woodpeckers may reach 400 hectares (1,000 acres) of mixed mature and old-growth forest with lots of snags. (R. Wayne Campbell)

British Columbia. To date, an estimated 60 percent of British Columbia's old-growth rain forest, 75 percent of Washington state's old-growth rain forest, 96 percent of Oregon's coastal rain forest and more than 96 percent of the great California state redwood forests have been logged. Obviously, this activity has affected bird species reliant on these habitats. A pair of Pileated Woodpeckers, for example, may require up to 400 hectares (1,000 acres) of continuous old-growth and mature forests to fulfill its foraging and nesting requirements.

Human-caused fragmentation of old-growth forests may also have an impact on the Brown Creeper, Townsend's Warbler, Pacific-slope Flycatcher, Northern Goshawk, Hairy Woodpecker and Varied Thrush, among other species. One cannot safely assume that these birds of the lower-elevation forests can simply relocate after vegetation in the valley bottoms has been altered. Studies reveal that there are significant differences not only between bird populations found in logged and unlogged forests, but between populations in the lower and higher elevations. A study completed in southwestern British Columbia analyzed the kinds and numbers of birds living in an old-growth western hemlock forest and in an adjacent higher-elevation old-growth mountain hemlock forest. Researchers found that, in general, the number and variety of bird species in the forest decreased with any increase in elevation. Researchers also found that the Red-tailed Hawk, Red-breasted Sapsucker, Pacific-slope Flycatcher, Steller's Jay, Common Raven, Swainson's Thrush, American Robin, Yellow-rumped Warbler, Black-headed Grosbeak and Purple Finch were found only in the western hemlock forest. At higher elevations, bird numbers fall because of lower plant diversity, which is caused by harsher living conditions: lower mean temperatures, more fog and cloud cover, more snow, more wind and less productive soils.

Presumably, cavity-dependent birds and other small animals will also be affected by the wide-

The Downy Woodpecker is smaller than the Hairy Woodpecker and has a proportionately smaller bill. The Downy also prefers younger mixed and deciduous forests. (Michael Wigle)

spread clearcutting of our coastal old-growth forests. In a typical coastal valley, you can expect to find about 25 species of birds that nest in snag cavities. When the forest is logged, many cavity-nesting birds must go elsewhere to find appropriate habitats. The common industrial practice of harvesting trees every 80 years means that forests never live long enough to produce the large snags that cavity-nesting birds require for their continued survival.

An obvious solution would be to leave more snags and nearby foraging areas intact when clearcutting forests. Unfortunately, however, snags are extremely dangerous to fallers and haulers because their branches are brittle and their bark can shatter at any time. Because they are dry and therefore flammable, snags also increase the risk of forest fires. As well, snags are valuable commodities in and of themselves: they can be salvaged for wood chip products and for firewood. Even if some snags were left standing in clearcut areas, studies have not yet been conducted to determine which species would be accommodated by the practice. Indeed, the task of preserving snags to satisfy the needs of various woodpecker and other cavity-dependent species would not be a simple one. To maintain populations of snag-dependent wildlife, forest managers would have to determine the appropriate number, species, size, age and distribution of snags. In order to maintain optimal population levels for our five coastal-valley woodpecker species (the Red-breasted Sapsucker, Downy and Hairy woodpeckers, Northern Flicker, Pileated and Three-toed woodpeckers), we would have to set aside an estimated 313 snags for every 40 hectares logged. To accommodate the needs of the Red-breasted Sapsucker and Pileated Woodpecker, 57 of these snags would have to be middle-aged (or hard); to accommodate the Downy Woodpecker, Hairy Woodpecker and Northern Flicker, 256 would have to be older (or soft). Furthermore, to satisfy the Downy Woodpecker's snag requirements, 16 snags would need to have a breast-height diameter of 27 centimetres (11 inches) or more; to serve the Hairy Woodpecker's habitat needs, 192 snags would have to be soft while at the same time having a breast-height diameter of 38 centimetres (15 inches) or more. But the list of avian habitat requirements does not end here. For the Red-breasted Sapsucker, 45 snags would have to be hard and have a breast-height diameter of 38 centimetres (15 inches) or more; for the Northern Flicker, 48 snags would have to be soft and have a diameter of 43 centimetres (17 inches) or more at the same height, and six snags would have to be hard and have a breast-height diameter of at least 43 centimetres (17 inches). Finally, for the Pileated Woodpecker, we would have to leave six hard snags with a breast-height diameter of 63 centimetres (25 inches). Even if we elected to manage forests in a way that would sustain minimal woodpecker densities (at, say, 10 percent of current population levels), and if we assumed that woodpeckers would share some snags, and if we assumed that woodpeckers would use snags left in clearcuts—our forest managers would have to leave 31 snags in every 40 hectares (100 acres) logged.

In the autumn of each year, a seemingly endless series of storms brings torrential rain from the Pacific Ocean to the coastal valleys, replenishing and revivifying the mountain streams. On all of the lower mountain slopes, you will see white ribbons of flowing water where bubbling streams and waterfalls send the plentiful rainfall back to the ocean. If the tempestuous weather breaks and the clouds dissipate, you will also see newly fallen snow shining clean and white upon the high shoulders of the mountains, a sure sign that winter has returned to the alpine country.

If you can tolerate the uncertainty of the weather, October is a fine month to search for birds by

Melting lakes and glaciers and seasonal storms provide water for the numerous streams and waterfalls of the raincoast. (R. Wayne Campbell)

visiting old-growth forests along salmon rivers. This is the time, fortuitously for many wildlife species, when scales covering many conifer cones open to release their seeds to the wind. Containing about 7,000 calories per kilogram of dry weight, the seeds thus released are a particularly important and nutritious food resource. Their high caloric value comes from their high fat content. Not surprisingly, conifer seeds are much sought after by myriad insects, birds and small mammals, each species having devised its own unique seed-obtaining strategy.

The best place to see these seed eaters in action is an old-growth forest. It may not be obvious at first glance, but much wildlife activity at this time of year revolves around the gathering and storing of conifer seeds. Many of the less visible seed eaters are insects. Adult cone beetles, for example, chew their way into the stems of developing pine cones in order to feed on the seeds, Coreid seed bugs use their long mouth parts to suck up the liquefied contents of developing and mature cone seeds, and the developing larvae of a whole host of fly species (including maggots, moths, worms and wasps) mine their way through the scales of maturing cones to feed upon the nutritious seeds within.

If you hear or see cones falling from the sky, look up—and look out. Chances are that in the boughs of a nearby tree, a red squirrel is methodically chewing off whole cones from branches and letting them fall to the ground. Later the squirrel will gather these harvested cones, eating some of the seeds immediately, but storing the vast majority of cones and seeds in large piles called middens. Squirrels locate their middens in shady, humid sites, presumably to prevent the cones from drying out and dropping their seeds too early. Generally squirrels use the same storage sites year after year; thus, over time, middens can become quite large—up to 48 cubic metres (62 cubic yards) in volume. Squirrels resort to these cone caches each year to survive the winter months.

Chipmunks are another local but rare seed-eating species residing along the extreme south mainland coast and at the heads of some deep inlets. Cautious and furtive, these small mammals make their way to fallen cones, stuffing the seeds into their cheek pouches and carrying them to food caches located under rocks, logs and roots. Like red squirrels, chipmunks seem to be constantly at work finding and storing food for the winter. Studies have shown that chipmunks store up to 70,000 seeds, nuts, plant tubers and dried insects in a single cache site.

The Hairy Woodpecker feeds soft animal foods to its growing young. Once fledged, the family eats a variety of berries, fruits, insects and seeds. (Mark Nyhof)

When night descends, other kinds of cone-eating mammals venture out into the darkness, including the northern flying squirrel, deer mouse and southern red-backed voles. Like squirrels and chipmunks, these nocturnal creatures work tirelessly to store seeds in small, scattered caches for use during the winter months.

Many different bird species also feed on conifer seeds, including nuthatches, chickadees, jays, nutcrackers, siskins and crossbills. Even woodpeckers resort to eating conifer seeds as a nutritious dietary supplement. The Hairy Woodpecker, for example, will try to open cone scales in order to obtain the seeds within; if unsuccessful, it will hammer away at the cone with its hard, sharp beak, shredding the cone to expose the seeds. Studies have shown that the Hairy Woodpecker is unique among coastal woodpecker species, spending as much time extracting cone seeds as it does searching for insects.

The Red-breasted Nuthatch, with its more slender bill, tends to be much more successful at removing seeds from the partially opened scales of Douglas-fir cones. Among the world's various nuthatches, our Red-breasted species is the only one that is truly dependent on conifer seeds in the winter. Often during the winter months, nuthatches flock together with chickadees; when food is scarce, these furtive creatures will snatch seeds right out of your hand before flying off to eat them.

Like the nuthatch, the Steller's Jay—our provincial bird—is quite adept at extracting seeds from cones. Fairly common along the coast, including our valleys, the Steller's Jay is a dark blue, strikingly handsome bird. In stature it is larger and more robust than a robin. The prominently crested head, upper chest, back and primary feathers are almost black, and the rest of the plumage is a deep, vivid blue. When sunshine reflects off this jay's prismatic plumage, the feathers on its wings, lower back and tail shine bluer than the flame of a welder's torch.

The coastal Steller's Jay lacks the white eyebrow found on the Steller's Jay that inhabits the interior of British Columbia. (Michael Wigle)

From late autumn to early spring, Steller's Jays are a familiar sight around towns and gardens. They usually gather in loud, raucous parties of three or four birds, shouting *shack-shack-shack* as they rove about. Around April, however, they disappear, pairing up with mates and retreating to coniferous forests near logging slash, streams and avalanche areas. During the breeding season they are notoriously secretive and shy.

Campbell Fact

During severe winter weather the Dark-eyed Junco must put on a layer of fat to insulate it and keep it warm. A junco may burn off as much as 15 percent of its body weight while roosting at night. When it awakens, the bird promptly starts feeding to regain the lost weight. The Dark-eyed Junco is the most common feeder bird in North America and our bird feeders certainly help prevent starvation during cold weather.

The Steller's Jay nest is built flat on a conifer branch (often a Douglas-fir) 2.5 to 5 metres (9 to 16 feet) above the ground. The nest consists of an outer bowl of twigs, rootlets and grasses plastered together with mud; it is lined with finer grasses, root fibres, leaves, pine needles, feathers and animal fur. In April or early May the female lays three to five greenish blue eggs whose shells may be adorned with small brownish spots or dots. The incubation period is 16 to 17 days in length, during which time the female incubates the eggs alone.

In the autumn, these jays make their way back to favourite human habitations, feeding on conifer seeds or whatever else they can find as they travel. Being active seasonal planners, they do not eat all of their food immediately; rather, they cache some in branch crotches, in crevices of bark or under rocks deep in the forest, for use at a later date.

Both Dark-eyed Juncos and Varied Thrushes are fond of seeds picked from aging cones lying on the ground. Indeed, studies have shown that up to 50 percent of the entire winter diet may consist of conifer seeds, their favourites coming from Douglas-fir cones. Juncos are among the bird species that have benefited from human activities. Throughout the year they can be found in logging slash areas, feeding on seeds from conifers, shrubs, grasses and forbs. Within five years of logging, junco densities will increase two to three times. As many as 40 seeds have been found in the gullet of a single junco, and it is estimated that these birds can consume up to 20 percent of all available conifer seeds. If you do the math, you will be impressed by their dietary intake: .6 bird per hectare (2.5 acres) times 40

Except for the white outer tail feathers, this juvenile Dark-eyed Junco does not look much like the dark-hooded adult. (Michael Wigle)

seeds per bird per day times 270 days equals 6,480 seeds per hectare per year. Remarkably, juncos and other seed-eating animals consume so many Douglas-fir seeds that they can affect local reforestation activities.

The Chestnut-backed Chickadee also feeds on cone seeds during the autumn and winter months. The conifer cone of choice for these small birds is the tiny one produced by the western hemlock. It is fun to watch them use their little bills to probe and pry seeds from these cones. Like the Steller's Jay, the Chestnut-backed Chickadee caches seeds for later meals. Chickadees are known as year-round omnivores, but they do depend heavily on conifer seeds during the winter months. It is estimated, indeed, that as much as half of their winter diet may consist of hemlock seeds. For an animal with such a tiny brain, the chickadee has a remarkably good memory: although it stashes surplus foods in all kinds of places, it seems to have no difficulty finding these caches throughout the year or even the following year.

When visiting the conifer forests of our coastal region, be sure to watch and listen for the arrival of a noisy, tightly bunched flock of Pine Siskins. In unison, the birds swoop down into the upper branches of a western redcedar tree to search for cones. The available seeds are extracted directly from partially opened hanging cones, the birds themselves often hanging upside down in order to carry out this work. As seed gatherers, Pine Siskins work in a deliberate and systematic manner: once a branch has been worked over, the flock moves down to the next branch and repeats the process. After a few

The Pine Siskin wanders across North America in search of edible cone crops. One bird banded in British Columbia was recovered in New York, and later in Texas. (Michael Wigle)

minutes, the flock moves on, leaving you in silence once again. Pine Siskins are small, heavily streaked, brownish grey finches that are easily recognized at a distance by their flocking behaviour and by their distinctive, questioning, wheezy *shreee*. The males and females of the species are similar in appearance. Look for subtly beautiful yellow edging across the base of the wing and tail feathers. Unlike chickadees, Pine Siskins are primarily seed eaters, favouring especially seeds of red alder, western hemlock, birches and dandelions. Studies suggest that western redcedar seeds are a crucial part of the bird's diet in the late autumn, winter and early spring. The Pine Siskin is a regular autumn and winter visitor to coastal valleys. An admirer of this bird, the renowned Canadian nature poet Archibald Lampman memorialized its winter foraging behaviour in a charming 19th-century couplet: "a rustle comes from a dusky clump, where the busy siskins feed, / And scatter the dimpled sheet of snow with the shells of the cedar-seed." Like other coastal finches, the Pine Siskin is an erratic wanderer; in some years it is commonly seen in the coastal valleys, but in other years it may be completely absent.

When you visit the older coniferous forests, be on the lookout for a noisy flock of sparrow-sized birds flying in an undulating fashion or exploring the upper branches of large Douglas-firs. If the birds announce their arrival with loud, sharp, repeating *jip-jip* notes, you may be certain that you have encountered a flock of Red Crossbills. These birds appear as dark silhouettes against the bright sky, their collective movements reminiscent of a parrot flock working its way through the jungle. Red Crossbills come here to feed upon Douglas-fir cones. Some of them will be seen picking cones from branches; others cling tightly to the hanging cones with their rather short legs and oversized feet. Some, as if emulating the Pine Siskin, will even hang upside down to feed, using their large bills to pry open cone scales. Within minutes of their arrival, you will likely be showered by debris from their frantic feeding activities.

Peering through binoculars, you will notice that Red Crossbill flocks contain two differently coloured birds. The adult males are mostly brick red, with blackish brown wings and tails and grey abdomens. The females are mostly greyish olive, with blackish brown wings and tails. The wings of both sexes lack any white markings. The curved upper and lower bills cross so that the tips overlap. Hence the bird's denomination.

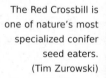

The Red Crossbill is one of nature's most specialized conifer seed eaters. (Tim Zurowski)

A nomadic finch, the crossbill travels in flocks that roam at will over northern coniferous forests, searching for mature cone seeds to feed upon. Depending on the season and the state of coniferous cone crops, the crossbill will also feed on alder, birch and willow seeds, as well as orchard fruit and even insects. But it is the crossbill's ability to extract seeds from conifer cones that makes it one our most fascinating and specialized forest birds.

The crossbill's uniquely shaped bill enables it to extract and eat conifer seeds with remarkable efficiency. It begins by putting its bill just under the tough cone scale. Then, by opening its jaw and bill, it is able to pry the scale up off the cone, exposing the seed. Finally, the crossbill uses its long, muscular tongue to scoop out the seed. It may swallow the seed immediately or store it in a special seed sac, called an *oesophageal diverticulum*, at the back of its throat. Seeds stored here can be regurgitated later when the bird is resting in a sheltered spot. A crossbill may eat up to 3,000 seeds in a single day.

As a species, crossbills do not appear to follow any kind of predictable migration pattern; instead, they wander from valley to valley and forest to forest looking for food. The flocks that arrive on British Columbia's coast may have come from hundreds or even thousands of kilometres east or south of the region. Red Crossbills don't stay for long, so enjoy them while you can.

When cones are abundant, the Red Crossbill stays and nests. It has one of the longest breeding periods of all coastal birds: courtship, breeding and nesting may take place anytime between early February and mid-August. This reproductive flexibility allows crossbills to take advantage of cone-rich areas, because in some years the food supply is not sufficient for the raising of a family.

Three to five eggs, coloured a pale bluish white with brownish specks and blotches, is the normal clutch size for this boreal species. The female sits on these eggs for 12 to 15 days; during this time the male occasionally assists with incubation duties and he regularly feeds his nesting mate.

Newly hatched young are fed by both of their parents, who work together to bring them a delectable regurgitated porridge of seeds, insects and intestinal fluids. Growing rapidly, the hatchlings will be ready to join the wandering flocks at about 17 days of age. In particularly good cone years, a pair of Red Crossbills may raise two broods.

Recent scientific studies indicate that the Red Crossbills of western North America may in fact represent nine separate species. Each discrete sub-population appears to specialize in feeding preferences, each has its own unique call, breeding varies, and there are subtle bill and skull differences between groups. The Red Crossbill species as a whole thus provides a notable example of the process of natural selection, by which creatures evolve to suit their particular niches.

One of the Red Crossbill subspecies is a large bird that prefers to feed in ponderosa pine forests; a slightly smaller form is found in coastal Douglas-fir forests; another frequents lodgepole pine woods; yet another form feeds mainly on tiny cones of the western hemlock; finally, there is a form that prefers cones found in Sitka spruce forests.

Apart from the whitebark pine, which enjoys a unique symbiotic relationship with the Clark's Nutcracker, most conifer trees are quite vulnerable in relation to the species their seeds support. At

A conifer heavily laden with cones. (R. Wayne Campbell)

first glance it may even seem that conifers have few options in protecting themselves from seed-hungry predators. But scientists hypothesize that over hundreds of millions of years conifers have in fact evolved some ingenious strategies of self-protection. One obvious defence is to cover the delicate seeds with an armour of tough, tight-fitting woody scales; another is to protect the cones by covering them with sticky resin, thus making the handling and eating of seeds more difficult. It is worth noting that most of our conifer species, especially those having larger and more nutritious seeds, such as firs, whitebark pine, Douglas-fir and Engelmann spruce, have resin-coated cones.

Another protective strategy involves physically reinforcing cones against seed predators. For example, the Douglas-fir's cone scales are thickest and hardest where squirrels normally bite them off. Since squirrels also bite off cones at their base or stem, cones tend to develop a lot of thickened woody armour here as well. The lodgepole pine has arguably the toughest cone for any mammal to chew through or any bird to open up. On the east side of the Coast Mountains, lodgepole pines produce cones that are practically impenetrable, requiring fire to melt the pitch sealing their seed scales inside. In contrast, cones produced by pines located on the most westerly slopes, where fire is a much less common occurrence, are much softer and contain a greater number of seeds.

Yet another protective strategy is reflected in the fact that each kind of conifer tree produces cones unique in size, shape and method of seed dispersal. In some years, cones may not be produced. But in good years, predators are swamped with more food than they can possibly consume.

All of the conifer species—including Douglas-fir, grand fir, western hemlock, western redcedar, Sitka spruce and coastal lodgepole pine—tend to have alternating years of abundant and meagre cone production. Interestingly, rates of cone production among all of these species follow the same general patterns or phases, the highest and lowest cone-producing seasons occurring simultaneously for all conifers.

The large, luscious spring cones of the Sitka spruce. (Michael Wigle)

Two factors seem to work together to determine the unpredictable variation of conifer tree cone production. The first is the fact that conifers cannot usually produce large numbers of cones for two years in a row. Presumably they require more than one growing season to accumulate the energy reserves necessary to produce a large cone crop. The second factor is the inherent unpredictability of the weather itself. Good cone-producing years are often associated with low rainfall in late spring and early summer, and little or no spring frost.

Studies have shown that in years of abundant cone production, animal predators take from one to 10 percent of the crop. In contrast, during low cone-producing years, seed predators can consume a much larger portion of the harvest. During years of low cone production, the affected animals must adapt by finding an alternative food source. Low cone-production years tend to coincide with low populations of seed predators, especially squirrels.

Some mammals deal with cone shortages by storing seeds during times of plenty or by switching to other kinds of food when necessary. Although red squirrels prefer Douglas-fir and Sitka spruce seeds, they can supplement their diets with such food items as deciduous seeds, conifer sprouts and buds, berries, bird eggs, nestlings, mushrooms, sap and insects. Mice, voles, chipmunks and other mammals also change their diet, depending more directly upon vegetation when cone seed supplies are low.

Unlike seed-storing mammals, most bird species do not store conifer seeds for future use. Instead, some species, like Pine Siskins, may travel thousands of kilometres to find a conifer forest rich with food. Other species that move about looking for conifer seeds include the Common Redpoll, Purple Finch, Evening Grosbeak and Pine Grosbeak.

Studies have shown that old-growth Douglas-fir forests produce 20 to 30 times more cones than similar-sized second-growth forests 50 to 100 years old. They start producing cones at 20 to 30 years of age and reach a maximum output at 90. In the interest of promoting animal welfare, humans must consider the conservation of cone forests.

A male Evening Grosbeak. Like the Pine Siskin and Red Crossbill, the Evening Grosbeak travels widely across North America in search of edible buds and seeds. (Michael Wigle)

6
Birds of the Second-Growth Deciduous Forest

Previous pages:
Black-capped
Chickadee.
(R. Wayne Campbell)

In the month of April, valleys on the raincoast undergo a remarkable trans-formation. As winter withdraws, a patchy carpet of green begins to cover the ground and a faint, hazy green halo surrounds the tips of tree branches. Then, quite suddenly, spring arrives in full force. Emerging leaf buds open wide and bright green foliage begins to grow rapidly. In and along the forest edges, all kinds of herbaceous plants spring from the ground, unfolding before your eyes; and on the clifftops, lush carpets of rain-soaked mosses take on a brilliant, almost fluorescent shade of green.

With the arrival of early May, the skeletal remains of last year's plants are barely visible among the new growth, which springs up from well-established perennial root systems, or from annual seeds deposited the year before. Coastal valley fields and lawns are now dressed in various shades of lively green. A lush ground cover of forbs and shoots forms over the valley floor. The shoots, leaves and stems of these young, fast-growing plants are perfect bird food: succulent, easily digestible and nutritious. The emergence of all this greenery coincides, in turn, with the arrival of billions of plant-eating insects, which emerge from winter hiding places or from eggs deposited the year before.

Above: The emergence of new green leaves along the raincoast coincides with the arrival of many different kinds of greenish yellow insect-eating birds. (Michael Wigle)

This explosion of plant and insect life attracts myriad greenish yellow insect-eating birds, which migrate to our coastal valleys from Central and South America. At this time of year there are enough insects to feed the migrating birds and help later to feed their rapidly growing young. These summer visitants join the year-round resident birds that have managed to survive the long, harsh winter. These birds all fill different niches for breeding, feeding and resting. The pace of life is hectic, as if the birds know instinctively that they must race against time to court, mate and raise young before autumn comes and food supplies change.

Campbell Fact

The amount of time a bird spends incubating or brooding in the nest varies from 60 to 85 percent. During its reproductive period, the Song Sparrow spends 75 percent of its time sitting (average shifts of nine minutes off and 29 minutes on), and the American Robin spends 80 percent (11 minutes off and 44 minutes on).

Over the course of their evolution, birds have developed diverse and ingenious ways of capturing insects. Most flycatchers sit patiently on tree perches, waiting for insects to fly past; when a winged morsel is sighted, the bird quickly intercepts it and then returns to the same spot to wait for another feeding foray. Cedar Waxwings, American Kestrels and even tiny Northern Pygmy-Owls hunt insects in a similar fashion. In contrast, the American Robin, Varied Thrush and the spotted brown thrushes all forage for insects on the ground. In the forest, woodpeckers, nuthatches and creepers search for insects hiding deep in the furrows and crevices of tree trunks and large branches. Some warblers, for their part, tirelessly pluck tiny insects from around newly opened leaves and colourful blossoms, sharing trees with vireos, which feed on larger insects gleaned from the undersides of leaves and from crevices in the bark. Chickadees, kinglets, Winter Wrens and Western Tanagers carefully search leaves and branches for insects as well.

The only insects that songbirds have not been able to utilize to any great extent are the nocturnal species, those insects that wait until night falls to begin their mating and feeding flights. But this does not mean that nighttime insects are safe from predators; on the contrary, when darkness descends and the feathered insectivores retire to rest, many kinds of bats take possession of the skies.

A female Mountain Bluebird. This bluebird is a rare spring and autumn visitor to the raincoast. Look for it around airports, log-littered beaches, farm fields and other open areas adjacent to mixed deciduous forests.
(R. Wayne Campbell)

Because they consume enormous quantities of insects, avian predators function as an important local natural pesticide in the forest ecosystem. Recent studies have shown that when birds are kept out of a deciduous forest, each tree harbours twice as many leaf-eating insects. In only one year, these expanded insect populations will consume twice the amount of available leaf biomass, causing deciduous trees to slow noticeably in their annual growth. Researchers have also concluded that thriving bird populations enhance the growth of some trees (especially juvenile oaks) by consuming leaf-damaging insects.

Many male birds establish breeding territories in the same general areas year after year, and perhaps generation after generation. One study found that more than 70 percent of male Red-winged Blackbirds, upon returning to our coastal marshes, reclaim the same territory they held the year before. This annual territorial return makes perfect sense: why would a bird gamble on raising a family in a totally new breeding territory when it could simply go back to a site that is both familiar and proven?

This male Red-winged Blackbird has staked out his territory and is now defending it with song and display on a small woodland pond. (Michael Wigle)

The size of the breeding territory varies from species to species and usually reflects the minimum amount of habitat needed to raise a family. Breeding swallows require a small nesting territory—usually the area just around their nests. The summer breeding and foraging territory of the American Robin, Dark-eyed Junco, and most sparrows, warblers and vireos appears to be less than .8 hectare (2 acres). The Winter Wren's breeding territory is slightly larger, comprising less than 1.2 hectares (3 acres); the Dusky Flycatcher requires 1.2 to 2.4 hectares (3 to 6 acres), the Downy Woodpecker requires 2.8 hectares (7 acres) and the Black-capped Chickadee 4 hectares (10 acres). The living space required for bigger birds ranges from 8 hectares (20 acres) for the Northern Flicker to 400 hectares (1,000 acres) for the Pileated Woodpecker and larger owls. Remarkably, the Northern Goshawk's total home range can be 39 square kilometres (15 square miles) in size—a veritable macrocosm of forest terrain.

Some female birds arrive in the coastal valleys to find the males singing their hearts out, assertively establishing their breeding territories. To determine which territories will be the best child-rearing sites, females can deploy two modes of inquiry: they can inspect each territory to assess the quality of its nesting habitat and available food, or they can investigate the "fitness" of the male who is claiming

the territory. Most female birds appear to do the latter, listening to the male's song, inspecting his appearance, even dancing with him before determining his appropriateness as a mate. The female's freedom to choose her mate, then, appears to account for all the bird songs issuing from the forest, and at the same time to explain why some male birds are dressed so brightly and dance so exquisitely each spring.

A female Purple Finch. (Michael Wigle)

Because each bird species has its own unique (although variable) song, female birds can easily identify and locate male birds of their own species. Once a female has identified a prospective mate, she listens carefully to his song, for the strongest and most robust males tend to be the ones who can sing the longest and loudest. Therefore, the virtuoso singers are the most successful at attracting mates.

Before mating can successfully occur, however, the male must deploy other courtship strategies as well. In many songbird species, the courting male shows off his plumage. Exactly what the female finds attractive about ostentatious plumage displays seems to vary from species to species. Some females appear to favour the most colourful male suitors, a preference that helps to account for the bright red heads of the Purple Finch, Pine Grosbeak, Western Tanager and Red Crossbill. Females of other species seem more interested in the size of the male's ornamentation, which helps to explain the long, deeply forked tail of the Barn Swallow and the extravagant plumes adorning the head of the Great Blue Heron.

At the end of the mating season, many males lose their colourful breeding plumage because it is no longer needed, and they can blend into the forest background more easily during the non-breeding season. Because nesting females need to be inconspicuous when sitting on their eggs, their plumage tends to be comparatively plain, drab, or more subtly coloured than that of their male counterparts.

In most songbird species, the female chooses the nesting site. No one knows why this is the case. Usually she also does most of the nest building. Nests vary in size, shape and construction, but each species has a unique kind of nest, so by studying a nest's form, materials and location, experienced naturalists can determine the species that built the nest—sometimes long after the family has left. Nests are essential to bird welfare and survival, providing a safe location for fragile and delicate eggs and helping to keep them sheltered during incubation.

The nests of the Mallard and most other dabbling ducks are down-lined hollows or depressions in the grassy ground near the edge of the water. The nests of the Ruffed Grouse, Killdeer and Spotted Sandpiper are also simple hollows in the ground lined with grasses, leaves and sometimes a few feathers for comfort and warmth. Loons, grebes and coots nest on platforms of mud, reeds and other debris, on islets or among reeds and cattails along the margins of lakes. Thrushes, including the American Robin and Varied Thrush, construct bulky cups of mosses, grasses, rootlets, twigs and mud. The waxwings, jays and nutcrackers also make bowl-shaped nests but use mostly twigs and rootlets. The nest of the flycatcher is a neat and compact cup of mosses, rootlets and grasses and is usually located in the fork of a shrub or out on a branch.

Vireo nests are neat basket-like cups that hang from forked twigs on trees or bushes. The nests of the American Dipper and kinglet look like bulky balls of mosses; those belonging to the wood-warblers and some of our sparrows are neat feather-lined cups made of plant stems, plant down, grasses, mosses and fine bark.

Unlike domestic poultry, songbirds lay eggs only during a well-defined breeding season. The number of eggs per clutch varies depending on the species. Most of the smaller birds lay one egg per day until the clutch is complete. Larger birds such as the Great Blue Heron lay one egg every second day. Ducks typically lay six to 12 eggs, shorebirds four, songbirds between four and six and hummingbirds two eggs per clutch.

Ground-nesting birds such as grouse, Killdeer, sandpipers, nighthawks and gulls all have buff- or brown-speckled eggs that are nicely camouflaged and therefore difficult for predators to detect. Songbird species building cup-shaped nests usually produce eggs adorned with spots and speckles. The eggs of burrow nesters, like some swallows and the Belted Kingfisher, are pure white.

Male songbirds are among the most devoted and loyal fathers in the animal kingdom. Among our coastal perching birds, only the Winter Wren, Red-winged Blackbird and Brewer's Blackbird are polygamous. Male birds from the other 70 or so species appear to bond with a single female for the entire nesting period. But this monogamy does not necessarily entail sexual fidelity. As in many human societies, extramarital "affairs" are not uncommon, and studies suggest that both male and female birds often sneak away to mate with attractive neighbours. The American Redstart, Common

The Killdeer, like many ground-nesting birds, has well-camouflaged eggs and chicks. (R. Wayne Campbell)

Yellowthroat, Violet-green Swallow, Hermit Thrush, American Robin, Dark-eyed Junco, Song Sparrow and White-crowned Sparrow are known to have engaged in such behaviour. However, their mates usually change from year to year.

Males of most songbird species participate in nest building. They may also share in the labour of egg incubation and care of young. Some male songbirds also feed their female partners during the incubation period; these include the Olive-sided Flycatcher, Pacific-slope Flycatcher, Northern Rough-winged Swallow, Tree Swallow, Violet-green Swallow, Steller's Jay, Common Raven, Black-capped Chickadee, American Dipper, Red-breasted Nuthatch, Brown Creeper, Winter Wren, Hermit Thrush, American Robin, Cassin's Vireo, Red-eyed Vireo, Wilson's Warbler, Common Yellowthroat, Brewer's Blackbird, Western Tanager, Pine Siskin, Red Crossbill and Song Sparrow.

Most males of single families stand guard while their mates take time off from incubation and child-rearing activities, thus helping the females replenish energy reserves used up while laying the eggs. Among polygamous songbirds, males accompany foraging females far less often; not surprisingly, the

The Yellow Warbler breeds near water in mixed deciduous forests. This species is showing population declines due to loss of its wetland habitats. (R. Wayne Campbell)

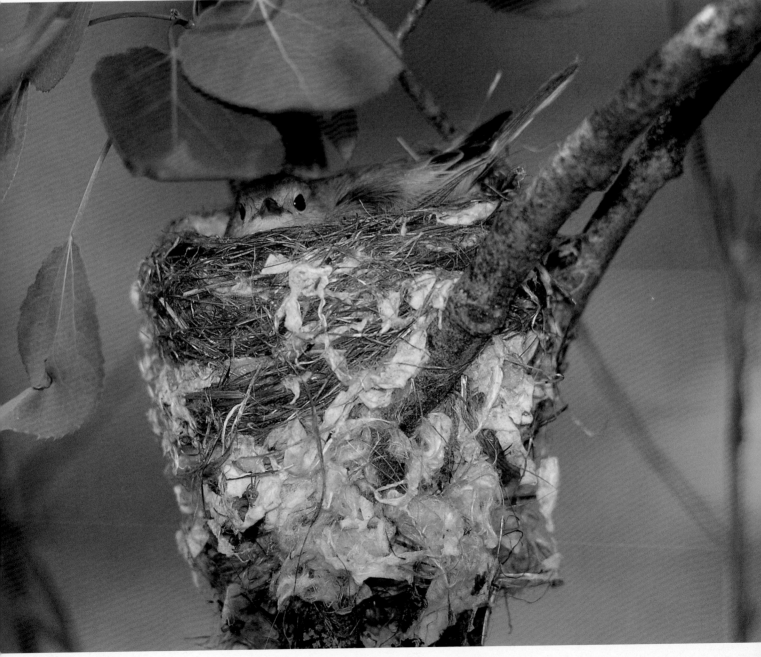

females of these species are more likely to be preyed upon. Studies have shown that survival rates for offspring are much higher when both parents participate in the rearing of their young.

Among species in which the sexes are different colours, known as sexually dimorphic songbirds (the Western Tanager, Red-winged Blackbird, wood-warblers and others), males appear to be much less helpful in nesting and child-rearing activities than the males of species whose colours do not differ between the sexes. Presumably we can infer that because brightly coloured males are more likely to draw attention to nesting sites, it makes good sense for them to stay away.

In the interval between the laying and hatching of eggs, female birds spend most of their time incubating their future offspring. A songbird's body temperature averages about 37.8°C (100°F); by using a bare incubation patch on her lower belly, the female can constantly keep her eggs warm and thus help them to develop. The incubation period for most of our songbirds ranges from 11 to 14 days. By comparison, waterbirds sit on their eggs for longer periods, usually four to five weeks. When an egg is ready to hatch, the chick pecks its way out of the shell using a small "tooth" on top of its bill. Songbird chicks tend to be born bare, blind and helpless, needing constant brooding and care before they can face the world. In contrast, grouse, plover and shorebird chicks are able to run around within hours of hatching.

By June, most songbirds along the coast are busy constructing nests, laying and incubating eggs, or feeding youngsters. Birdsong fills the woods less often as the nesting season progresses, for the male singers become more secretive and devote more time to feeding their young. Many predators search for helpless nestlings. Among the most versatile nest robbers are the ravens, crows, jays, squirrels, hawks and martens. Surrounded by such predators, songbirds raise their young as quickly as possible; indeed, such pressures may help to explain why songbird parents devote so much time to feeding their hungry offspring during daylight hours. Most songbird nestlings grow quickly and leave their protective nest at two to three weeks of age. Young warblers develop even more swiftly, leaving the nest after only eight to 10 days. In contrast, young flickers may stay in the nest for as long as 27 days before attempting their first flight.

A recently fledged Black-capped Chickadee waits to be fed. This is the chickadee species most frequently seen foraging in raincoast deciduous forests. (R. Wayne Campbell)

The Song Sparrow, American Robin, Common Yellowthroat, Dark-eyed Junco, Barn Swallow, Golden-crowned Kinglet, Yellow-rumped Warbler, Red-winged Blackbird, White-crowned Sparrow, Warbling Vireo and Swainson's Thrush are among the few birds that continue to sing throughout the summer months. Their summer residence in our coastal regions is also more protracted than that of other migrant birds. These species typically raise two broods of young per year. It is likely no coincidence, then, that they are among our most common and widespread summer visitants.

May is the best month for birdwatchers to visit a second-growth deciduous or mixed deciduous-coniferous forest. Such forests are plentiful, for most coastal valleys have been logged off at least once. Here, stands of red alder, black cottonwood, young western hemlock, Douglas-fir, spruce and western redcedar are dominant. More than 50 kinds of birds feed and nest in these diverse coastal forests.

When visiting second-growth areas in the early springtime, listen for chickadees calling from the tops of alder and cottonwood trees. It is not uncommon to see whole flocks of these birds foraging busily among the new foliage. These birds hunt for spiders, insect eggs and larvae, grubs and caterpillars.

Studies indicate that one chickadee can eat several hundred insect larvae in a single day.

Four species of chickadee visit our coastal forests, but only two are often seen: the Black-capped and Chestnut-backed chickadees, both of which can be seen year-round. Occasionally the Mountain Chickadee and Boreal Chickadee wander to the coast, visiting only during the winter when very cold weather forces them into valley bottoms. As their names suggest, the Mountain Chickadee is a bird of high-elevation, semi-open coniferous forests, and the Boreal Chickadee lives mostly in boreal spruce forests located to the east of the Coast Mountains.

Male and female chickadees look alike and are the most recognizable and familiar of our birds. They are small, active sparrow-sized birds with short, stubby bills; short, rounded wings; and long, slender tails. The Black-capped Chickadee, to quote John Burroughs, wears the colours of "ashes and jet." Its crown, neck, throat and bib are jet black; its cheeks, neck sides and undersides are white; and its wings and tail are a solid slate grey. The Chestnut-backed Chickadee displays rich chestnut-brown back and flanks.

In addition to differences in colouring, chickadee species can be distinguished by their foraging habits. The Black-capped Chickadee instinctively forages in crevices in the bark of deciduous trees, and the Chestnut-backed Chickadee prefers to forage in open clusters of conifer needles. Despite these differences, it is not unusual to see Chestnut-backed and Black-capped Chickadees coexisting in the same forest. Research has shown that when such coexistence occurs, the Chestnut-backed species feeds higher in the tree and more often on outer branches than its Black-capped relative.

Throughout Canada, the Black-capped Chickadee has garnered a variety of sonic folk-names (names inspired by the sound of its call). In Newfoundland it is sometimes called a "pig-a-pee"; in agrarian Nova Scotia it occasionally goes by the name "sow the wheat"; in Quebec one of its folk-names is a questioning "qui es tu?" ("who are you?"); and in some parts of western Canada it is called

Campbell Fact
During its life, the Black-capped Chickadee must face threats from predators, harsh weather, food shortages, diseases, accidents and a host of other hazards. Researchers know from studying banded birds that nearly half of the population dies each year and that on average the lifespan of this diminutive bird is about two years. It is a rare chickadee that lives to its maximum age of nine years!

A maturing second-growth deciduous forest, showing the layering of shrubs and trees that attracts a variety of foraging and nesting species.
(Michael Wigle)

a "phoebe." Since all of these names are onomatopoeic or sonic, the Black-capped Chickadee is living proof that different cultural and linguistic groups hear things differently and that language, far from being rooted in nature, is a highly conventional and arbitrary social phenomenon.

During the greater part of the year, chickadees can be seen travelling in small flocks. Just before the nesting season starts, however, these flocks break up as each nesting pair goes off to establish its own safe breeding territory. If you are lucky, you might, with the help of a flashlight, find a brooding chickadee sitting in a nesting cavity in a rotting tree. If the bird feels threatened, she may quickly open her mouth and hiss loudly at you, all the while moving her head back and forth. Her sounds and movements, reminiscent of gestures made by a threatened or threatening snake, may be a defence mechanism to scare away any squirrels or weasels looking for an easy meal.

In trees where wood is particularly punky, chickadees excavate their own nests; otherwise they use abandoned woodpecker nests and naturally occurring cavities. Chickadees line the bottom of their nesting holes with mosses and other soft materials, including mammal fur or bird feathers. In April and May, the female lays six or seven eggs, which are lightly dotted with reddish brown spots. Although the female is responsible for all incubation duties, her mate helps to feed the young once they have hatched. The chickadee's incubation period lasts for 12 to 14 days. The young develop rapidly, leaving the safety of the nest in about 15 days. Two broods may be raised in a single year.

The Black-capped Chickadee lays five to 10 eggs, which are white with reddish brown spots and always placed on soft mosses. (R. Wayne Campbell)

Listen for the Swainson's Thrush in late May and early June, soon after it arrives from wintering grounds in Mexico, Peru, Bolivia, Paraguay and western Brazil. Among the last of our summer songbirds to return to the British Columbia coast each spring, the Swainson's Thrush is something of a "Johnny-come-lately." Like the Varied Thrush, this bird is fond of mature coniferous forests growing in coastal valley bottoms; but it is also commonly sighted near towns, along the edges of fields and pastures, and among red alder and willow thickets. Its song consists of a distinctive, upwardly spiralling series of flute-like notes repeated eight to 14 times per minute and sometimes introduced by a quick introductory note sounding like *whit.*

From up in the conifers, the Ruby-crowned Kinglet sings *tee-tee-tee tew tew-tew-tew tidadee ti-dadee ti-dadee.* According to some listeners, this song sounds like *liberty liberty tout suite.* As in the

Winter Wren, the Ruby-crowned Kinglet's song is surprisingly loud for such a tiny bird. In addition to its diminutive size, its identifying physical characteristics include a short tail and a fine, black, pointed bill. Repeatedly flicking its wings as if unable to decide whether to fly away, the Ruby-crowned Kinglet is a rather anxious-looking bird, and its alarm call is a husky sounding *did-it*. As for its plumage colouring, its upper parts are painted an olive grey and its lower parts display a whitish buff hue. In addition the kinglet has a conspicuous white eye-ring and a pair of white wing bars. If you are fortunate, you may catch a passing glimpse of a partially concealed scarlet patch on the top of the bird's head.

Unlike the Golden-crowned Kinglet, which confines its springtime activities to the late mature and old-growth forest canopy, the Ruby-crowned Kinglet is likely to be found in more deciduous habitats. This bird often frequents the edges of mature and second-growth forests, as well as thickets of tall willow and red alder shrubbery, but it is particularly fond of large Sitka spruce trees, which are among its favourite nesting sites.

The nest of the Ruby-crowned Kinglet resembles a thick, deep cup looking somewhat like a globular ball of mosses. A skilled builder, this bird loosely weaves together mosses, lichens, fine barks and other botanical matter to form the ball; then it uses spider webs and plant fibres to bind these materials together. On the inside, the nest is lined with animal hair or feathers. Generally it is tucked under the tip of a coniferous branch, well off the ground. On average, six to nine spotted eggs are laid in each nest. The incubation and fledging periods are each about 12 days in duration. When the young are born, both parents tend them, busily providing them with such delicacies as spiders, leaf bugs, leafhoppers, aphids, flies, insect eggs, larvae and pupae.

A hardy creature, the Golden-crowned Kinglet is a year-round resident who doesn't seem to mind our cold, damp coastal winters; in contrast, its Ruby-crowned cousin prefers to migrate to warmer southerly climates (although a few may spend the winter in extreme southwestern British Columbia). Nevertheless, the Ruby-crowned Kinglet is one of our earliest spring migrants. In some years its loud song can be heard as early as late March.

Warbling Vireos sing incessantly, even from the nest while sitting on their eggs. All vireo nests look like small hanging baskets. (R. Wayne Campbell)

Another common and vocal songbird is the Warbling Vireo. Its song is a long, continuous musical warble consisting of a rapid series of *twees* that gradually rise in pitch and intensity. The song is reminiscent of the Purple Finch's, but it is less energetic, more hoarse and not as loud. The Warbling Vireo is a small, rather plain-looking sparrow-sized bird. Its colouring—greenish grey above and whitish below—matches the deciduous foliage in which it forages; thus, it can be difficult to spot. Distinctive features include a broad, white eye stripe and dark brown eyes. A vociferous creature, it tends to sing incessantly.

Warbling Vireos arrive from their wintering grounds in El Salvador, Guatemala, Mexico and other Central American locations. They love to frequent mature deciduous forests, where they can forage for crawling insects hidden among the leaves of the high canopy.

After an elaborate courtship display, mating occurs and nest construction begins. In its hanging nest, the female lays three to five dull white eggs whose shells are sparsely dotted with brown near the large end. The incubation process, carried out by both sexes, takes from 12 to 14 days. This bird is easy to find in the summer, because it warbles from the nest while sitting on its eggs.

The Warbling Vireo's nest, located far out on a branch, is a delicate structure made of bark strips, leaves, grasses, mosses and lichens that are all bound together with spider webbing. It is always

The Ruby-crowned Kinglet (above) and Warbling Vireo (left) are two very vocal songbirds that are commonly seen in second-growth deciduous forests. (Top: Tim Zurowski; bottom: Michael I. Preston)

Above: Cassin's Vireo
was formerly known
as the Solitary Vireo.
(Tim Zurowski)

Right: The song of
the Red-eyed Vireo
is sometimes con-
fused with that of
the American Robin.
(Edgar T. Jones)

suspended by its rim from a small forked branch. When exchanging incubation duties, the birds hop from branch to branch, flicking their wings and tails, indicating that it is time for a change.

The Warbling Vireo is one of three kinds of vireo that one can expect to see along the coast. The others are the rare Cassin's Vireo and Red-eyed Vireo. These birds resemble some of the duller-coloured warblers, but upon close examination you will notice that the vireo's bill is comparatively shorter, thicker and heavier, having a tiny hook at the end. In contrast to wood-warblers, vireo males and females look alike: both sexes are plain-coloured, usually displaying dull olive green plumage above and greyish white plumage below. With the exception of the Cassin's Vireo, which has whitish eye-stripes or eye-rings and light wing bars, vireos have no streaking or spotting on the plumage.

Vireos spend most of their time among the outer branches of deciduous trees and shrubs, searching the bark and foliage for caterpillars and slow-crawling insects. These birds move through the foliage in a more deliberate, less hurried fashion than the wood-warblers.

When the experienced birder thinks of the moist forests of successional red alder and black cottonwood, the Warbling Vireo inevitably comes to mind. But when contemplating the more mature coniferous forests, one might think of the rarer Cassin's Vireo. This is the vireo species most likely to be associated with coniferous forests, for it nests almost exclusively in conifers, generally within 4.5 metres (15 feet) of the forest floor. Like other coastal vireos, the female Cassin's lays three to five eggs having brownish spots, mostly at the large end. Common summer visitors to many of our coastal valleys, Cassin's Vireos first arrive in late April and early May after completing arduous journeys from wintering grounds ranging from California to Nicaragua. A sparrow-sized, dull-coloured songbird, the Cassin's Vireo may be identified by several features: its back, rump and upper tail are a dull olive colour; its sides and flanks have a yellow tinge; and its underparts are greyish white. The bird's distinctive field marks include a blue-grey head, bold white eye-rings and pale wing bars. The song of the Cassin's Vireo is somewhat reminiscent of the robin's, consisting of short, slurred, whistled phrases. Its song is also similar to, but lower-pitched and less varied than, that of the Red-eyed Vireo.

To see the Red-eyed Vireo, turn your gaze inland toward the drier eastern parts of our long coastal inlets. Like its Warbling relative, the Red-eyed Vireo migrates in the autumn to South America, where its wintering grounds extend from Colombia and Venezuela to eastern Peru and western Brazil. The Red-eyed Vireo's song is sometimes confused with the robin's, sounding a bit like *See me, hear me, see you, vireo* repeated over and over again. The short, abrupt phrases are punctuated with pauses, giving the impression that the bird is asking questions and then answering them itself. Renowned for its excessively vociferous and exuberant singing style, the Red-eyed Vireo is sometimes known by the folk-name "preacher."

Singing is important in the lives of all birds but the Red-eyed Vireo seems particularly vocal. Researchers found that one Red-eyed Vireo sang 22,197 songs in a single day to woo a mate.

Surprisingly, the fairly large Red-eyed Vireo can be hard to see as it searches the foliage for slow-crawling insects. If you manage to get close to one of these birds, you will notice that it lacks white wing bars and wears a solid grey crown. You will also notice that it has a prominent pale white stripe above the eye, as well as a dusty stripe running through it. As for the eyes themselves, they are a dramatic ruby red.

Another group of birds you are sure to see in the mixed deciduous-coniferous forests are the wood-warblers. Learning to recognize them is a challenging but rewarding task. Expect to see at least eight kinds of wood-warblers along the coast, including the Yellow-rumped Warbler, Black-throated Gray Warbler, MacGillivray's Warbler, Orange-crowned Warbler, Townsend's Warbler, Wilson's Warbler, Yellow Warbler and Common Yellowthroat.

Dressed in greys and olive browns and adorned with boldly contrasting black, yellow and orange feathers, male wood-warblers are among the most beautiful North American birds. They are also among the most vocal of our songbirds, repeating their lively songs over and over, hour after hour and day after day.

In appearance, female wood-warblers tend to be much less distinctive and much duller than their male counterparts. They are also very shy and elusive, which makes them especially hard to locate once nesting season gets underway. The wood-warbler's nest is a cup-shaped structure built by the female with little or no help from her mate; it is usually situated in a tree or shrub. Some species, like the Orange-crowned Warbler, nest on the ground. The female lays between two and six white or cream-coloured eggs, the shells of which are variously spotted or blotched in shades of brown, chestnut, lilac or black. The incubation period lasts from 12 to 14 days. In most wood-warbler species, the female sits on her eggs for less than half an hour at a time, frequently leaving for one to 10 minutes to feed and drink. Although the male does not help with incubation, he occasionally feeds his mate while she sits on the nest. He also helps to feed the nestlings.

In the springtime, the ubiquitous Yellow-rumped Warbler is among the first to arrive, making its annual appearance sometime after the first week of April. The Orange-crowned Warbler is next, usually arriving after the second week of April. The Wilson's Warblers begin to arrive a week or so later, and the first Yellow Warblers, MacGillivray's Warblers, Townsend's Warblers, Common Yellowthroats and Black-throated Gray Warblers arrive in May.

Despite apparent similarities in the diet and feeding habits of warblers, biologists have learned that there is very little competition between warbler species. Indeed, the various warblers divide the habitat into smaller areas and niches, and there are differences in where they find food and how they catch it. Some of these differences are obvious; others are much more subtle. Also, each species builds its nest in different sites.

The absence of distinctive markings is one of the identifying features of the Orange-crowned Warbler. (Donald E. Waite)

The Common Yellowthroat can be found foraging on or near the ground among riparian bushes and thickets bordering streams and ponds. The Common Yellowthroat is particularly numerous in the estuaries. The Wilson's Warbler, MacGillivray's Warbler, Orange-crowned Warbler and Yellow Warbler forage in associations of willows, black cottonwoods and other shrubby edge areas. The Wilson's Warbler, for its part, seems particularly adept at catching flying insects. The Yellow Warbler prefers to forage and nest near water; the American Redstart and Black-throated Gray Warbler seek food higher up in second-growth trees. Both the Townsend's Warbler and the Yellow-rumped Warbler seem to prefer foraging among the high branches of older and larger trees. The Yellow-rumped Warbler will most likely be seen among the large deciduous trees of mixed woodlands. The Townsend's Warbler's preferred habitat is clearly the old-growth coniferous forests. In the upper reaches of some of our coastal valleys you will see yet another kind of wood-warbler: the elusive Northern Waterthrush. Of the various wood-warblers, this one is most closely associated with water. Look for it on or near the ground in and among alder and willow thickets bordering streams.

Small green caterpillars appear to be the Black-throated Gray Warbler's favourite food. In contrast, the Townsend's Warbler has a marked preference for beetles, especially weevils (also known as snout-beetles) and engraver beetles.

The well-concealed nests of the Orange-crowned Warbler and Wilson's Warbler are usually found on or near the ground in small clumps of grasses, low bushes or shrubs. The MacGillivray's Warbler typically locates its nest in dense brush or amid tall weeds or ferns, usually within 60 centimetres (2 feet) of the ground. Yellow Warblers tend to build their nests in the forks of willows, dogwoods, alders

A young MacGillivray's Warbler perches on a cow parsnip in late summer. This species prefers the brushy edges of deciduous forests. (Michael Wigle)

or young cottonwood trees, most often 60 to 100 centimetres (2 or 3 feet) off the ground. The Yellow-rumped Warbler, by contrast, usually nests in coniferous trees, generally building 1 to 1.5 metres (3 to 5 feet) above the ground. As for the Black-throated Gray Warbler, it nests almost exclusively in coniferous trees, generally 1 to 3 metres (3 to 10 feet) above the ground, but sometimes as high as 15 metres (50 feet). The highest nester, the Townsend's Warbler, may be found near the tops of 60-metre (200-foot) coniferous trees.

The easiest way to identify wood-warblers in a mixed deciduous-coniferous forest is to learn their songs and know where they live. For example, if you hear an unhurried, sweet-sounding trill issuing from the branches of a large cottonwood or alder tree, you are likely listening to a Yellow-rumped Warbler's serenade. Adult members of this species dress in an elegant combination of blue-grey and black and white, and can be seen flitting from branch to branch, inspecting leaves, leafy buds and catkins. The adult male Yellow-rumped Warbler is fairly distinctive in appearance, having a black mask, grey head and yellow on its shoulders, neck and rump; it also has a solid black chest and heavy black streaks on the back, breasts, sides and flanks. It is impressive to see how well this bird's bright yellow plumage blends in with the yellow-green leaves of its habitat, not to mention how nicely its

The preservation of streamside shrubbery is crucial to ensuring healthy populations of Yellow Warblers. (Michael Wigle)

greys and blacks match the deeply furrowed pale grey bark of the cottonwood and alder trees. In size and shape, the Yellow-rumped Warbler is slightly smaller and trimmer than a sparrow. Its bill is thin, straight and pointed and its tail is rounded.

The Yellow-rumped Warbler is the most abundant of our wood-warblers. At one time birders recognized two distinct species: the "Audubon's" Warbler and the "Myrtle's" Warbler. Today they are considered races. Both of these birds have mostly bluish grey upper parts, and their bodies are decorated here and there with similar patches of yellow. They can be distinguished, however, by differences in throat colouring and wing pattern: the "Audubon's" Warbler has a yellow throat and the "Myrtle's" Warbler has a white throat.

The "Audubon's" Warbler breeds in the forests of coastal, central and southern British Columbia; the "Myrtle's" Warbler breeds across northern British Columbia and into Alaska. Hybridization occurs where the ranges overlap. Flocks of "Myrtle's" Warblers are found in the eastern parts of coastal valleys during migration. It is the "Audubon's" Warbler that one sees during the breeding season.

At the end of the summer, the Yellow-rumped Warbler lingers for a while in British Columbia; it is, in fact, the last of the warblers to return to its wintering grounds. Its ability to feed on seeds and small fruits is unique among the insect-eating warblers, enabling it to stay in the valleys until late autumn. Each year a few of the hardiest Yellow-rumped Warblers will even try to spend the winter in southwestern British Columbia.

From the topmost droopy branches of western redcedar and western hemlock trees, the Black-throated Gray Warbler sings its rapid and lisping *zee-zee zee zee su zy*. A small bird with a black crown, mask and throat, a bluish grey back and whitish underparts, this warbler sports a white stripe above and below its face mask. Close examination reveals a very small yellow spot between its black bill and dark eyes. The Bella Coola valley marks the northern limit of its breeding range in British Columbia.

If you are hiking near willow thickets along a stream, be certain to listen for the cheerful, lively warbling *tsee tsee tsee tsee titi wee* of the Yellow Warbler. This song has also been translated as *sweet-sweet-sweet-sue-so-sweet*, which is a pretty good approximation of its sound. Despite its loud song, it remains almost invisible among the yellow-green leaves. Its upper parts are yellow-green and the sides of its head and underparts are bright yellow, making it a well-camouflaged sojourner among the willow's foliage.

Issuing from the shade of the devil's club, salmonberry, salal and wild gooseberry shrubs, the two-part *sweet sweet sweet sugar sugar* trill of the MacGillivray's Warbler may be heard. Between songs, the male utters frequent *cheks* in alarm. To view this warbler, make your way through the dense shrubbery as silently as possible. The adult male MacGillivray's Warbler is notable for his extensive slate grey hood. Above and below his eye is a partial white eye-ring. The back, wings and tail are a dull olive green above and bright yellow below. Singing males will allow you to come surprisingly close.

The extremely shy Orange-crowned Warbler, a bird of open deciduous woods, brushy field edges and dense thickets, prefers to forage in low trees and brush. Its overall colour is a rather drab and inconspicuous olive grey, though its plumage also boasts various subtle greens (the greens of its upper parts tending toward olive and those of its underparts more toward yellow). The Orange-crowned Warbler's bill is dark grey, its legs olive grey. If you could capture a male and hold it in your hand you would understand the derivation of the bird's name, for at such close quarters you would discover an almost hidden patch of burnt-orange on the top of its head. Generally speaking, however, you are more likely to hear this warbler than to see it. Listen for its characteristic song issuing from the thick foliage: a weak, rapidly

Many songbirds depend on fruit during their short summer stay in British Columbia. These salmonberries are ripe and ready to eat. (Michael Wigle)

Right: Wood-warblers like this Orange-crowned Warbler are referred to as neotropical migrants because they winter in Central America. (R. Wayne Campbell)

delivered, trilling *si-si-si-si* that decreases in pitch and tempo toward the end. The song reminds one of a wind-up music box whose melody begins with force, then slowly runs out of steam.

If you see a small, black-capped yellow warbler nervously flitting near the ground in a dewy patch of shrubbery, you are most likely looking at an adult male Wilson's Warbler. Its upper parts are yellow-green, its undersides a bright golden yellow. Unlike some of the other warblers, it has no wing bars, black stripes or breast streaks, and it is comparatively short in stature. As with most of the wood-warblers, the female is a much duller version of the male—the black cap hardly noticeable. This bird's insect-catching skills are so impressive that it is sometimes known as the "black-capped fly-catching warbler." This bird has a spirited but short chattering trill, which drops in pitch near the end. A creature of the damp and dense underbrush, it feels especially at home among willow thickets and in the lower strata of alder and cottonwood.

The Common Yellowthroat is another wood-warbler that prefers to stay on the lower branches of dense riparian trees and shrubs. The male's clear and distinctive song sounds like *witch, teer, witch i teer, witchiteer, witchiteer*. Remarkably, at the height of the courtship period, males can be heard calling as many as 250 times an hour. When you hear a Common Yellowthroat singing, sit down and utter a few squeaking notes in reply; chances are that one of these inquisitive little fellows will make its way into view. As its name indicates, the male Common Yellowthroat has a bright yellow throat and

Look for the Common Yellow-throat in thickets and low bushes around wet places within second-growth deciduous forests. Elsewhere, they breed mainly in marshes. (Michael Wigle)

upper breast. Like a feathered masquerader, it also wears a nicely decorative jet black mask bordered by white above. A solid olive green colouring on its wings, back and tail makes it one of the most easily recognized warblers.

The Common Yellowthroat is particularly fond of coastal estuaries, where it can be seen on or near the ground, foraging among tall grasses or in the willows and sweet gale shrubbery. Farther upstream it frequents low bushes and thickets bordering streams, ponds, sloughs, brushy damp pastures and old wet fields.

At the end of deeper, larger coastal valleys, where deciduous scrub is abundant, listen for the song of the rare American Redstart, a distinctive ditty composed of a series of loud, slow, high-pitched *teetsy* notes sung in varying patterns, each of which ends with a note slurred either up or down. When you hear one of these birds, you may want to imitate a pygmy-owl's call. This immediately attracts the bird's attention. If interested, it will pop out of the greenery, revealing its boldly coloured body. Like Common Yellowthroats, redstarts are very inquisitive birds. They feed like little flycatchers, darting out after craneflies and other slow-flying insects, hovering momentarily with tails fanned and wings aflutter, and plucking food right out of the air. Dressed in a strikingly bold pattern of black, orange and white, the American Redstart is sometimes appropriately called the "butterfly bird." Except for a white belly and orange-red patches on its side, wings and tail, the male is dressed entirely in glossy, coal-black plumage.

The nondescript *Empidonax* flycatcher is another kind of insect-eating bird you will see in the mixed forests during the spring and summer months. If you notice a small bird that is plain olive

grey above and a lighter colour below, and if it is sitting atop a sun-whitened snag or broken branch overlooking a clearing, you are probably looking at one of the *Empidonax* flycatchers. Watch it nervously twitch its tail while it waits for insects to fly past. If it darts out, catches a fly and then returns to its perch, you will know for certain that you are watching a flycatcher.

Unfortunately, the *Empidonax* flycatchers are among the most challenging songbirds to identify by species. At least five kinds of these flycatchers can be found along the coast: the Pacific-slope Flycatcher, Hammond's Flycatcher, Alder Flycatcher, Willow Flycatcher and Dusky Flycatcher.

As in the case of the wood-warblers, habitat considerations may help you to identify the species. The rare Alder and Willow flycatchers prefer to reside in successional forests of red alder and black cottonwood, especially those containing dense thickets of red-osier dogwood, wild rose and willow shrubbery, usually near water. The Pacific-slope Flycatcher prefers mature valley-bottom forests of Douglas-fir, western hemlock and western redcedar. The Hammond's Flycatcher hangs out in higher-elevation forests of mature Engelmann spruce, fir and lodgepole pine. Another *Empidonax* flycatcher rarely seen on the coast is the Dusky Flycatcher, which appears to nest primarily in British Columbia's central and southern Interior regions.

If you find yourself in a mixed second-growth forest and you spot a flycatcher at close quarters, look for a white eye-ring. If the bird has one, chances are you are looking at either an Alder Flycatcher or a Willow Flycatcher. The only way to distinguish them is by listening to their voices. The Alder Flycatcher's song sounds like a raspy *fee-bee-oh* or *rrree-beep*; the Willow Flycatcher's sounds more like *fitz-bew*. To complicate matters, however, some birdwatchers claim to have heard the same bird

Although the Dusky Flycatcher is very rare along the rain-coast, a nesting pair was recently discovered on the north mainland coast. (R. Wayne Campbell)

The Western Wood-Pewee, a fairly common bird in mixed deciduous forests, winters from Panama south to Bolivia. Healthy populations therefore depend on healthy habitats in both North and South America. (R. Wayne Campbell)

singing both songs. The calls of the Alder Flycatcher include *pit* and *wee-oo*; those of the Willow Flycatcher sound like *wit*. If the bird utters a call note sounding more like *peep*, then you will leave as confused as we all do. A good guess, without even waiting to hear the flycatcher's song, is to assume that you are looking at a Willow Flycatcher, for in our coastal regions the Willow Flycatcher is by far the most common.

In addition to the *Empidonax* flycatchers, one can expect to see the Western Wood-Pewee and Olive-sided Flycatcher. These two species are collectively known as *Contopus* flycatchers. They resemble the *Empidonax* group in general coloration, but they differ in size, having larger, sparrow-sized bodies with larger heads, heavier bills and shorter tails. Male and female *Contopus* flycatchers look the same. Their bills are long, stout and dark. The Olive-sided Flycatcher's head, neck, back and sides are a drab olive grey. The throat, central breast spots and bellies are off-white, contrasting sharply with the olive-coloured sides. Compared to the Olive-sided Flycatcher, the Western Wood-Pewee is a bit smaller, paler and longer-tailed.

The Western Wood-Pewee, like the Willow Flycatcher, appears to thrive in successional forests. Quoting the American poet Trowbridge, Burroughs calls it "my forest bird,—/ The peewee of the loneliest woods." In most of our coastal valleys, the Western Wood-Pewee is fairly common. In contrast, the Olive-sided Flycatcher is an uncommon summer visitant and is most often sighted in the dry eastern parts of the valleys. The Western Wood-Pewee usually nests in deciduous trees, and the Olive-sided Flycatcher prefers to raise its family from nests in coniferous trees. The nests of both species are located well out on a horizontal branch.

The best way to distinguish the two *Contopus* flycatchers is by listening to their songs. The Western Wood-Pewee has a distinctive song—a nasal, descending call sounding like its name. In a poem entitled "The Wood Peewee," the Canadian poet Duncan Campbell Scott expressed a strong admiration for this bird and its song: "At dawning when the cool air floats, / When dove-wing tints are streaming, / He, earliest of the early throats, / Begins his song adreaming." Though perhaps less poetic, the whistled song of the Olive-sided Flycatcher seems admirably practical, attention-catching and to the point, sounding like *Quick three beers*. As living proof of the power of suggestion, one might get thirsty when hearing this song.

A female Blue Grouse. This species is locally common during the summer, in open shrubby and grassy areas in and adjacent to deciduous woodlands. In the winter it migrates to lower-elevation conifer forests to feed and roost.
(R. Wayne Campbell)

Like the *Empidonax* flycatchers, *Contopus* flycatchers hunt insects from tree perches. One study has shown that in some regions the Western Wood-Pewee and the Hammond's Flycatcher both tend to feed in the forest's middle canopy. However, subsequent feeding studies revealed that the Western Wood-Pewee prefers longer, more robust and heavier insects than the Hammond's Flycatcher. In particular, whereas adult and juvenile moths and butterflies are the most important food in the Western Wood-Pewee's diet, beetles are of central dietary importance to the Hammond's Flycatcher. This study suggests that the *Empidonax* and *Contopus* flycatchers are able to coexist in the same forest because they feed on different insects and nest in different sites.

Along the coast, the Western Wood-Pewee's spring migration reaches its peak in May. This bird doesn't stay for long; after only a couple of months it returns to its wintering grounds in Central and South America. The peak of the autumn migration occurs in mid- to late August, and by early September most pewees have departed. The Olive-sided Flycatcher arrives a little later, sometime after the middle of May, but it also leaves for warmer climes by early September.

The grouse inhabiting our steep coastal valleys and forests is the frequently heard but seldom seen Blue Grouse. This handsome bird is most commonly encountered at higher elevations, preferring the drier Douglas-fir forests where the male can perch in and "hoot" from the branches of scraggy fir trees. Here the female can rear her young in relative seclusion and safety, foraging with them for insects,

In another 10 days or so, this Blue Grouse chick will be able to fly well. (R. Wayne Campbell)

seeds, young fir needles and buds, all of which may be found on the ground in adjacent natural clearings or in previously burned or logged-off areas. Uttered from the high branches, the Blue Grouse's courtship call consists of a series of five to seven deep, muffled notes or hoots (hence two of the bird's folk-names: "hooter" and "timber grouse"). Under the right conditions, the Blue Grouse's booming call, produced by the release of air from inflated sacs in the bird's neck, can be heard several miles away. Interestingly enough, the Blue Grouse's call notes sound similar to the hooting call of one of the grouse's mortal enemies, the Great Horned Owl (only the grouse's call is about an octave lower on the musical scale).

The Blue Grouse looks a bit like a big, fluffy chicken. The male's plumage is a mottled grey-blue, matching the deeply furrowed grey bark of the trees it hides among. Close observation reveals an orange or yellow patch of skin above the eye. A ruff of erectile white feathers outlines another yellowish patch of thick, gelatinous skin on either side of the grouse's neck. The female's plumage is a darker greyish brown colour. Because the Blue Grouse tends, possibly at its peril, to be unsuspicious of humans, it has sometimes been dubbed a "fool hen."

If you are looking for woodpeckers in the mixed deciduous coastal forests, keep your eyes open for the handsome Red-breasted Sapsucker. It is a shy, quiet and strikingly beautiful bird. Its head, throat and upper breast are a deep crimson red, and the rest of its upper parts are black and white. Its underside is white with dusky markings. Though sapsuckers live year-round in our coastal valleys, those from more northerly areas migrate southward in the winter.

Campbell Fact

The amount of time woodpeckers spend incubating their eggs is short compared to other birds. This adaptation appears to be related to the low oxygen content and high carbon dioxide levels in the bottom of the nest chamber. Eggs must hatch early so that the young can grow a bit before the air in the nest becomes unbreathable.

The Red-breasted Sapsucker is a fascinating bird. Unlike other woodpeckers, sapsuckers do not chisel out holes in trees in order to get at insect eggs or larvae. Rather, as their name suggests, they drill holes into trunks and limbs in order to get at the tree's sap, a substance consisting primarily of water and sugar. Typically the sap holes are squarish in shape and drilled in parallel rows, often on the sunny side of a tree trunk. After drilling, the sapsucker returns to the tree's food supply every few days to lap up the sweet flowing sap and feed on nearby insects. One biologist has estimated that 38 different mammals and birds, as well as numerous insects, feed on the sugar-rich sap flowing from these sapsucker larders. Northern Flying Squirrels, red squirrels, martens, warblers, hummingbirds and the common butterflies (mourning cloak, spring azure and anglewing) are a few such animals. Sap wells can be found in ash, aspen, apple, birch, maple, red alder, willow, western hemlock and young lodgepole pine trees. Red-breasted Sapsuckers may drill up to 20 new "sap wells" in the trunks of western hemlocks, western redcedars, red alders and willows each day.

In a late-May excursion through the deciduous forest, you may be attracted to a peculiar buzzing sound coming from a sapsucker nesting hole in a dead deciduous or coniferous tree. Approaching the tree, you may be duly rewarded, for if the young sapsuckers are sufficiently grown, they will stick their heads out of the hole to inspect you curiously. The buzzing sound they make is common in all three sapsucker species, making their nests easy for humans to locate. Each year, in the shelter of her nesting cavity, the female sapsucker lays a clutch of three to six round white eggs.

Opposite: A Red-breasted Sapsucker delivers food to its vocal nestlings. (Mark Nyhof)

The sparrow-sized, black-and-white Downy Woodpecker is the smallest woodpecker found along

the coast and the smallest of Canada's 13 woodpecker species. The Downy's beak is smaller and weaker than that of its larger pileated relative, and rather than functioning like a chisel to break through a tree's bark, it gently probes existing crevices in the bark. Furthermore, the Downy Woodpecker frequently searches for insects on older, smaller snags having softer wood than those preferred by the Pileated. It is not unusual to see a male and female Downy feeding together on the same snag. Unlike the female, the male has a vivid red patch on the back part of his head.

The lush deciduous riparian growth of some coastal streams provides great habitat for many bird species. (Michael Wigle)

Observations have shown that male Downy Woodpeckers tend to glean insects from the upper branches of trees, but females prefer to work the trunk and lower branches. Unlike Hairy Woodpeckers, Downy Woodpeckers prefer deciduous and mixed deciduous and coniferous valley-bottom woods. People are often impressed by how well the Downy's colours match those of the bark and lichen patches found on black cottonwood and other deciduous trees. This woodpecker has a black-and-white-striped head. Elsewhere its upper parts are black (except for a white stripe in the centre of its back and some white spots on its wings), and its underparts are white. The Downy Woodpecker's call is a rapid and rattling *ki-ki-ki-ki-ki*—a call easily mistaken for that of the Kingfisher.

Although Downy Woodpeckers usually excavate nest cavities in dead deciduous trees (including aspen, red alder, black cottonwood, water birch and even Pacific crabapple), they occasionally choose dead conifer snags as well. Typically these nest cavities are located one to 5 metres (3 to 16 feet) above the ground. The nest's entrance hole is 2 to 3 centimetres (3/4 to 1 1/4 inches) wide, extending down the middle of the trunk 20 to 30 centimetres (8 to 12 inches). Egg laying can begin as early as late April, but most females lay four or five small white eggs in May or June. The incubation period averages 12 days, the fledging period 21 to 26 days.

A real treat to find in the mixed deciduous forests hugging the eastern tip of long inlets and valleys is the Black-headed Grosbeak. The colourful males arrive in mid-May, the buff-brown females later in the month. These birds have flown all the way from wintering grounds in the southern United States and Mexico.

The male Black-headed Grosbeak is a large coastal songbird. His song is similar to the American Robin's, but it contains more sliding notes and is delivered with greater speed and energy. Unlike birds that sing primarily for courting and territorial purposes, the Black-headed Grosbeak seems to enjoy singing while he searches for food. Roughly the size of a robin, the male has a thick conical bill that is well designed for crushing fruit and seeds. His head and chin are jet black, as are his back, wings and tail (though the plumage of these latter parts displays numerous bold white markings); his lower belly is white; and his chest, upper belly, neck and rump are a bright cinnamon brown. Females are much duller, being largely brown with streaks, but they sport the same bills as their male companions. To date, no nests have been found.

By late September, when summer's greenery has given way to autumn's dramatic golds and yellows, the majority of our summer visitants have left for warmer southern climates. Most pass the winter in California, Central America, Guatemala and Costa Rica. Sadly, some North American songbird populations are declining at a rate of up to five percent per year. The reasons for this decline include loss of habitat, especially on the wintering grounds, habitat fragmentation, urbanization, pesticide spraying in wintering areas and even ecotourism. Furthermore, hunting by domestic cats and the

dangers posed by windows and fast-moving automobiles, contribute greatly to loss of life.

Scientists believe that the destruction of Central and South American habitat has had a particularly strong adverse impact on the lives of songbirds. Nowadays it is common knowledge that the western hemisphere's tropical forests are being cleared at a frightening rate to meet local human needs and world demands for tropical hardwoods, inexpensive beef, bananas, coffee, cotton and cane sugar. It has been estimated that nearly half of the original land base in Latin America has been altered.

Bird species that summer on the Pacific raincoast and winter in the tropics include the Vaux's Swift, Eastern Kingbird, Western Wood-Pewee, Pacific-slope Flycatcher, Hammond's Flycatcher, Black-headed Grosbeak, Western Tanager, Red-eyed Vireo, Warbling Vireo, Orange-crowned Warbler, Yellow Warbler, Wilson's Warbler, Veery and Swainson's Thrush. Seasonal migrants breeding widely along the British Columbia coast but having less than half of their wintering range in the southern United States include the Rufous Hummingbird, Dusky Flycatcher, Lincoln's Sparrow, Violet-green Swallow, Northern Rough-winged Swallow, Cassin's Vireo, Yellow-rumped Warbler, Black-throated Gray Warbler, Townsend's Warbler and Common Yellowthroat. Saving habitat is the key to enjoying these birds in the future.

The Black-headed Grosbeak regularly nests in second-growth deciduous forests in southern portions of the raincoast.
(Mark Nyhof)

7
Birds of Town, Garden & Glade

At the end of a long, grey winter, spring announces its annual reappearance in many ways. The sun's warmth melts the high-country snows, swelling the streams and rivers; hibernators awaken in their nests and caves and emerge into the open air; and, amidst an abundant array of fresh greens, the season's first floral blossoms unfold, adorning the landscape with colour and delicate grace. Between the first flush of spring and the warmer days of early June, an impressive assortment of wildflowers blossoms in the valleys.

Above and right: The lush vegetation of the raincoast includes an abundance of flowers such as the Indian rice root, which attract many hummingbirds. (Michael Wigle)

Orchids, lilies, honeysuckles, buttercups, daisies, currants, heather, figworts, mint, mustard, clover, lupine, strawberries, roses, raspberries, saxifrage, violets and wintergreen are just a few of the colourful plants that are in bloom at this time of year. Their blooms take a wide variety of forms, including simple bowl-shaped, long tube-shaped and intricate flag-shaped petal arrangements. Some flowers are sweet smelling, some smell horrible and others are odourless.

The lily-of-the-valley, yellow violet and lilac are among the flowers whose agreeable fragrance perfumes the valley air, drawing bees, hummingbirds and butterflies. The comparatively unpleasant odours of mountain ash and chocolate lily also play an important role in the valley's ecosystem, attracting flies and beetles.

There are several hundred different kinds of flowering plants in Pacific coastal valleys. If you watch any of these flowers long enough, you will be struck by the number of pollinators congregating around them. Bumblebees, honeybees, solitary bees, syrphid flies, butterflies, moths, beetles and birds all play a role in spreading the life of flowering plants. Symbiotic associations between animal pollinators and flowers have been evolving for nearly 135 million years.

Pollinators visit flowers to collect food: usually they consume the nectar, but many eat pollen as well. Nectar is a sugary liquid solution containing 25 to 75 percent simple sugars (glucose, fructose and saccharose) and variable amounts of amino acids and lipids. Plants have no trouble manufacturing and producing controlled quantities of nectar, thus providing animals with a high-energy food that is easy to gather and simple to digest. Pollen satisfies a diverse array of dietary requirements. A rich source of protein (between 16 and 30 percent of its content), it also contains starch (one to seven percent), fat (three to 10 percent), ash (one to nine percent) and a variety of vitamins and minerals.

Not surprisingly, most insects play a part in pollination. Beetles are among the oldest of the insect pollinators, but their chewing mouthparts, clumsy movements and relatively smooth body surface make them inefficient at this task. Butterflies and moths also pollinate flowers, but they do so rather sporadically. (Butterflies, one should note, differ from moths insofar as they are active only during the day, have a well-developed sense of colour vision and do not hover.) Flies, ants and wasps also pollinate flowers, but the most important and versatile pollinating insects are bees.

The tiny jewel-like hummingbird—which the English poet Charlotte Smith appropriately

A female Rufous Hummingbird feeds at a garden honeysuckle. (Michael Wigle)

denominated the "lovely Bee-bird" on account of its diminutive size—is another important west coast pollinator. The best time to see this bird is between late April and early June, when the most abundant assortment of flowers is in bloom. Flitting from flower to flower all day long, the Rufous Hummingbird feeds by hovering in front of a flower, inserting its long, narrow black bill deep into the blossom and then using its extrusible tongue to lick up the nectar. As the bird feeds, pollen from within the flower adheres to its crown, chin, throat and bill. When it moves along to visit another flower of the same species, therefore, it inadvertently deposits some of this pollen, thus fertilizing the flower. Since the typical hummingbird flower has no scent, it is appropriate that hummingbirds have no sense of smell. Their preferred flowers are long and tubular in shape, open during the day and sturdily constructed. Usually the blooms are orange or red, colours that cannot be seen by insects. Hummingbirds have a passion for the blooms of salmonberry, black twinberry, columbine, lupine, orange honeysuckle, Mexican hedge-nettle, lilac and trumpet creeper.

Remarkably, a hummingbird can beat its wings 75 to nearly 200 times per second and can fly for short stints as fast as 88 km/h (55 mph). An impressive aerial acrobat, it has developed the ability to

169

hover motionlessly, fly backwards and sideways and even turn somersaults. Its energy requirements are therefore high. To get through a single day, an average 4-gram (.14 oz) hummingbird must consume half its body weight in nectar and insects, a level of consumption that would be roughly equivalent to a human eating 100,000 calories in a day (the average person consumes only about 2,000 calories daily). Not surprisingly, a hummingbird must feed frequently—five to eight times per hour—but even at this rate the little bird does not secure enough nectar to burn through the night. To compensate for this deficiency, the hummingbird's metabolism slows as darkness falls, and it enters a state of temporary hibernation called torpor. Its body temperature drops about 6°C (10°F) and its heart rate decreases by two-thirds to about one beat per second.

The salmonberry is an important food for migrating and nesting songbirds in early spring. (R. Wayne Campbell)

A Rufous Hummingbird feeds at bee balm, a summer-blooming garden flower. (Michael Wigle)

When feeders are available, hummingbirds congregate around them throughout the spring and early summer. Feeder concentrations of half sugar and half water are preferred.

These amazing tiny birds measure only 8.5 to 9.5 centimetres (3 1/2 to 3 3/4 inches) from bill to tail, weighing less than 5 grams (.17 oz) when fully grown. Despite their diminutive size, hummingbirds easily travel all the way from South America to breed in British Columbia. The males arrive first, in April, followed shortly by females. Of the world's 320 hummingbird species, only the Rufous Hummingbird makes its temporary home in British Columbia's coastal forests and valleys.

Naturalists have noted that the Rufous Hummingbird arrives at about the same time the salmonberry plant begins to bloom. A good way to spot the first hummingbirds of the year, therefore, is to visit a patch of flowering salmonberry in mid-April. It won't be long before the little birds announce their arrival with the unmistakable *whirrrr* of their rapidly beating wings. The male Rufous

Hummingbird is easily recognized by his metallic copper-coloured throat, or gorget. In the sunlight this gorget flashes scarlet red, looking, as Duncan Campbell Scott remarked, like a "dew encrusted jewel." Hovering in front of a blossoming salmonberry shrub, the hummingbird inserts its long slender bill down into the tube-shaped flowers and then sucks up the nectar through a straw-like tongue. If salmonberry or gooseberry blossoms are not plentiful, the little bird will supplement its diet with nectar collected from pussy willows and black twinberry blossoms. It will also search out and feed on tree sap oozing from holes drilled by sapsuckers, and of course there are always insects to eat.

A week or two after the first male hummingbirds arrive, the females, with their plain throats and green backs, appear. At this time the hummingbird's intricate mating ritual begins. The male Rufous Hummingbird's dazzling courtship display is delightful to watch. Showing off for a potential mate, he flies straight up into the air, as high as 30 metres (100 feet). At the zenith of his ascent, he flashes his copper-red throat feathers and then dives rapidly back toward the earth. Just before pulling out of his impressive 80 km/h (50 mph) nose dive, he screams *dit-di-dit-deeee*, as if proclaiming his eminence among hummingbirds.

While her mate is busy courting and feeding, the female hummingbird begins constructing her nest. First she builds a delicate little bowl out of spider webs, lichens, bark and mosses, all of which she glues together with saliva. Next she lines the inner bowl with mosses, fine grasses and soft cottonwood down. Usually she locates her nest out on a large conifer branch (preferably one belonging to a western redcedar, Douglas-fir or western hemlock). The occasional female, however, chooses to nest in such deciduous trees as the black cottonwood, trembling aspen and paper birch or in shrubs like the huckleberry and juniper. The nest is usually 4 to 6 centimetres (1 1/2 to 2 1/2 inches) across and 3 centimetres (1 1/4 inches) deep; it can be found up to 18 metres (60 feet) above the ground, but most are built at elevations of 1 to 3 metres (3 to 10 feet).

Just before completing her nest, the female hummingbird seeks a mate. If more than one male is available, she will choose the one that conducts the most impressive courtship display. The male

The tiny nest of the Rufous Hummingbird is made of mosses, lichens, bark and even spiderwebs, glued together with saliva.
(R. Wayne Campbell)

shows little interest in domestic duties and, after mating, most males leave the family and head to alpine areas.

Generally the female hummingbird lays two white eggs requiring a two-week incubation period. Her newborns are blind, featherless and extremely small, about the size of a bumblebee; she feeds them by thrusting her long sword-like beak down their throats, regurgitating nectar and partially digested insects. To obtain insects, she snatches them out of the air in the manner of a flycatcher, or picks them off of flowers she happens to be feeding on. Insects are an important dietary supplement, providing protein, minerals, fats and vitamins not present in nectar. As the nestlings grow, their eyes open and their feathers gradually develop. After about 20 to 26 days, the nestlings are fully feathered and ready to leave the nest. For the rest of the summer and early autumn, these youngsters feed voraciously in preparation for their impending southward migration to the mountains of central Mexico and northern Guatemala.

After mating season ends in the first half of June, male hummingbirds leave their breeding territories in lower elevations and head up nearby mountains in search of flowers blooming in the wake of the receding snowline. Here, among the clearcut openings, subalpine and alpine meadows, avalanche gullies and rocky scree and talus slopes, they will find Indian paintbrush, red columbine flowers, red monkey flowers, wild roses and fireweed. Some female hummingbirds and their young also move to these higher-elevation sites, but usually not until July.

Campbell Fact

Every year birds must replace old, worn feathers at least once. During the moult, feathers are dropped and new ones grow in. As a general rule moult is related to feather wear. Birds that migrate long distances or live in harsh, scratchy environments have two moults a year; resident species and those living in open habitat have only one. Some species, such as ptarmigan and the Long-tailed Duck, have four different plumages in their lives. Feathers drop out in a very symmetrical pattern so as not to interfere with the bird's day-to-day activities.

In late August the evenings become colder and the mountain wildflowers start to fade and wither. Sensing the coming demise of summer, hummingbirds begin their migratory journey south to Mexico. Most will proceed via high-elevation routes, leapfrogging from mountain meadow to mountain meadow and staying no longer than a week or so at each location; a few will follow low-elevation coastal routes.

When contemplating flowers and birds, the experienced naturalist often thinks about the Purple Finch. Unlike the hummingbird, this large and colourful sparrow-like bird does not pollinate flowers; it eats them. Purple Finches usually arrive along the South Coast by late April. They are particularly fond of feeding on fruit tree blossoms: every spring you can watch them eating the light pinkish purple flowers of the introduced Japanese plum tree. When feeding thus, these birds can be difficult to see, for their plumage matches the plum blossoms' colouring.

The upper parts of the male Purple Finch, particularly the head and rump, are bright raspberry red. The throat, breast and flanks are a duller red colour; the eye and ear region, as well as the back, tail and wings, are brown; and the lower belly is white. As for the tail, it is well notched, and the finch-like bill is heavy, short and conical. Adult females, first-year males and immature birds all lack the mature male's red coloration. Their upper parts, wings and tail are olive brown; their throats and upper breasts are off-white adorned with numerous brown streaks. These birds also sport dark brown ear patches, light eyebrow stripes and light cheek stripes.

In the springtime, male Purple Finches are incessant singers, delivering a fast, lively, rich warble with slurred notes that drift in pitch as the song progresses downward. This song is commonly heard around houses, farm woodlots and in open mixed deciduous and coniferous woodlands. During courtship, the male dances as he sings, strutting on the ground with fluffed-up body feathers, cocked tail feathers and rapidly fluttering wings. During this ostentatious display he makes short vertical flights of a few feet as well.

The typical Purple Finch's nest is a well-hidden, cup-shaped structure composed of twigs, grasses,

The Rufous
Hummingbird
(above) and Purple
Finch (left) live in the
same environments
as humans.
(Michael Wigle)

rootlets and fine roots. It is typically located three to 6 metres (10 to 20 feet) above the ground in a coniferous tree. The female lays four to six speckled, greenish blue eggs requiring an incubation period of about 13 days. Although the female performs most of the incubation herself, the male helps her to feed the new hatchlings. At roughly 14 days of age, the young are ready to fly.

During their early seasonal sojourn along the coast, Purple Finches eat flower blossoms, buds, insects and seeds. When summer arrives, they supplement their diets with fruits like twinberries and blackberries; in the autumn and winter, they will depend increasingly upon seeds from grasses and weeds. When their migratory cycle comes full circle, Purple Finches take to the skies once more, travelling to wintering grounds extending from southern Canada and south to Mexico.

Spring is a season of visual delight: along the pathways, roadsides and forest edges, countless colourful blossoms appear, transforming even the meanest vine into an exuberant work of floral art. By the time June arrives, however, many early blossoms will already have shed their delicate petals and the year's first berry crops—including wild strawberry, black twinberry, salmonberry, thimbleberry, huckleberry and salal—will begin to grow and ripen. Wherever these berries appear, of course, one will also find a variety of berry-eating creatures.

For hundreds of millions of years, berries and berry-eating animals have coexisted, evolving together in dynamic ecological association. Like symbiotic relationships between other coastal plants and animals (the pollinator and the flower, the woodpecker and the snag, the nutcracker and the pine seed, etc.), the connection between fruit eater and fruit is ecologically important.

One of the major challenges facing plants is the distribution of seeds. Because plants are immobile, they need their seeds to be spread by others. One strategy of dissemination involves the harnessing of wind power. The smaller the seed, the better it can be pushed about. The tiny seeds of the wild orchid, for example, can literally float through the air like balloons. Larger seeds are sometimes equipped with "parachutes" or "wings" that help them to remain airborne. The parachutes found on cattail, dandelion and milkweed seeds are especially effective—so effective, indeed, that these plants can distribute their seeds across hundreds of miles.

Lacking the capacity to send their seeds aloft, however, most plants rely upon animals to help them propagate, in one of three basic ways. First, seeds may stick to an animal's body, hitching a ride on the bills and feathers of birds or on the fur of mammals.

Top: A summer berry crop on salal bushes. (R. Wayne Campbell)

Above: Chipmunks are residents in southern portions of the raincoast. (R. Wayne Campbell)

Second, animals may distribute seeds by storing them for future use. For example, jays, chickadees, nuthatches, chipmunks and squirrels often transport seeds to storage sites, and sometimes they never return to eat them. Under favourable conditions, some of the unused seeds germinate the following year. Third, animals eat fruits and disperse the seeds in their droppings.

A fruit may contain one or more hard seeds, surrounded by a nutritious outer substance. Along the coast, commonly recognized seed-bearing fruits include salal, wild strawberries, raspberries, gooseberries, huckleberries and blueberries, as well as apples, pears, currants and cherries. Because these fruits are fleshy, nutritious and tasty, many birds and mammals love to eat them. The seeds, however, are designed to resist being digested; thus, when fruit-eaters defecate, seeds are deposited intact, and if the conditions are right, some of them will germinate. Only a few birds, including sparrows, finches, grouse and ducks, are able to crush and digest fruit seeds.

From the animal's perspective, the best fruits are those that are good tasting, nutritious and easy to obtain. From the plant's perspective, the best animals are those that eat their fruits when they are ripe and distribute the seeds to favourable new growing sites. To ensure that they are not preyed upon prematurely, immature fruits often contain toxic or repulsive chemicals like tannins, alkaloids and sour acids. As the fruits ripen, however, these chemicals slowly disappear and are replaced by tasty sugars. As well, ripe fruits are usually boldly coloured in shades of red, blue or black, making them easy for fruit eaters to locate. It is no coincidence that a fruit is at its most delicious, most nutritious and most colourful when its seeds are ripe.

Fruiting plants accommodate avian frugivores in a number of ways. First, the fruit on each plant ripens asynchronously: it can take up to a month for all the berries on one bush to ripen. This gradual ripening is good for both plants and fruit-eating animals, giving seeds a better chance for anchoring, growth and effective distribution by a variety of animals.

Second, different plants bear fruit at different times, further ensuring the overall availability of

Berries, especially in the autumn, are an integral part of the diet of many migrating birds. (R. Wayne Campbell)

In spring, dandelions are a favourite food of black bears. (R. Wayne Campbell)

175

Cedar Waxwings are frugivorous birds, meaning that they depend on wild fruit for their survival. (Michael Wigle)

By the time young Cedar Waxwings are ready to leave the nest in midsummer, the fruit of the black twinberry is ready to eat. (R. Wayne Campbell)

fruit for frugivore consumption, and at the same time minimizing competition between plants. Fruit ripening is as predictable as the changing of the seasons. Along the coast, salmonberries are ready to eat first, followed by thimbleberries, black twinberries, blue huckleberries, red huckleberries and salal. As autumn approaches in mid-September, Pacific crabapples are ripe for the picking; by the middle of October, wild rose hips are ready to eat.

The fruit of subalpine and alpine plants ripens in a slightly different way. If you hike to the treeline in early September, you will encounter a veritable Eden of berry-laden bushes. At high elevations, berry production is much more synchronous than it is in valley bottoms: on crowberry, dwarf blue- berry, dwarf blueberry, bog blueberry, kinnikinnick, black mountain blueberry and Alaska blueberry plants, almost all the berries are ripe and ready to eat at the same time. Upon first consideration, this synchronic fruit ripening seems very wasteful, and undoubtedly it would cause problems at lower elevations. But in subalpine and alpine areas, this ripening schedule is ecologically effective. At the time when high-elevation berries are ready to eat, summer resident birds are just beginning their autumn migrations to southerly wintering areas. As they pass over the coastal mountains, hundreds of thou- sands of birds stop to feed on the abundant supply of high-country berries. If you hike up to the treeline at this time of year, you will encounter all kinds of fruit-eating thrushes, jays, grouse, sparrows, warblers and vireos—not to mention the voracious berry-eating black bears, chipmunks and mice. After resting and replenishing their nutrient and energy reserves, the birds are ready to resume their migratory journeys, depositing seeds along the way.

Coastal fruits contain varying amounts of water and sugar. Early-season fruits like strawberries, salmonberries and huckleberries are invariably succulent, bursting with sugar and water. Although they are extremely tasty, they don't last very long, succumbing quickly to rot or insect destruction.

Mid-season fruits like bunchberries, huckleberries and mountain ash berries tend to be pulpier, drier and tougher than the earlier-ripening fruits. Because they contain less sugar, these fruits are not as tasty; but they are more nutritious, containing more fat and vitamins. Late-season fruits such as rose hips and crab apples are waxy and nearly tasteless. Because they contain so little water, however, they are not as vulnerable to the winter cold as earlier fruits; indeed, many survive the winter without rotting.

When the first edible berries ripen during the month of June, one may expect to see the year's first Cedar Waxwings, wild pigeons, Western Tanagers and spotted thrushes (including the Swainson's Thrush and Hermit Thrush). These birds specialize in feeding upon fruits and berries. Birds that eat mainly fruits are known as major frugivores. Because of their dietary specialization, major frugivores are among the last of the summer visitant birds to arrive in our coastal valleys each year.

The Cedar Waxwing arrives by June, flying in close flocks of up to two dozen birds. These birds are particularly fond of the black twinberries and orange-red salmonberries that are now in full fruit. Gentle and gregarious creatures, Cedar Waxwings seem to enjoy human presence. Not only do their flocks tolerate a close approach; sometimes these birds will actively surround human passers-by, flitting from tree to tree and calling softly in their high-pitched, lisping voices. Though their individual voices are barely audible, waxwings produce a distinctive buzzing noise when many of them call out in concert. If you are lucky, you will see a waxwing, its face stained bluish black, hovering in front of a black twinberry branch, knocking loose a shiny black berry with its bill and deftly catching it in mid-air.

The Cedar Waxwing is larger than a sparrow but smaller than a robin. An elegant-looking crested bird, it sports a satiny black mask and silky, smooth cinnamon-brown plumage. The waxwing's chin and throat are black, and the narrow black mask is lined with white. The black bill is stout, flattened near the base, pointed and slightly hooked. The crest is narrow, sharply pointed and swept backwards. On the belly and flanks, the bird's warm brown colouring fades to a pale yellow; on the rump, wings and tail, the same colouring shades to grey. Across the tip of the squared-off tail is a broad, bright yellow band. The wings lack white bars, but the wing tips are bright red, as though the bird had dipped its wings in red sealing wax. In flight, waxwings resemble starlings as they alternate between periods of rapid wing beating and short, arching glides.

Ripe berries along the raincoast are usually red, blue or black in colour. (R. Wayne Campbell)

Not long after their spring arrival in coastal British Columbia, migrating flocks of Cedar Waxwings break up into mating pairs. They are noted for being fruit and berry eaters, but their growing young require more protein during nesting season than fruit can provide. For this reason it is not uncommon to see a waxwing hunting flying insects like a flycatcher, all summer long. As they grow and develop, waxwing youngsters change to a diet of berries.

The Cedar Waxwing's nest is a bulky, shallow, open cup usually located well out on a horizontal branch in a coniferous or deciduous tree. It is 4.5 to 6 metres (15 to 20 feet) off the ground and placed flat on a crotch of the branch. The outer part of the nest is made of twigs, bark, mosses and lichens; the inside is lined with fine rootlets, fine grasses and plant down. The waxwing lays three to five bluish grey or bluish green eggs, which are irregularly flecked with small dark brown or black spots. The female incubates her eggs for about two weeks; after hatching occurs, the male helps to feed the young. About 18 days after they are born, the young are ready to leave the nest.

Following their arrival on the coast, the waxwing flocks do not form again until August, when far-

flung mated pairs will gather together in anticipation of the autumn migration. Leaving our coastal valleys, they head for wintering grounds extending from southern British Columbia, through the western United States, to Central America. The last stragglers depart as late as early November.

If you see a waxwing in the winter months, you are probably looking at a rare Bohemian Waxwing. This bird infrequently comes to our coast from nesting grounds in northern Canada and Alaska. The Bohemian Waxwing is a larger, greyer version of its Cedar Waxwing cousin; it can be distinguished from the latter by the black, yellow and white markings visible on its darker wings, and by red colouring under the tail. These birds share a similar-sounding call, though that of the Bohemian Waxwing is rougher, lower and buzzier.

Bohemian Waxwings are a delight to watch. Rivalling the most devoted human epicures in the zeal with which they feed, these birds gorge themselves on mountain ash berries, yew berries and crab-apples. By the time Bohemian Waxwings arrive to feast upon these fruits, some berries are partially fermented. It is thus not unusual for one to find intoxicated waxwings that have crashed into the sides of buildings or come to rest on the ground in a drunken stupor. If you leave these little bacchanalians alone, they usually sober up quickly and get on their way.

Glaciation is believed to have played a role in the evolutionary development of our two waxwing subspecies. Thousands of years ago, an immense icefield covering the northern hemisphere effectively separated North American waxwings from Eurasian ones. The Bohemian Waxwing developed in Asia and Europe, while the Cedar Waxwing was coming into its own in North America. When the glaciers retreated, the birds from Asia and Europe moved down through Alaska into North America, at which time the separated waxwing cousins began once again to share the same continental territory. A similar historical process of glacial separation and subsequent post-glacial reunion might help to explain the existence of other closely related species, including Boreal Owls, Northern Saw-whet Owls, Northern Shrikes and Loggerhead Shrikes.

Like waxwings, thrushes are also extremely fond of eating fruit. Our coastal forests are in fact home to at least seven kinds of thrushes: the common American Robin, Varied Thrush, Hermit Thrush, Swainson's Thrush, and rarer Townsend's Solitaire, Mountain Bluebird and Veery. Thrushes are medium-sized birds with rather slender bills and fairly stout legs and feet. They are mainly tree dwellers, but they will often descend to feed on the ground. The group as a whole seems best adapted for particular edge habitats: thrushes especially love to reside in areas where forests are juxtaposed with areas of shrubbery or open grass. Their food consists largely of adult and larval insects, worms, snails, fruit and berries. Most thrushes nest in cup-like nests of mud, grasses, mosses and rootlets, which they build in small trees. Thrushes can be found in every habitat from the ocean shores to the highest alpine meadows. By choice, each species of thrush feeds and nests in a slightly different kind of habitat.

The robin—the North American version of John Clare's "sweet little bird in a russet coat"—inhabits lawns, fields, estuaries and open forests. As a rule, this bird avoids heavily forested lands. Because of its orange-brown breast, the Varied Thrush is something of a robin look-alike; hence it has acquired such folk-names as the "Alaskan robin" or "swamp robin." Unlike the robin, however, the Varied Thrush has a broad grey-to-black band running across the breast as well as an orange-buff line above and behind the eye. The Varied Thrush also differs from the robin in its choice of habitat, being a bird of shady, damp, old-growth and mature woods. As its name suggests, the Mountain Bluebird is seen most commonly upon mountainous terrain in autumn, preferring especially to reside in open country bordering mixed forests of Engelmann spruce and lodgepole pine. Mountain Bluebirds are generally sparrow-sized bluish birds with black bills and black feet. The male, in particular, may be justly praised as one of our most beautiful birds. Its upper parts are a bright sky blue, its underparts a lighter blue, and its lower belly is more whitish than blue. The female is less intense in colour, wearing smoky grey plumage with bluish shadings most obvious on the wings, rump and tail. Comparatively plain looking, the brownish grey Townsend's Solitaire is a thrush that prefers to reside in the open and in broken habitats at high elevations.

The Townsend's Solitaire is found throughout the year in some parts of the raincoast, but it is a very rare breeder. (R. Wayne Campbell)

The Townsend's Solitaire and the Mountain Bluebird usually visit the lower parts of coastal valleys only during spring migrations and move to higher-elevation nesting areas in the Interior. In valleys between Alaska and Washington, these species are frequently seen in early April, having migrated northward from wintering grounds as far away as northern Mexico.

The Hermit Thrush, Swainson's Thrush and less common Veery are often called wood thrushes. Although their songs are commonly heard, these shy, elusive and well-camouflaged birds are rarely seen. They reside among the shadows of both deciduous and coniferous forests, especially those areas exhibiting a luxuriant undergrowth of shrubs and forbs. The all-brownish birds are about the same size, ranging in length from 16 to 19.5 centimetres (6 1/2 to 7 3/4 inches). Their sides and backs range from grey to brown in colour, their underparts are lighter and paler and their breasts are spotted. Subtle differences like the presence or absence of an eye-ring, the patterning of breast spots or the colour of the tail and rump helps one to identify them. The best way to distinguish them, however, is to learn their various songs and calls.

The Swainson's Thrush is most commonly found in valleys. It can regularly be heard and seen in wooded areas of towns, along edges of fields and pastures and among thickets of red alder and willow. In early summer it can be seen singing from perches on the branches of large Sitka spruce or western redcedar trees. Its song consists of a distinctive upwardly spiralling series of flute-like notes repeated eight to 14 times per minute, sometimes with a quick introductory *whit* note. Because wood thrush songs in general have a flute-like quality, these birds are sometimes called "*flûtes*" in the French-speaking regions of eastern Canada.

Male Mountain Bluebird carrying food to its young in the lower Fraser River valley. (R. Wayne Campbell)

The Swainson's Thrush is the most common thrush and the most widely distributed songbird on the raincoast during the summer. (Donald E. Waite)

The Veery, a rare bird anywhere along the coast, seems to favour the drier, more easterly regions. In particular it prefers shrubbery habitats located along rivers and streams. This spotted thrush's song consists of a downwardly spiralling series of breezy, flute-like notes sounding a bit like *view view view.* Occasionally this song begins with an introductory *wu* note.

During the summer, the Hermit Thrush lives higher up the side valleys along the edges of logged clearings, or among stunted tree growth bordering subalpine meadows. Like its fellow wood thrushes, the Hermit fills the woods with strikingly beautiful flute-like music. In its song a long introductory note is followed by a rapid series of rising and falling notes; according to some rather fanciful listeners, the Hermit Thrush sings *Hey Sweet-heart, Hey Sweety-heart!* After a pause, the bird begins its song anew, though often in a different pitch. At the height of the breeding season, the song is repeated as often as 15 times per minute.

Early in the summer, small flocks of our only remaining wild pigeon, the Band-tailed Pigeon, often congregate around elderberry bushes, feeding voraciously on the small, bright red berries. These birds can be a bit noisy as they thrash through the shrubbery, but their cooing is a gentle and calming *oo-whoo, whoo-oo-whoo.* In appearance, the Band-tailed Pigeon is a predominantly bluish grey bird with a conspicuous white crescent on the back of its neck. Stout and grouse-sized, it has a short neck, small head and slender rounded bill. When its tail is fanned, a conspicuous pale terminal band becomes visible. When Band-tailed Pigeons are frightened, they fly to the shelter of a nearby tree and perch there until the threat of danger has subsided, all the while continuing their characteristic cooing.

Like its various pigeon relatives, the Band-tailed Pigeon is a strong and swift flyer capable of covering long distances in a short time. Its folk-names include "wild pigeon" and "wood pigeon," and it has sometimes been mistakenly called a Passenger Pigeon in allusion to the extinct bird that formerly bore this name. A somewhat nomadic bird, the Band-tailed Pigeon flies from place to place in search of food, especially berries, nuts and acorns. When food is located, pigeons will stay for a while and may even nest and raise their young in the vicinity. Although most pairs raise only one chick at a time, they may nest again later in the season. Nests are usually built in coniferous trees, especially Douglas-fir, western redcedar and Sitka spruce, but they have also been found in birches, red alder and Pacific crabapple trees.

The Band-tailed Pigeon is the largest pigeon in North America and weighs about 340 grams (12 ounces). Band-tailed Pigeon nests are flimsy, frail, saucer-like concatenations of loose twigs. They are generally built out near the ends of horizontal branches between three and 45 metres (10 to 150 feet) above the ground. The female usually lays a single egg, though she may lay as many as three. Her baby, known as a squab, hatches in a couple of weeks; for the early part of its life she will feed it a substance known as pigeon's milk, a nutritious white liquid secreted from her throat lining. After a nestling period of about 18 days, scattered nesting pairs somehow get together again to search for food, all the while exploring other parts of British Columbia. Once the cooler autumn weather arrives, these flocks embark upon their autumn migrations, flying south to winter in areas as near as Victoria or as far away as Central and South America.

Pacific crabapple blossoms. (Michael Wigle)

The strikingly beautiful Western Tanager is another summer visitor with a particular fondness for fruit. Although tanagers are classified as minor frugivores, they are often associated with cherries; the best place to get a close look at them along the coast is in woodlands surrounding local cherry

orchards. Look and listen for this red-headed bird in the upper branches of larger black cottonwood trees. Larger than a sparrow, the Western Tanager is a brilliant yellow bird with black wings, black tail and a reddish orange face. A pair of pale yellow wing bars is visible on its black wings. Its dusky grey beak looks like a cross between the slender, pointed beak of the warbler and the massive conical bill of the grosbeak. Because of its brightly coloured plumage and striking red head, birdwatchers love to catch a glimpse of the male Western Tanager. The female is not so brilliantly dressed as her male partner, but she is nonetheless easily recognized as a tanager.

The Western Tanager's song is composed of wheezy whistles; it is similar to the song of an American Robin but shorter in duration and hoarser in tone. When nervous, the bird often stops singing, quietly moves out of sight and bleats out a slurred note sounding like *pit-tick*.

The Western Tanager builds its nest on a horizontal coniferous branch. A loosely constructed cup of twigs, rootlets and grasses, the nest is lined with hair and fine rootlets for added comfort and security. The nesting female lays three to five pale blue eggs speckled with various browns, and she incubates them for about 13 days. Young Western Tanagers are raised on a mixed diet of ants, bees, caterpillars, small fruits and berries. By early September most tanagers depart for various wintering grounds ranging from central Mexico, to Guatemala, El Salvador and Costa Rica.

The song of the Western Tanager resembles that of the American Robin. (Tim Zurowski)

8
Birds of
the Alpine &
Subalpine

Few outdoor activities can rival a mid-summer's hike across the pristine spaces of high-elevation meadows above the raincoast. Where not long ago a deep blanket of snow covered the ground, countless wildflowers are starting to bloom, colouring the landscape with a dazzling assortment of natural hues. As you move along, small rivulets and waterfalls splash and tumble across your path, carrying meltwaters from remaining patches of alpine snow to the river valleys far below. Now and then, the Hoary Marmot's haunting whistle may be heard above the sound of rushing winds and tumbling streams. No matter how difficult and tiring the climb to reach this place may have been, you notice only a sense of exhilaration as, rounding the mountain's shoulder, you behold the dazzling prospect of neighbouring peaks or, to the west, the sparkling waters of the sun-swept Pacific. Like the mountain birds that visit this place, you may not remain here for long, but lasting memories of your excursion will accompany you well into the future.

One of many beautiful alpine lakes located along British Columbia's raincoast. (Michael Wigle)

It is easy to romanticize the high-elevation country, whose reality can be harsh indeed. From 1,500 to 1,700 metres (4,950 to 5,600 feet) above sea level, depending on where you are along the coast, living conditions can be so difficult that often not even the hardiest subalpine fir, amabilis fir, mountain hemlock, Engelmann spruce, or yellow cedar can grow. This is the alpine tundra, a windswept place of long, cold winters and extremely short and cool growing seasons. At night, the heat that has accumulated during the day is rapidly lost, and frost is possible all year-round. There is little or no soil here, and snow covers much of the ground even into early July. Some of the highest side valleys are still occupied by slowly retreating glaciers, veritable rivers of ice leaving bare rock, rubble and little vegetation in their wakes.

Despite these adverse conditions, numerous plants manage to flourish in the alpine and upper subalpine regions. Red algae grows on the snow itself, sometimes staining the ice crystals a pinkish red. Hardy green and black lichens cover the bare rocks, and the crevices harbour an assortment of alpine sedges, rushes, grasses and moss campion. With the passing of time a succession of low-growing herbs and shrubs eventually gives way to such sub-climax species as partridgefoot, white mountain heather, alpine speedwell and Tolmie's saxifrage; and climax plant species like pink mountain heather, alpine clubmoss and dwarfed willow and juniper trees appear.

During the brief growing season, an amazing kaleidoscope of flowering plants blooms in the moist mountain meadows. Along with the white flowers of Tolmie's saxifrage and white mountain heather, almost all of the colours of the rainbow are represented here. Look for the rose-red flowers of the pink monkey, pink mountain heather and moss campion; the red flowers of common red paintbrush, the orange-red flowers of the western columbine and the orange flowers of the orange agoseris. Numerous yellow flowering plants can also be seen, including the yellow mountain heather, subalpine buttercup, yellow monkey flower, mountain sagewart, broad-leafed arnica, hairy arnica, arrow-leafed groundsel and spotted saxifrage. Green flowering plants include the false Indian hellebore, crowberry and mountain sorrel. Finally, at the far end of the spectrum you will see the blue

Left: The Hoary Marmot, also called "whistler," lives in rock rubble and scree slopes with a lush, abundant supply of vegetation. (R. Wayne Campbell)

Below: The White-tailed Ptarmigan is the most common of the three ptarmigan species on the raincoast. It is well adapted for living year-round at high elevations. (R. Wayne Campbell)

One of the best places to see mule deer is at the edge of a subalpine meadow in late summer and early autumn. (R. Wayne Campbell)

flowers of the bluebell and mountain monkshood; the pale blue flowers of the snowy Jacob's ladder and alpine speedwell; the bluish purple flowers of the dwarf mountain lupine and the subalpine broad-leafed lupine; and the reddish purple flowers of the subalpine daisy.

The subalpine meadows are also a good place to see an array of different mountain butterflies flitting from place to place. The small grey-and-white grizzled skipper, the whitish apollo, the small blue silvery blue, the brownish yellow brown arctic and the brownish orange purple bog fritillary are among the species found here. These mountain butterflies, some of which stop to feed on the wild-flowers, tend to be smaller, hairier and darker than their valley-bottom counterparts.

A female mountain goat and kid feed in the subalpine. (R. Wayne Campbell)

Hoary marmots, American pikas, voles, mule deer and mountain goats are among the various mammals that may be seen in the high country. Hoary marmots are usually heard before they are seen, because the distinctive sound of their high-pitched whistles can travel a great distance. Marmots spend the summer feasting on grasses, leaves, flowers, fruit and insects, becoming extremely corpulent by early autumn. In October, the last of them waddle into their burrows, their furry bellies dragging on the ground beneath them; then, knowing that winter is fast approaching, they plug their entrance holes with earth, curl up into tight balls and begin another long season of hibernation.

When you visit the high country, you may have the good fortune to see a large mule deer grazing at the edge of a sub-alpine meadow; or you may spot a small herd of mountain goats feeding along the steep granitic cliffs, apparently untroubled by the perilous abysses yawning below. These animals come here to fatten themselves on a rich diet of nutritious forbs, grasses and shrubbery and to prepare for the rut that will take place in the coming months.

During the summer in the high country you will also observe bird species that cannot be seen

During the summer months, the White-crowned Sparrow breeds in brushy subalpine areas. (Michael Wigle)

elsewhere along the coast at this time of year. The White-tailed Ptarmigan, Gray-crowned Rosy-Finch, Townsend's Solitaire and White-crowned Sparrow all specialize in high-elevation alpine living. After nesting in the valley bottom, some birds venture up to subalpine mountain meadows to feed in late summer and autumn. The most common of these birds include the American Robin, Townsend's Warbler, Ruby-crowned Kinglet, Golden-crowned Kinglet, Pine Siskin, Dark-eyed Junco, Winter Wren, Yellow-rumped Warbler, Varied Thrush and Hermit Thrush. Other birds you can expect to see in subalpine regions are the Red-breasted Nuthatch, Red Crossbill, Blue Grouse and sometimes a Clark's Nutcracker. Surprisingly, you may even see a Spotted Sandpiper, American Dipper, Northern Waterthrush, American Kestrel and Sharp-shinned Hawk foraging and hunting along one of the many streams and ponds.

Look for the rare Golden-crowned or common White-crowned sparrows in open habitat among willow, alder and streamside shrubs. This sparrow conceals its nest on the ground or in low shrubs or dwarfed trees. The nest is usually a thick, bulky structure made of small twigs, rootlets, fern fronds, coarse grass stems and bits of bark, mosses and dead leaves; on the inside it is lined with finer insulating plant materials, mammal hairs and feathers. The normal clutch is four or five eggs, which are pale green in colour and speckled with brown. After 12 to 14 days, the young hatch; 10 days later they are strong enough to leave the nest and fly off.

The few Golden-crowned Sparrows that nest in high-elevation parts of subalpine environments are on their way south by September, though some of them may begin their exodus in the waning

At subalpine altitudes in the eastern parts of the larger coastal valleys, the Clark's Nutcracker can be seen foraging for whitebark pine cones. (R. Wayne Campbell)

summer days of late August. Instead of retracing their springtime migration route over the coastal lowlands, these birds appear to travel south along the Coast, Cascade and Sierra Nevada mountain ranges to reach their various wintering grounds. Most of them pass the winter along the Pacific coast from southwestern British Columbia to northern Baja California. The White-crowned Sparrow winters in the same general area, but it will stray as far south as central Mexico.

In whitebark pine habitats in subalpine regions, be sure to listen for the loud, repetitive and rather grating *khrraaa ... khrraaa* of the Clark's Nutcrackers, cousins of the Steller's Jay, and then watch them foraging for cone seeds in the scrubby-looking whitebark pine trees. The Clark's Nutcracker is a pigeon-sized, smoky grey bird with a pointed black bill, black wings, white outer tail feathers and large white wing patches. In appearance, it is a cross between a woodpecker and a crow. In flight, this bird characteristically alternates between rapid wing beats and glides.

The Clark's Nutcracker is commonly seen in subalpine areas located along the more eastern parts of coastal valleys, where it feeds on conifer seeds, insects and occasionally berries. The bird nests early in the springtime, sometimes as early as March, when a deep layer of snow still covers the ground. The nest is a very bulky construction of twigs lined with grasses, shredded bark, hair and feathers; generally it is located on the branches of a dense coniferous tree. The eggs, numbering two or three, are pale green flecked with small, pale brownish spots.

The seed-eating and -storing habits of this bird actually benefit its conifer of choice, the whitebark pine, providing another example of a mutually beneficial or symbiotic association between particular plant and animal species. This relationship is likely a very old one. Indeed, over the course of natural history the Clark's Nutcracker and whitebark pine appear to have become dependent on each other. The nutcracker benefits in several ways. First, the tree's ripe seeds do not fall out of their cones but stay in until later in the year, making them easier to transport and store. Second, the whitebark seed contains more calories than any other conifer seed, making it highly nutritious. Third, the whitebark seed has a thick skin that protects it from being damaged while the nutcracker extracts, handles and buries it. All of these characteristics appear to be ecological adaptations acquired, over the course of evolution, to accommodate the foraging nutcracker. In turn, the whitebark pine relies on the nutcracker to spread its seeds, which are notably wingless and cannot be dispersed by the wind.

Each year, sometime after mid-August, look for nutcrackers harvesting and storing ripe whitebark pine seeds in the subalpine country. Because of their rather noisy exuberance, foraging nutcracker flocks are usually easy to locate. Up close you can watch a bird extract a whole seed by inserting its long, sturdy, slightly decurved beak into openings between ripening cone scales and then lifting out the seeds hidden inside.

Nutcrackers have evolved a unique seed-storage pouch for transporting seeds to cache sites. This pouch is a sac-like extension on the floor of the bird's mouth, and apparently it can hold between 80 and 100 whitebark pine seeds.

Like a wise investor who avoids placing all his or her savings in a single stock or fund, the Clark's Nutcracker caches small numbers of seeds in a multitude of promising sites. The number of seeds stored in a single cache ranges from one to 15, but the average cache contains only three seeds. Scientists believe that this mode of caching benefits the whitebark pine because the smaller the cache, the less competition there is for moisture, space and light among seedlings; hence, the nutcracker's storage habits minimize the pine's reproductive loss.

The Clark's Nutcracker prefers to cache its seeds in open areas on steep south-facing slopes. Such areas experience a relatively early snow melt, which means that seeds will be available when other foods are in short supply. This is a good strategy, because whitebark pine seeds germinate best in open areas where there is less shade and less root competition. Also, the trees develop larger crowns in open areas, enabling them to produce larger seed crops than pines growing in dense mixed spruce–pine forests.

Nutcrackers continue to harvest and store clusters of ripe pine seeds until late October, when the birds become dependent on stored seeds until the new cone crop is ready for harvesting the following summer. Nutcrackers may spend up to five hours per day harvesting and storing seeds. They are most active shortly after sunrise and in the late afternoon. On

Typical subalpine habitat on the raincoast. (Michael Wigle)

a busy day, one nutcracker can store about 850 seeds. In a single season, it stores up to 35,000 seeds in some 9,500 different cache sites. Clearly, in order to find their stored seeds, birds of this species must possess a remarkable memory. Researchers have watched nutcrackers peck through many centimetres of snow to recover seeds they stored several months earlier. One would think that Mnemosyne, the mythological titan of memory herself, had smiled upon these busy little creatures.

Studies suggest that nutcrackers will only breed if there is a good supply of seeds. Even after the food requirements for raising a family are taken into account, 35,000 stored seeds represent only three to five times the nutcracker's annual energy requirement. Assuming a nutcracker requires only 7,000 to 12,000 seeds per year for sustenance, a lot of seeds will be left over to germinate and grow into trees. In the remarkable symbiotic association of nutcrackers and pine trees, everyone wins.

The other kind of jay one commonly sees in subalpine and alpine settings is the Gray Jay or

"whiskey jack." The adult is a fluffy grey robin-sized bird. Its upper parts are dark grey, its head and underparts a lighter shade of the same colour. On the back of the head and neck there is a distinctively darker grey area, appearing somewhat like a black patch extending around to the eye. The dark bill is short and pointed; the tail is relatively long. Young of the year have all-dark, slate-coloured bodies.

Like all jays, the Gray Jay is omnivorous, eating all the food it comes across, including seeds, meats, carrion, insects and fruit. If it finds more food than it can eat at once, it often caches the excess away in trees to help it survive periods of extreme weather. This is why Gray Jays keep coming back when you feed them. If you happen to encounter a troop of these fearless and feisty birds while camping or picnicking in the high country, you will quickly learn why they are sometimes called "camp robbers." It is not uncommon for them to land on pots of porridge or soup you have set aside to cool. If you offer them anything to eat, they will even land on your hat, shoulder or outstretched hand in the hope of obtaining another handout. These companionable tricksters always seem to have a mischievous and playful glint in their eyes, making them a welcome sight wherever they are encountered.

The Gray Jay's favoured nesting habitat is in secluded flooded swamps that extend into the subalpine country. Like the Clark's Nutcracker, this species gets an early start on the nesting season, usually courting during March when the air temperature along British Columbia's Central Coast routinely drops to below freezing. Gray Jay nests are usually located on conifer branches close to the tree trunk, between 1 and 3 metres (3 to 10 feet) above the snow's surface. The nests are relatively large, presumably to help protect the eggs and young from frigid nighttime temperatures. To build its nest, the Gray Jay fashions coarse and fine twigs, bark, leaves and grasses into a bowl-shaped structure, which it subsequently insulates with a thick lining of hair, feathers, fine grasses, plant down, lichens and needles. Three or four finely spotted greyish olive eggs are incubated by the female for 16 to 18 days. The male helps to feed both the female and the young. Once their feathers have grown, however, the nestlings are often left unattended while their parents search for food.

In all likelihood you will encounter a third member of the corvid family in the high-elevation meadows, namely the ubiquitous and clever Common Raven. Look into the sky to see this large black bird soaring, playing and circling on high. The raven is sometimes mistaken for a crow because of its similar shape and all-black colouring. Seen at close quarters, however, the raven's larger size, heavier and more powerful bill and shaggy throat plumage easily distinguish it from the crow.

In flight, the raven's wings are broader and more rounded toward the tips than a crow's, and whereas the raven's tail is wedge-shaped, the crow's tail generally takes the shape of a fan. The raven's most common call is a low, guttural, croaking *krock*, but its voice is as varied as the life of the bird itself.

A Common Raven
flies (left), and its
mate calls from its
perch far below.
(R. Wayne Campbell)

Campbell Fact

First Nations tribes in the Pacific Northwest revered the Common Raven for its cunning. One legend tells of a raven flying across a great body of water to bring the sun to their people. Concerned about the vast distance it had to fly, the raven cleverly carried pebbles in its bill and dropped them into the water whenever it tired. The pebbles became islands on which the bird could land and rest.

In the Atlantic provinces, early Gaelic settlers are said to have called the raven a "fang" in allusion to its carrion-eating tendencies. Here on the west coast, ravens are the vultures of the high country, always scavenging for dead creatures, but they will follow their food sources throughout the year. In the early spring when the eulachon arrive, in autumn and winter when the salmon are spawning and any time the dump contains scraps of cow, deer and moose, ravens may move down to the valley bottoms to scavenge. But during the spring and summer months, many ravens prefer to live in the high country, where they nest upon ledges or on rocky cliffs under overhanging rocks. Like jays, ravens sometimes nest in large trees or under bridges.

The Common Raven's nest consists of a large, intricately woven mass of sticks and twigs arranged into a bowl shape and then lined with grasses, rootlets, hair, feathers and mosses. As early as April, the female lays a clutch of three to five eggs, incubating them for about three weeks. By early June, the first young are already airborne. Unlike many bird families, the raven family stays together right through the winter. Like crows, ravens may band together to form larger foraging and roosting flocks during the late autumn and through the winter.

Higher up, in the treeless and boulder-strewn alpine terrain, the birds to look for include the rare Gray-crowned Rosy-Finch, Townsend's Solitaire, American Pipit and ptarmigan.

A chunky, grey-headed, short-tailed bird, the Gray-crowned Rosy-Finch can be thought of as a large alpine sparrow. This is an amazingly tame creature, which feeds on a variety of plant seeds and

A Gray-crowned Rosy-Finch stretches its wings over an ants' nest. The benefits of such behaviour are not yet known. (R. Wayne Campbell)

insects gleaned from the ground and snow banks. It repeatedly calls out a soft, high-pitched *chew chew*, but this call is hard to hear from a distance. Before and after nesting season, Rosy-Finches gather into large, roving flocks, which from a distance are easy to mistake for flocks of juncos. The males and females look alike, though the females are a bit duller in colour. The head is grey with a black forehead and cap; the remainder of the body is a brownish hue. Close examination of the plumage reveals a pinkish tinge on the wings, rump and belly.

Very few nests have ever been found. A couple have been seen deep within crevices, or on ledges and rocks in the rocky terrain. A cup-shaped structure made of grasses, mosses and rootlets, the Gray-crowned Rosy-Finch's nest is lined with feathers, fur, lichens and finer dry grasses. During the month of June, four or five unmarked white eggs are laid, requiring 12 to 14 days of incubation. The female incubates the eggs alone, but her mate helps her to feed the young. In late autumn and winter, Rosy-Finches can sometimes be found foraging in valley bottoms.

Although it nests readily at lower elevations, the Townsend's Solitaire can be thought of as an alpine thrush. Seen from a distance it looks like a small, slender robin. Male and female solitaires look alike, sporting brownish grey plumage above and pale grey plumage below. If you get close to one of them, you will notice its stubby black bill, conspicuous white eye-ring and buffy white wing stripe and tail tip. The buff wing stripe and white outer tail feathers are most apparent when the solitaire is in flight.

As for its song, the solitaire delivers a loud, long, melodious series of warbling notes as rapidly as those sung by the Winter Wren and sounding a lot like the song of the Purple Finch. In contrast to its tuneful song, the solitaire's call is a loud and abrupt *eek*.

The Townsend's Solitaire feeds on the usual thrush foods: caterpillars, beetles, flies, moths and

The Townsend's Solitaire is sometimes referred to as the "Alpine Thrush." (R. Wayne Campbell)

other invertebrates, as well as berries and seeds. Often this bird will be seen catching insects in fly-catcher fashion.

The Townsend's Solitaire usually builds its nest on or near the ground. Favourite nesting sites include cutbanks and cliffs, the bases of stumps or trees and sheltered areas formed by overhanging banks. In the alpine country, the solitaire nests under the protective overhang of large boulders. The typical nest is a bowl-shaped cavity lined with twigs, pine needles and/or coarse grasses. The female lays three to five eggs with dull white shells flecked with brownish markings, and she incubates them for about two weeks. Most mated pairs raise one brood, but in southern areas of British Columbia some solitaires raise two broods before the season's end. Because they rove about in search of juniper and other berries, Townsend's Solitaires have erratic winter movements. When weather conditions are favourable, one may expect to see them in coastal valleys until late autumn.

The plumage of nestling Townsend's Solitaires appears scaly with buffy spots, quite unlike the all-over grey-brown attire of their parents. (R. Wayne Campbell)

Many species of birds in the raincoast nest only to the limits of trees, shrubs and grasses in subalpine habitats. (R. Wayne Campbell)

The American Pipit is sometimes referred to as the "Alpine Wood-warbler." The white outer tail feathers are an important identifying feature.
(Edgar T. Jones)

During your visit to the alpine country, don't forget to look for the American Pipit, often thought of as an alpine wood-warbler. A slender, sparrow-sized bird with a thin, pointed bill, the American Pipit has relatively long, slim legs and a long tail edged with yellow or white. The male and female birds look alike, having dark greyish brown plumage above and paler, lightly streaked plumage below. The pipit's call sounds like a sharp, thin *pippit* or *tsip-tsip*.

A ground feeder, the American Pipit dines mainly upon insects, spiders, seeds and small fruits. As it moves about, it does not hop; rather, it walks, all the while wagging its white-edged tail. In the low-elevation regions, be on the lookout for migrating American Pipit flocks in late April and early May, when they are commonly seen feeding in the fields. But these flocks stay in the low country only for a brief period; as the snow recedes, they move to nesting sites in the alpine meadows. Here the pipit nests on the ground, usually under cover of a rock, a low plant like heather or a cutbank near a bush. The nest is constructed of grasses and twigs; the eggs, numbering four or five per clutch, are greyish white with heavy brown spots. Although the female incubates the eggs by herself for about 14 days, her mate helps her to feed and raise the young. About two weeks after hatching, these new arrivals are ready to leave the nest. In the autumn the American Pipit bids us a temporary farewell, migrating to wintering grounds located from extreme southwestern British Columbia all the way to Mexico.

Adapted to a rigorous and demanding mountain existence, ptarmigan are basically alpine grouse. Their preferred foods include leaves, buds, conifer needles, insects, seeds, berries and other small fruits. One can expect to see three kinds of ptarmigan in the coastal alpine meadows: the common White-tailed Ptarmigan, the rare Willow Ptarmigan and the rarer Rock Ptarmigan. The Willow Ptarmigan tends to be the largest of the three species, the White-tailed the smallest and most common. But there is little difference in stature, and size distinctions are not particularly helpful to the

task of identification. Although our three ptarmigan species are year-round residents, they undertake some downhill movement during severe winter months.

Ptarmigan are renowned for their two distinctive seasonal plumages, which look the same in males and females. In winter they are mainly white; in summer they shade to brown and grey; in spring and autumn their attire exhibits an interesting mix of the winter and summer appearances.

In winter, Willow and Rock Ptarmigan are all white except for their black-tipped tail feathers, and the White-tailed Ptarmigan's plumage is entirely white and unmarked. Often the Rock Ptarmigan, the rarest and highest dwelling of the three, has a conspicuous black line running from the bill through the eye. Unfortunately this eye-line is not always present in the males and never present in the females, so Willow and Rock ptarmigan cannot always be distinguished easily during the winter months.

In the summer, the adult male Willow Ptarmigan develops a white eye-ring and a conspicuous crimson comb. The head, neck and breast are a solid, dark chocolatey red; the tail feathers are black; the wings and belly are white. As for the rest of the body, it combines black and

The eggs of all three species of ptarmigan are well camouflaged and difficult to spot. (R. Wayne Campbell)

brown barring with some interspersed white colouring.

At first glance, the male Rock Ptarmigan and male White-tailed Ptarmigan look alike: both lack the Willow Ptarmigan's conspicuous red comb and chocolate-brown head, neck and breast; both are mainly brown, displaying prominent dark brown or black barring interspersed with white; and both have white wings and bellies as well as small red eye combs. But the White-tailed Ptarmigan lacks the

A female Rock Ptarmigan incubates her eggs. Ptarmigan are so confident in their camouflage that they are known to allow people to walk up and touch them. (R. Wayne Campbell)

black outer tail feathers seen in both its Willow and Rock relatives. In all our ptarmigan species, the tail colouring is most noticeable when the birds are flying.

Female Willow Ptarmigan, Rock Ptarmigan and White-tailed Ptarmigan resemble one another very closely; therefore, it is not easy to distinguish one species from the next. All are cryptically coloured in blacks, browns, greys and whites.

The Willow Ptarmigan's call is a series of loud, deep, nasal *kyow* notes, which from a distance sound like *go-out, go-out* or *go-back, go-back.* The Rock Ptarmigan's call is a harsh, croaking *karr-ke-karr kikikikik;* when you hear this call, you will understand why its owner has occasionally been referred to by the folk-name "croaker." As for the White-tailed Ptarmigan, it is less vocal than the other two birds, having a call consisting of cackling notes, clucks and low, soft hoots.

Over the course of their evolutionary development, the three ptarmigan species have acquired distinctive habitat preferences that can help in identifying them. The Willow Ptarmigan favours willow thickets and dwarf birch thickets in meadows, along stream edges and around the timberline. The Rock Ptarmigan nests higher on the mountain slopes, where the terrain is rockier, drier and less vegetated. The White-tailed Ptarmigan prefers an alpine habitat somewhere between these two extremes. In the late spring, winter flocks break up and breeding pairs are formed. These ground-nesting birds usually breed in May and June, concealing their nests in and around vegetation or among rocks on a scree slope. To build their nests, ptarmigan dig a bowl-shaped hollow in the ground, then line it with grasses, leaves, feathers or mosses. Sometimes pebbles are added. In the nest's relative safety and comfort, the female lays about seven buff-coloured, variously spotted eggs requiring an incubation period of about 21 days. It is always surprising to see how well camouflaged she is when sitting on eggs in open treeless country. Within a few hours of hatching, young ptarmigans are capable of running around with their parents; after another 12 days or so they test their wings and fly short distances.

The male Willow Ptarmigan often stays with the growing family. An intrepid bird, he is famous for defending them against all invaders, even including bears. In contrast, male Rock and White-tailed ptarmigan leave their families shortly after mating occurs. In late August and September, however, these ptarmigan families reunite to form flocks that pass the winter together. Most such flocks consist of 20 to 200 birds or more.

9
Birds of
Winter

Previous pages: The ubiquitous Song Sparrow occurs throughout the rain-coast at lower elevations. (Michael Wigle)

Below: Coastal valleys such as the Bella Coola can become starkly still during the winter months. (Michael Wigle)

A Dark-eyed Junco finds food on a cold winter day. (Michael Wigle)

As autumn gives way to inevitable winter, the snow that had previously fallen only on the mountaintops gradually makes its way downhill, threatening to cover the valley bottoms and coastal strands. Bereft of their colourful autumn foliage, deciduous trees stand skeletal and barren against the slate-grey sky and near-silence reigns where the gentle rustling of windblown leaves once filled the forest. Dark, inscrutable and starkly beautiful, the coastal winter landscape makes one long for the warmth of a crackling fire.

Winter can be long, cold and unforgiving in our river valleys. Despite the tempering effect of the Pacific Ocean, which makes coastal climates warmer than Interior climates at similar latitudes, coastal valley air temperatures can still fall to –15°C (5°F). Indeed, when you account for the wind-chill factor produced by east winds blowing at 25 knots or more, temperatures can plunge as low as –30°C (–22°F). At these times, ice forms on the rivers and streams and snow blankets the ground. For year-round resident animals, food that was once readily available in the water and on the ground suddenly becomes inaccessible; and freezing to death is not out of the question. Under these harsh conditions, surviving the winter is a life-and-death struggle in which many animals perish.

It is no wonder, then, that millions of birds go elsewhere in the autumn, forsaking our coastal valleys and shores to travel to warmer southern climates. The observant birdwatcher will notice that the Tree Swallow, Warbling Vireo, Townsend's Warbler, MacGillivray's Warbler, Yellow Warbler, Brown-headed Cowbird, Rufous Hummingbird, Pacific-slope Flycatcher, Vaux's Swift, Black-headed Grosbeak, Western Tanager, Swainson's Thrush, Common Nighthawk and other species leave our environs as early as August. Other migrant species undertake their annual autumn journeys from September through November.

Autumn is the time of year John Keats celebrated as the "Season of mists and mellow fruitfulness," a time when the "redbreast whistles from a garden croft; / And gathering swallows twitter in the skies" as they prepare to embark upon their southerly migrations. Along the coastal shores and in the forests south of the Alaska Panhandle, decreasing daylight hours, dwindling food supplies and cool evening temperatures trigger a massive exodus that rapidly moves southward. Most birds depart rather quietly. Some migrate only at night and are therefore not as obvious as other migrants passing through. But the larger, more vocal ducks, geese and swans are highly noticeable as they pass overhead, reminding us that winter is coming and the busy autumn migration is underway. Of the 90 or so summer visitors commonly found in our coastal valleys, roughly 55 depart before winter descends.

Although some birds, including American Robins and European Starlings, are content to spend their winters in the extreme southwestern corner of British Columbia, most of the warblers, swallows and flycatchers winter in southerly areas extending from California to Central America. Others,

Trumpeter Swans in flight.
(R. Wayne Campbell)

like the Osprey, Pectoral Sandpiper, American Golden-Plover, Northern Rough-winged Swallow, Barn Swallow, Cliff Swallow, Spotted Sandpiper and Common Nighthawk, may travel as far south as Argentina and Chile to spend the winter. The rare American Golden-Plover, one of the world's more ambitious migrants, makes an amazing non-stop journey of 3,700 kilometres (2,220 miles) across the Pacific Ocean from Alaska to Hawaii.

Obviously it takes a lot of energy to fly such long distances. Indeed, many birds lose as much as 50 percent of their original body weight by the time they reach their winter destinations. The autumn migration is usually more protracted than its springtime counterpart, when there is a mad dash to reach northerly breeding grounds. Estimates suggest that some species, cruising at a speed of 35 km/h (21 mph), can fly as far as 2,000 kilometres (1,200 miles) before they must land and refuel.

In the avian world, long-distance migration is a risky business. Predators follow and hunt some migrants as they travel, and storms, lights, windows and fog disorient many travelling birds, causing them to crash into buildings, wires and windows. Every year, hundreds of millions of birds, especially songbirds, perish en route to their seasonal destinations.

When the songbirds depart in the autumn, the coastal valleys and shores become noticeably quieter. Nevertheless, during the winter months one will still hear the calls of year-round resident birds, including the *chick-a-dee-dee-dee* of the Black-capped Chickadee, the *yank yank yank* call of the Red-breasted Nuthatch, the raucous *shack-shack-shack* of the Steller's Jay and the loud *caw caw caw* of the Northwestern Crow.

Other birds that spend the winter in coastal valleys include such year-round residents as the Bald Eagle, Dark-eyed Junco, Brown Creeper and Varied Thrush, as well as various species of grouse,

Campbell Fact

On cold winter nights, songbirds seek out the warmest and most protected spots possible to avoid life-sapping wind chill and maintain critical body temperatures. Birds' favourite sleeping places include the dense foliage of evergreen shrubs and trees, the lee side of logs and buildings, old woodpecker cavities, deep rock crevices and disused birds' nests. Some species roost alone; others are more social. In BC, 23 Winter Wrens spent several very cold days crammed into a nest box 15 centimetres (6 inches) square, on top of each other for warmth!

woodpeckers and owls. If the weather is not too cold, birds like the Fox Sparrow, Pine Siskin, Brewer's Blackbird, European Starling and Winter Wren may attempt to pass part or all of the winter. If the mild winter weather suddenly becomes frigid, however, they will leave. The odd Red-winged Blackbird, Song Sparrow, American Robin, Spotted Towhee and Sharp-shinned Hawk may also enliven birdwatching in winter.

One should note that some winter visitors deliberately spend the cold months in our coastal valleys and stay until the following spring, when warmer weather allows them to return to their more northerly summer homes. Birds like the rare Common Redpoll and Bohemian Waxwing and the more frequent Northern Shrike come to us from nesting grounds situated far to the north; others, like the Evening Grosbeak, Purple Finch, Boreal Owl, Red Crossbill, Three-toed Woodpecker, Gray Jay, Pine Grosbeak, Gray-crowned Rosy-Finch, Boreal Chickadee and Mountain Chickadee, sometimes visit to get away from bad weather or seasonal food shortages, common at higher altitudes.

A winter visitor, the Northern Shrike specializes in living on songbirds, small mammals and large insects. It is one of nature's more unusual predators, for among the perching group (known as passerines) it is the only true "bird of prey." Shrikes are rare birds, but keep an eye out for them in winter and early spring. Sometimes in March and early April, a Northern Shrike can be heard singing in the branches of trees. The song is a surprisingly pleasant medley of disjointed warbles and whistles, the singer a grey-and-black robin-sized bird with a conspicuously long, frequently flicking tail. The Northern Shrike wears a sinister black eye mask and sports a stout, sharply hooked black bill. In flight it beats its wings rapidly, moving up and down and flashing white wing patches as it propels itself through the air. Few people ever actually see a Northern Shrike, let alone hear its wonderful song.

The Northern Shrike does not have sharp claws or a razor-sharp bill, so it has a more difficult time killing prey than other raptors. Undaunted by its physical shortcomings, however, this feathered thug often secures prey by knocking its victim to the ground and then hammering at its head. After the

The Varied Thrush gives a splash of colour to an otherwise dreary winter landscape. (Michael Wigle)

victim has been killed, it is frequently hung on a thorn, barbed-wire fence, branch crotch or other object to facilitate feeding. In allusion to its dramatic, violent predatory and feeding practices, the Northern Shrike has earned such folk-names as "butcher bird," "devil's bird" and "joy-killer."

In order to survive, our winter birds possess a host of specialized physical, physiological and behavioural characteristics and abilities. Because they are warm-blooded creatures, birds have a metabolism designed to operate most efficiently at high body temperatures, making them particularly vulnerable to cold weather. Like other warm-blooded animals, they deploy a couple of basic strategies to ensure winter survival.

The first survival strategy is to become inactive, to pass the winter in a state of deep and prolonged slumber known as hibernation. Bears, marmots, jumping mice, reptiles and bats are other good hibernators. Their metabolic rates drop measurably; respiration and heart rate slow significantly. Hibernators survive the winter by living off the fat stores they accumulated in autumn. When the little brown bat goes into hibernation, its heart rate drops from 100 beats or more per minute to around five or 10 beats per minute; and its body temperature drops from 40°C (104°F) to 5°C (41°F). As for birds, scientists have recently discovered that some goatsucker species, to which the Common Nighthawk belongs, may become inactive for up to three months during the winter, thus exhibiting a form of hibernation. But this practice seems to occur only in the southern United States, where temperate weather conditions are conducive to such hibernation.

Such animals as snowshoe hares, squirrels and mice do not hibernate. Some of the tiny birds, like the kinglets, nuthatches and chickadees, barely have enough fat to get them through one night, not to mention an entire winter. During periods of extreme cold, these small birds are capable of short hibernation-like naps, but they can sustain such states for a few days at most.

Another strategy that warm-blooded animals employ to cope with the cold is to eat a lot. Various physical adaptations also help them to stay warm and dry during adverse weather. As winter

approaches, for example, birds replace their thin summer plumage with thicker, denser feathers. By fluffing up their breast feathers, birds create and regulate a warm air layer close to their skin, their closely overlapping outer feathers functioning as an additional insulation layer. Finally, nuthatches, chickadees and small owls are known to huddle together to reduce heat loss. As many as 100 nuthatches are reported to have been found stuffed together inside a single tree cavity.

Among coastal resident birds, another interesting winter phenomenon is inter-species flocking. For much of the breeding season, nuthatches, creepers and woodpeckers live solitary lives, but in late autumn they often join up with chickadees, kinglets, juncos or other birds to form mixed foraging flocks. These flocks scour forest and field in search of foods such as insect eggs and pupae, conifer seeds, berries and weed seeds. Sometimes they check out bird feeders. But they don't stay long: when the weather begins to warm, the mixed flocks break up and disperse to nesting areas. Certain advantages attend mixed flocking behaviour. First, the more birds there are in a flock, the more likely it is that one of them will detect an approaching predator and warn its companions. Second, the chance of finding nourishment during times of scarcity seems to improve when numerous birds travel together. Individual birds alert others members of the flock when new food sources are discovered. As an added benefit, it is possible that these mixed flocks may help to control pestiferous insects locally.

A good way to attract mixed flocks of birds is to put out a bird feeder. Doing so may even help them get through the severest of winters. Depending on what you put in your feeder, you can expect to attract up to 25 different kinds of feathered visitors, including juncos, chickadees, siskins, nuthatches, thrushes, jays, crows, blackbirds, starlings, sparrows, finches, grosbeaks, woodpeckers, shrikes and even small hawks and falcons.

Of all our local birds, only grouse seem able to thrive without apparent hardship during the winter. Their preferred foods include coniferous buds, seeds, berries and needles. As the weather cools, the Ruffed Grouse moves from river-bottom groves of alder and cottonwood and from deciduous and coniferous mixed woodlands into coniferous forests. The Blue Grouse also migrates uphill into coniferous forests to pass the winter.

If you approach grouse in thickly treed areas, they will often conceal themselves until you get very close. At that point it is not uncommon to be startled by a grouse exploding suddenly and noisily out of the soft, deep snow. Resourceful creatures, grouse make use of the insulating properties of snow: like ptarmigan and even redpolls, they frequently bury themselves in the powder to stay warm on cold winter nights and during severe daytime storms. Indeed, if the snow is soft, they may fly right into it and then burrow down another 30 centimetres (12 inches) or so.

Under the snow, insulated from the chilling winds above, numerous animal species live and thrive, remaining warm, alert and surprisingly active. The space between the ground and snow blanket can be as much as 25 degrees warmer than the open air. Deer mice and red-backed voles—animals that

Opposite: An adult Bald Eagle and Common Raven search for food during the challenging winter months. (Michael Wigle)

Above: Bird feeders are great places to see birds. They also help birds survive the cold winter days. (R. Wayne Campbell)

A Great Horned Owl
with a freshly killed
Mallard.
(Michael Wigle)

sustain our wintering owls—live in tunnels under the snow. With their keen auditory sense, owls can actually hear these small mammals scurrying about in their tunnels. It is an amazing sight to see an owl suddenly crash into the snow with spread wings and open feet and then resurface with a squirming morsel in its talons. At this time of year, larger owls, like the Great Horned, will also kill snowshoe hares, as well as waterbirds that winter on the estuary.

Because finches and grosbeaks are so beautiful, birders are always delighted when they visit the coastal winter landscape en masse. The sudden appearance of large numbers of gaily coloured Common Redpolls, Pine Grosbeaks and Evening Grosbeaks is a phenomenon that occurs every few years. Among naturalists, such appearances are known as eruptions. Presumably this phenomenon takes place because food has become scarce in the Interior or northern boreal habitats where the birds usually reside.

Evening Grosbeaks are among the most beautiful of our winter birds. Elegant robin-sized creatures dressed in yellow, white and black, they sport very large, conical yellow-white bills. On the wing, they move through the air in an undulating or up-and-down fashion. Although male and female Evening Grosbeaks look similar, the females are duller in colour than the males. The boldly patterned males have black head crests, wings and tails, and their wings are adorned with large, conspicuous white patches. Beneath the crest, the bird's head is brownish olive in colour except for the eyebrow and forehead, which are yellow. The rump, back and belly are also bright yellow, making the bird highly visible against the pristine snow.

The Evening Grosbeak is so called because it was once thought to sing only near the close of day. This is not true, so the bird's elegant name is a misnomer. Its call is clear and crisp, sounding a bit like *cheeer*. If you keep a large supply of black-and-white sunflower seeds in your feeder, you are likely to have some of these lovely singers around your house for months at a time. Birds of all mixed and coniferous woodlands, Evening Grosbeaks feed in the wild on a wide variety of berries, fruit, pits and seeds. They also eat insects, especially when they are raising their young.

In most parts of British Columbia, the Evening Grosbeak is listed as an uncommon or locally erratic migrant. Some years it appears to be very common, with flocks numbering in the hundreds; other years it is remarkably scarce. Evening Grosbeaks do not follow traditional migration routes. Instead, these feathered gypsies wander the continent irregularly in search of food, sometimes roaming as far afield as the southern United States.

When food is plentiful, Evening Grosbeaks may spend the winter on the coast and breed here in the following spring. During courtship the male offers its mate food and shows off to her by posturing with his wings and tail. When the birds mate, they get along well, but they do not exactly find perfect matrimonial harmony: nuptial fights are common. The nest, a shallow bowl of twigs, is lined with rootlets, bark, grasses and lichens; it is usually built in a conifer tree up to 37 metres (125 feet) above the forest floor, where it may be well concealed among the thick green foliage. Two to five greenish blue eggs, variously marked with brown and grey blotches and lines, comprise the normal clutch. The female incubates them for 12 to 14 days. After hatching, the young remain in the nest for up to 14 days, during which time they are fed by both of their parents. Occasionally, if conditions are exceptionally good, the mated pair may raise a second brood of young during the same season.

Another robin-sized finch, the Pine Grosbeak, is a rare and unpredictable winter visitor to some coastal valleys. This beautiful and rather tame bird does at times, however, visit the rain forests from its home in the boreal forests. Both male and female Pine Grosbeaks have heavy, conical, dark-coloured bills, dark legs and feet, dark grey tails and wings, and conspicuous white wing bars. The adult male is rather showy and ostentatious, having a mostly red body. His female mate is a plain-coloured but subtly beautiful bird: her head and rump are yellow-olive in colour and her plumage is grey. The male Pine Grosbeak looks like a large male Purple Finch (though the finch lacks the grosbeak's two white wing bars).

During the summer months, the Pine Grosbeak feeds mainly on seeds, buds and fruit, while supplementing its diet with insects; in the winter it relies heavily on spruce seeds for sustenance. When these seeds are scarce, the Pine Grosbeak wanders across the winter countryside looking for other seeds and fruit to feed upon.

During the breeding season, the Pine Grosbeak utters a warbling song similar to but less energetic than the Purple Finch's song; its call sounds like a high-pitched, whistled *pew-pew-pew*. Pine Grosbeaks prefer to breed in high-elevation boreal forests. During an elaborate courtship ritual, the male feeds the female, perhaps to demonstrate his skills as a provider. Built in the crotch of a conifer or fir branch 1 to 9 metres (3 to 30 feet) above the ground, the Pine Grosbeak's nest is a bulky cup-shaped structure made of twigs, fibres and lichens. The inside is lined with fine rootlets, grasses, mosses and mammal hair.

The normal clutch is four eggs, but two to five eggs have been found. They are bluish green with numerous dark spots and blotches concentrated at the larger end. The female incubates her eggs for about 14 days, after which time the male helps her feed the hatchlings. At a mere 11 to 14 days of age, the young fledglings are able to fly from the nest.

Another regular winter sojourner is the Common Redpoll, who visits us from the northern forests and Arctic tundra. It is fun to watch flocks of these little finches flutter excitedly through the branches, feeding voraciously on tiny birch-cone seeds. Like the Red Crossbill and the Clark's Nutcracker, the

When the winter ground is frozen, Canada Geese feed along the edges of flowing and ebbing tides. (R. Wayne Campbell)

Common Redpoll has a diverticulum—a pouch halfway down its gullet in which it can store seeds. When the pouch is full, the bird can fly away to a nighttime roost and feed in safety.

A sparrow-sized bird, the Common Redpoll has greyish brown upper plumage that is streaked with white. Its distinctive forehead and crown patch are pinkish red in colour; its belly is whitish and its chin black, and it has a sharp, stubby conical bill. Its call, which is frequently voiced in flight, sounds like a hoarse *chit-chit-chit*. Because it is so tame, the Common Redpoll is a favourite feeder bird. Scientists are not sure why it is so tame; perhaps it is because the bird was raised in the scarcely populated North and has not yet learned to fear people.

If you wish to see a variety of waterbirds in winter, visit the estuary, where you may find the Trumpeter Swan, Common Goldeneye, Bufflehead, Mallard and Canada Goose. These wintering waterfowl spend their time resting and feeding near the edges of the flowing and ebbing tide. Here, relatively warm incoming tidal waters thaw frozen mud and vegetation, making food available to birds. At low tide, some waterfowl feed on green algae such as sea lettuce and rock weed scattered over the mud flats and river channels. At high tide, these waterfowl graze on sedges, grasses, clovers, silverweed roots and other vascular plants. The dabbling ducks also snack on insect larvae and snails, small clams and other marine invertebrates. After a warm and heavy winter rain, dabbling ducks like the Mallard and American Wigeon supplement their estuary diets by feeding in and around flooded pastures farther up the valley. During cold spells, however, these fields freeze and food supplies become inaccessible.

Competition for food has been minimized by the evolution of different dietary preferences among ducks and geese. Whereas ducks display a definite preference for wild clover roots, the Canada Goose prefers to feed upon the roots of silverweed.

Bald Eagles can perch for many hours at a stretch with their feathers fluffed to conserve heat and energy during the coldest days of winter. (Michael Wigle)

Trumpeter Swans spend their winters in coastal estuaries as well as open-water areas of ponds, sloughs and agricultural fields. (Michael Wigle)

Other birds frequenting the estuary in winter include the Belted Kingfisher, American Dipper and Great Blue Heron. It is always surprising to watch these birds fly across the skyline and then suddenly disappear against the mottled background of dark grey granitic cliffs. Their dark blue-grey feathers harmonize beautifully with the colours of the west coast backdrop.

Over the course of the winter, the Bald Eagle, Glaucous-winged Gull, Herring Gull, Northwestern Crow and Common Raven are daily visitors to the estuary and its muddy shores.

One of the most beautiful and elegant birds to grace the coastal estuaries in the winter is the Trumpeter Swan. At this time of year, your chances of seeing this bird are reasonably good, for at least half of the world's Trumpeter Swans feed in estuaries along the coast. For many birders, early November is a time of anticipation, for this is when wintering Trumpeters usually arrive. Although people often regard swans as symbols of elegance and grace, they are in fact very hardy creatures: no matter how cold the east wind blows, they remain in the estuary all winter long.

Herbivorous birds, Trumpeter Swans thrive on a diet of underwater vegetation, shore grasses and grass roots. Generally they feed during the day, but when tidal conditions are favourable they also feed at night. Their preferred foods include arrowgrass and the dense mat-like roots of the bulrush. Watching swans dine in shallow water can be quite entertaining. They begin by rapidly paddling their feet in the soft muck to loosen the rhizome substrate. Then, dipping their heads and necks into the

water, they tug at and pull up rhizomes with their bills, making craters in the mud as they go. After a period of this activity, the shoreline can look a bit like a moonscape when the tide recedes.

Estuaries, even in winter, are places of life. Soon spring will signal its impending return; upstream in the quiet spawning beds, the salmon fry will start to emerge, and gulls, mergansers and even robins will begin to feast on them in the shallows. As the days grow longer, more bird species will come flocking back to the forests and fields surrounding the rivers that define the coastal valleys of the Pacific rainforest. It is unlikely that all of the birds mentioned in this book will be encountered in a single season, even by the most diligent birdwatcher. It might even take a lifetime to check them all off a list. And certainly there are always new things to be discovered about the behaviour of our raincoast birds. Just learning about them and their habits can be an adventure—and a great excuse to explore coastal British Columbia.

A Glaucous-winged Gull sits out a snow-storm. (Michael Wigle)

ACKNOWLEDGEMENTS

Many people contributed to this book during the course of its research and preparation. We are grateful for help kindly offered by Ron Mayo, Lise and Tony Karup, Eva Mack, Patricia McKim-Fletcher, Paul Harris Jones and Mike Wigle, each of whom contributed information used in this book. Carol and Keri Thommasen assisted with the initial editing of the manuscript—as always, their helpful input is much appreciated. David Steele worked as a dedicated research assistant to Kevin Hutchings; Lisa Dickson provided an abundance of material and moral support; and Barry Booth was a source of insight and inspiration. The personal visions and encouragement of managers Stan Coleman (Weyerhaeuser) and Tom F. Bailey (BC Hydro) were appreciated and served as a source of inspiration in researching this book. Assistance in compiling the bird checklist was provided by Michael I. Preston (Data Manager, Wildlife Data Centre) at the Centre for Wildlife Studies in Victoria. For some of the discussions of common names, we are indebted to W.L. McAtee, author of an informative study entitled "Folk-Names of Canadian Birds" (*Natural Museum of Canada Bulletin* No. 149, Ottawa: 1957). *Birds of the Raincoast: Habits and Habitat* has been published with the assistance of a publishing grant provided by the University of Northern British Columbia; warmest thanks go out to Max Blouw, Catherine Foster and the UNBC Research Office for generous financial support. And finally, our thanks to everyone at Harbour Publishing, and in particular to Shyla Seller, Vici Johnstone and Mary Schendlinger for their gifted and professional handling of the manuscript.

This book is dedicated to our children, Amy, Keri, Sean, Tessa, Sahra, Emma and Claire, whose love of nature has inspired us.

Drawings by Amy Thommasen

NOTES ON THE AUTHORS

Harvey Thommasen is a country doctor and Adjunct Professor in the Community Health Program at the University of Northern British Columbia.

Kevin Hutchings, PhD, is an Assistant Professor, Department of English, at the University of Northern British Columbia.

Wayne Campbell, MSc, R.P. Bio, O.B.C., is Director, Centre for Wildlife Studies, in Victoria; and senior author of the four-volume *The Birds of British Columbia*.

Mark Hume is a national correspondent with *The Globe and Mail* in Vancouver and author of three books: *River of the Angry Moon, Run of the River* and *Adam's River*.

PROACTIVE CONSERVATION IN BRITISH COLUMBIA: THE WILDLIFE DATA CENTRE

There are more than 23,000 registered societies in British Columbia. Of these, over one-third have some interest in wildlife and the environment. They include a broad range of human interests, such as carving, sport fishing, canoeing and kayaking, gardening, mountain biking and hiking, eco-touring, hunting, photography, birdwatching and environmental stewardship. Some groups have only a few passionate and dedicated individuals, while others have membership that numbers in the tens of thousands. Most of these societies are locally distributed, and within their own mandate function independently of other groups. Collectively, however, these groups can become an influential voice for conservation issues in the province.

With this in mind, the Centre for Wildlife Studies has established the nation's first regional Wildlife Data Centre in British Columbia, as a non-profit, non-government organization. For the first time ever, residents will have access to a "one-stop" source for information on the province's amphibians, reptiles, birds and mammals. The information, gathered from naturalists, birdwatchers, professional biologists, universities, libraries, museum collections and various other sources, is stored in a set of newly designed databases. The advanced programs and queries allow for information to be summarized quickly and accurately for conservation and preservation initiatives.

The Wildlife Data Centre, situated in Victoria, has the largest regional wildlife library in Canada (65,000 articles), the largest computerized databases (5 million records), a wildlife image bank (over 100,000 images), and the largest and most actively used nest record scheme (180,000 records). We encourage everyone to support this visionary endeavour. The information we collect and preserve is critical in our quest to become the informed voice for wildlife in the province.

To obtain information about the Centre, or to support its activities by donation or membership, please contact:

Centre for Wildlife Studies
P.O. Box 6218, Station C
Victoria, BC V8P 5L5
The Centre for Wildlife Studies is a registered non-profit charitable organization.

Published by
Harbour Publishing Co. Ltd.
P.O. Box 219
Madeira Park, BC
V0N 2H0
www.harbourpublishing.com

Edited by Mary Schendlinger
Cover and text design by Roger Handling
Cover photograph by R. Wayne Campbell
Photography by Michael Wigle, R. Wayne Campbell, Donald E. Waite, Mark Nyhof, Edgar T. Jones courtesy of the Provincial Museum of Alberta, Tim Zurowski, Michael I. Preston, Glen Ryder and Michael Kawerninski.

Printed and bound in Canada

Harbour Publishing acknowledges financial support from the Government of Canada through the Book Publishing Industry Development Program and the Canada Council for the Arts, and from the Province of British Columbia through the British Columbia Arts Council and the Book Publisher's Tax Credit through the Ministry of Provincial Revenue.

Library and Archives Canada Cataloguing in Publication

Thommasen, Harvey, 1957-
Birds of the raincoast : habits and habitat / by Harvey Thommasen & Kevin Hutchings ; with R. Wayne Campbell & Mark Hume.

Includes index.
ISBN 1-55017-300-6

1. Birds—British Columbia—Pacific Coast. 2. Birds—Northwest Coast of North America. 3. Birds—British Columbia—Pacific Coast—Pictorial works. 4. Birds—Northwest Coast of North America—Pictorial works. I. Hutchings, Kevin D. (Kevin Douglas), 1960- II. Campbell, R. Wayne (Robert Wayne), 1942- III. Hume, Mark, 1950- IV. Title.
QL681.T49 2004 598'.09711 C2004-904915-1

BIRD CHECKLIST

Spring: March, April, May

Summer: June, July, August

Autumn: September, October, November

Winter: December, January, February

C: Common (seen on most visits)

U: Uncommon (not seen on every visit)

R: Rare (rarely seen)

*: breeds

Es: Estuary

Ri: River

FF: Field and Farmland

CF: Conifereous Forest

DF: Deciduous Forest

TG: Town, Garden and Glade

AS: Alpine and Subalpine

Birds (Taxonomic Order)		Sp	Su	Au	Wi	MH
Red-throated Loon*	RTLO	U	R	U	R	Es
Pacific Loon	PALO	R	R	R	R	Es
Common Loon*	COLO	C	U	C	U	Es
Yellow-billed Loon	YBLO	R	R	R	R	Es
Pied-billed Grebe	PBGR	R			R	Es
Horned Grebe	HOGR	R	R	U	R	Es
Red-necked Grebe	RNGR	U	R	U	R	Es
Western Grebe	WEGR	U	R	U	R	Es
Sooty Shearwater	SOSH	R	R	R		Es
Fork-tailed Storm-Petrel	FTSP	R	R	R		Es
Pelagic Cormorant	PECO	R		R		Es
Great Blue Heron*	GBHE	U	U	R	R	Es, Ri
Cattle Egret	CAEG			R	R	FF
Turkey Vulture	TUVU	R				Es, FF
Greater White-fronted Goose	GWFG	R		R		Es
Snow Goose	SNGO	R		R		Es
Canada Goose*	CAGO	C	R	C	R	Es, FF
Brant	BRAN	R	R			Es
Trumpeter Swan	TRUS	R		R	U	Es
Tundra Swan	TUSW	R		R		Es
Wood Duck	WODU	R				
Gadwall	GADW	R	R			Es
Eurasian Wigeon	EUWI	R				Es
American Wigeon	AMWI	U	R	U	R	Es, FF
Mallard*	MALL	C	R	C	U	Es, Ri
Blue-winged Teal	BWTE	R	R	R		Es, Ri
Cinnamon Teal	CITE	R				Es
Northern Shoveler	NOSL	R	R			Es
Northern Pintail	NOPI	R	R	U	R	Es
Green-winged Teal	GWTE	R	R	U	R	Es, Ri
Canvasback	CANV	R		R	R	Es
Ring-necked Duck	RNDU	R		R	R	Es, Ri
Greater Scaup	GRSC	R	R	R	U	Es
Lesser Scaup	LESC	R		R		Es
Harlequin Duck	HADU	R	U	U	R	Es
Surf Scoter	SUSC	C	R	R	U	Es
White-winged Scoter	WWSC	U	R	R	U	Es
Black Scoter	BLSC	R	R	R	R	Es
Long-tailed Duck	LTDU	R		R	R	Es
Bufflehead	BUFF	C	R	C	R	Es, Ri

Birds (Taxonomic Order)		Sp	Su	Au	Wi	MH
Common Goldeneye	COGO	R	R	U	U	Es, Ri
Barrow's Goldeneye	BAGO	U	R	U	R	Es
Hooded Merganser	HOME	R	R	R	R	Ri, Es
Common Merganser*	COME	U	R	U	R	Es, Ri
Red-breasted Merganser	RBME	R		R	R	Es
Osprey	OSPR		R			Es, Ri
Bald Eagle*	BAEA	C	C	C	C	Es, Ri
Northern Harrier	NOHA	R		R	R	FF, Es
Sharp-shinned Hawk	SSHA	R	R	R	R	FF, TG
Northern Goshawk	NOGO	R	R	R	R	FF, Es
Red-tailed Hawk*	RTHA	R	R	R	R	FF, AS
Rough-legged Hawk	RLHA			R		FF
Golden Eagle	GOEA	R	R			AS
American Kestrel*	AMKE	R	R	R		FF, TG
Merlin*	MERL	R	R	R	R	TG, CF
Peregrine Falcon*	PEFA	R	R	R	R	Es
Ruffed Grouse*	RUGR	U	U	R	R	DF, FF
Rock Ptarmigan	ROPT	R	R	R	R	AS
White-tailed Ptarmigan	WTPT	U	U	U	U	AS
Blue Grouse	BLGR	R	R	R	R	CF, AS
American Coot	AMCO	R	R	R		Es
Sandhill Crane*	SACR	R	R	R		FF, Es
Black-bellied Plover	BBPL	U	R	R		Es
American Golden-Plover	AGPL	R		R		Es
Pacific Golden-Plover	PGPL	R	R			Es
Semipalmated Plover	SEPL	R	R	R		Es
Killdeer*	KILL	R	R	R		FF, Es, Ri
Black Oystercatcher*	BLOY	R	R	R		Es
Greater Yellowlegs	GRYE	U	R	R		Es, Ri
Lesser Yellowlegs	LEYE	R	R			Es
Solitary Sandpiper	SOSA	R				Es, Ri
Wandering Tattler	WATA	R	R	R		Es
Spotted Sandpiper*	SPSA	U	C	U		Ri, Es
Whimbrel	WHIM	U	R	R		Es
Long-billed Curlew	LBCU	R				Es
Hudsonian Godwit	HUGO	R				Es
Marbled Godwit	MAGO	R		R		Es
Ruddy Turnstone	RUTU	R	R	R		Es
Black Turnstone	BLTU	U	R	U	U	Es
Surfbird	SURF	R	R	R	R	Es

Birds (Taxonomic Order)		Sp	Su	Au	Wi	MH
Red Knot	REKN	R				Es
Sanderling	SAND	R	R	U		Es
Semipalmated Sandpiper	SESA	R	R			Es
Western Sandpiper	WESA	U	R	U		Es
Least Sandpiper	LESA	U	R	U		Es
Baird's Sandpiper	BASA	R		R		Es
Pectoral Sandpiper	PESA	R	R	R		
Sharp-tailed Sandpiper	SHSA			R		Es
Rock Sandpiper	ROSA	R	R			Es
Dunlin	DUNL	U	R	U	R	Es
Short-billed Dowitcher	SBDO	U	R	U		Es
Long-billed Dowitcher	LBDO	R	R	R		Es
Wilson's Snipe	WISN	U	U	R	R	Es, FF
Red-necked Phalarope	RNPL		R	R		Es
Pomarine Jaeger	POJA		R	R		Es
Parasitic Jaeger	PAJA		R	R		Es
Long-tailed Jaeger	LTJA		R	R		Es
Bonaparte's Gull	BOGU	U	R	U		Es
Heermann's Gull	HEEG		R			Es
Mew Gull	MEGU	U	R	U		Es
Ring-billed Gull	RBGU	R		R		Es
California Gull	CAGU		R	U		Es
Herring Gull	HEGU	R	R	U	R	Es
Thayer's Gull	THGU	R		R		Es
Western Gull	WEGU	R			R	Es
Glaucous-winged Gull*	GWGU	C	C	C	C	Es, Ri
Glaucous Gull	GLGU	R		R	R	Es
Sabine's Gull	SAGU		R	R		Es
Black-legged Kittiwake	BLKI		R	R		Es
Caspian Tern	CATE		R			Es
Common Tern	COTE			R		Es
Arctic Tern	ARTE		R	R		Es
Common Murre	COMU	R	R	R		Es
Pigeon Guillemot*	PIGU		R			Es
Marbled Murrelet*	MAMU	U	U	R		Es, Ri
Cassin's Auklet	CAAU		R			Es
Rhinoceros Auklet	RHAU		R			Es
Rock Dove*	RODO	R	R	R	R	TG, FF
Band-tailed Pigeon	BTPI	R	R			DF, FF
Mourning Dove	MODO			R		FF
Western Screech-Owl*	WSOW	R	R			CF, DF
Great Horned Owl*	GHOW	U	U	U	R	CF, DF
Snowy Owl	SNOW			R	R	Es, FF
Northern Pygmy-Owl*	NPOW	R	R	R	R	CF, DF
Barred Owl*	BAOW	R	R	R	R	CF, DF
Short-eared Owl	SEOW			R		Es, FF
Northern Saw-whet Owl	NSWO	R	R	R	R	CF, DF
Common Nighthawk	CONI		U	R		FF, TG
Black Swift	BLSW		R			Es, Ri
Vaux's Swift	VASW	R	U			CF, DF
Anna's Hummingbird	ANHU	R	R	R	R	TG
Rufous Hummingbird*	RUHU	C	C	R		TG
Belted Kingfisher*	BEKI	U	U	U		Ri, Es
Red-breasted Sapsucker*	RBSA	U	U	U		DF, CF

Birds (Taxonomic Order)		Sp	Su	Au	Wi	MH
Downy Woodpecker	DOWO		R	R		DF, TG
Hairy Woodpecker*	HAWO	U	U	U	R	DF, TG
Three-toed Woodpecker	TTWO			R		CF
Northern Flicker*	NOFL	U	U	U	R	DF, TG
Pileated Woodpecker*	PIWO	U	U	U	R	CF, DF
Olive-sided Flycatcher	OSFL	U	U	R		Ri, CF
Western Wood-Pewee*	WWPE	U	U	R		CF, DF
Alder Flycatcher	ALFL		R			Ri, DF
Willow Flycatcher	WIFL		R			Ri, DF
Least Flycatcher	LEFL		R			DF
Hammond's Flycatcher*	HAFL	R	U			CF
Dusky Flycatcher*	DUFL	R	R			DF, Ri
Pacific-slope Flycatcher*	PSFL	U	U	R		CF, FF
Say's Phoebe	ATFL		R			FF
Western Kingbird	WEKI	R	R			FF
Eastern Kingbird	EAKI	R	R			FF
Northern Shrike	NOSH	R		U	R	FF, TG
Cassin's Vireo	CAVI	R	U			CF, DF
Hutton's Vireo	HUVI		R			CF
Warbling Vireo*	WAVI	U	C			DF, CF
Red-eyed Vireo*	REVI	U	U			DF
Gray Jay*	GRJA	R	U	U	U	AS, FF
Steller's Jay*	STJA	C	U	C	C	CF, TG
Clark's Nutcracker	CLNU	R	U	U	R	AS, CF
Black-billed Magpie	BBMA			R	R	FF
Northwestern Crow*	NOCR	C	C	C	C	Es, FF
Common Raven*	CORA	C	C	C	C	FF, AS, Es
Horned Lark	HOLA	R	U	R	R	FF, AS
Tree Swallow*	TRSW	C	C			FF, TG
Violet-green Swallow*	VGSW	U	U			FF, TG
Northern Rough-winged Swallow*	NRWS	U	U			Ri, Es
Bank Swallow	BKSW	R	R			Ri, FF
Cliff Swallow*	CLSW	U	U			FF, Ri
Barn Swallow*	BASW	C	C	R		FF, TG
Black-capped Chickadee*	BCCH	C	U	C	C	DF, TG
Mountain Chickadee	MOCH	R		R	R	CF, TG
Chestnut-backed Chickadee*	CBCH	U	U	R	R	CF, TG
Boreal Chickadee	BOCH		R		R	CF, TG
Red-breasted Nuthatch*	RBNU	C	U	C	R	CF, DF
White-breasted Nuthatch	WBNU				R	TG
Brown Creeper*	BRCR	U	U	U	R	CF, DF
Winter Wren*	WIWR	C	C	U	R	CF, DF
American Dipper*	AMDI	C	U	U	R	Ri, Es
Golden-crowned Kinglet*	GCKI	C	C	C	R	CF
Ruby-crowned Kinglet*	RCKI	C	C	U		CF, DF
Mountain Bluebird	MOBL	R	R			FF
Townsend's Solitaire	TOSO	R	R	R		AS, FF
Veery*	VEER	R	R			DF
Swainson's Thrush*	SWTH	U	C	R		CF, DF
Hermit Thrush*	HETH	U	C	U		DF, AS
American Robin*	AMRO	C	C	C	U	FF, TG
Varied Thrush*	VATH	C	U	U	R	CF, AS
Gray Catbird	GRCA	R	R			FF

Birds (Taxonomic Order)		Sp	Su	Au	Wi	MH
Northern Mockingbird	NOMO		R	R		FF, TG
European Starling*	EUST	C	C	C	U	FF, TG
American Pipit*	AMPI	U	C	U		FF, AS
Bohemian Waxwing	BOWA	R		R	R	TG, FF
Cedar Waxwing*	CEWA	R	U	U		TG, FF
Tennessee Warbler	TEWA	R	R	R		DF
Orange-crowned Warbler*	OCWA	C	U	R		DF, Ri
Nashville Warbler	NAWA		R			DF
Yellow Warbler*	YEWA	U	U	R		Ri, DF
Magnolia Warbler	MGNW	R	R	R		CF, DF
Yellow-rumped Warbler*	YRWA	C	C	U		CF, DF
Black-throated Gray Warbler	BTGW	U	U	R		DF
Townsend's Warbler*	TOWA	C	C	R		CF, AS
Hermit Warbler	HEWA	R				
Blackpoll Warbler	BKPW		R	R		DF, CF
Black-and-white Warbler	BAWW			R		DF, FF
American Redstart*	AMRE	R	R			DF, Ri
Northern Waterthrush	NOWA	R	R			Ri
MacGillivray's Warbler	MACW	R	U			DF
Common Yellowthroat	COYE	R	U			FF, Ri
Wilson's Warbler	WIWA	U	U	R		Ri, FF
Western Tanager	WETA	U	U	R		CF, DF
Spotted Towhee	SPTO	R	R	R	R	FF, TG
American Tree Sparrow	ATSP			R	R	FF, TG
Chipping Sparrow*	CHSP	U	U			FF, AS
Vesper Sparrow	VESP		R			FF
Lark Sparrow	LASP	R				FF
Savannah Sparrow	SAVS	U	R	U	R	FF, Es
Fox Sparrow	FOSP	U	U	U	R	DF, AS, FF
Song Sparrow*	SOSP	U	U	U	R	FF, TG

Birds (Taxonomic Order)		Sp	Su	Au	Wi	MH
Lincoln's Sparrow	LISP	U	R	R		FF
White-throated Sparrow	WTSP	R		R	R	FF, TG
Harris's Sparrow	HASP			R	R	FF. TG
White-crowned Sparrow	WCSP	U	R	U		FF, TG, AS
Golden-crowned Sparrow	GCSP	U	R	U	R	FF, TG, AS
Dark-eyed Junco*	DEJU	U	U	U	U	FF, TG, AS
Lapland Longspur	LALO	R				Es
Snow Bunting	SNBU	R			R	FF
Black-headed Grosbeak	BHGR		R			DF
Lazuli Bunting	LZBU	R	R			FF
Red-winged Blackbird*	RWBL	U	U	R	R	FF, TG
Western Meadowlark	WEME	R		R		FF, Es
Yellow-headed Blackbird	YHBL	R		R		FF
Rusty Blackbird	RUBL	R		R	R	FF
Brewer's Blackbird	BRBL	R	R	U	R	FF, TG
Brown-headed Cowbird	BHCO	R	R	R		FF, TG
Bullock's Oriole	BUOR			R		TG
Gray-crowned Rosy-Finch	GCRF			R	R	FF, AS
Pine Grosbeak	PIGR		R	R	R	DF, FF
Purple Finch	PUFI	R	R	R		CF, TG
House Finch	HOFI	R	R			TG, FF
Red Crossbill	RECR	U	U	R		CF
Common Redpoll	CORE				R	FF
Hoary Redpoll	HORE				R	FF
Pine Siskin	PISI	U	U	U	R	CF, TG
American Goldfinch	AMGO		R	R		TG, FF
Evening Grosbeak	EVGR	R	R	R	R	TG, DF
House Sparrow	HOSP			R		TG

INDEX

ADDITIONAL READING

More Great Photography Books From Harbour Publishing

The Wild Edge: Clayoquot, Long Beach and Barkley Sound
Jacqueline Windh
Jacqueline Windh has spent ten years photographing the Clayoquot-Pacific Rim in all its seasons and moods, studying its history and getting to know its people. In *The Wild Edge* she shares her findings in images and words, supplementing her unforgettable scenic photographs with a light-hearted but informative text that blends history and science with essential visitor guidance.
ISBN 1-55017-350-2 • 8 1/2 x 11 • 200 pages • colour photographs • hardcover • $34.95

Natural Light: Visions of British Columbia
David Nunuk
British Columbia's beauty has inspired many photo collections but none quite like David Nunuk's. From frosted mountain peaks to the low-lying farmlands of the Fraser Valley, from the Sahara-like sand dunes of Farwell Canyon to the dripping moss-bedecked rainforest of the Queen Charlotte Islands, the photographs in *Natural Light* capture the drama of British Columbia in a whole new light.
1-55017-273-5 • 14 x 11 • 120 pages • 120 colour photographs • hardcover • $49.95

Bella Coola: Life in the Heart of the Coast Mountains
Hans Granander and Michael Wigle
The Bella Coola Valley lies in the misty heart of British Columbia's West Coast, where the Pacific spills into the forest-clad cracks in the Coast Mountains. Through their light-hearted text and breathtaking photographs, Michael Wigle and Hans Granander introduce you to this wild country, its residents, animals and stunning beauty.
1-55017-305-7 • 8 1/2 x 11 • 160 pages • 160 colour photos • hardcover • $32.95

Visions of the Wild: A Voyage by Kayak Around Vancouver Island
Maria Coffey and Dag Goering
Brimming with breathtaking colour photos and compelling journal entries, an inspiring chronicle of the adventure of a lifetime.
1-55017-264-6 • 8 x 9 1/2 • 192 pages • colour photos • hardcover • $36.95

Ranchland: British Columbia's Cattle Country
Diana French and Rick Blacklaws
This exhilarating journey through British Columbia's historic cattle country takes the reader from the high Chilcotin meadows to the rich irrigated fields of the southern Okanagan, from cattle drives to modern marketing, from urban ranches to those tucked away in splendid isolation—all with spectacular full-colour photographs.
1-55017-232-8 • 11 x 8 1/2 • 208 pages • 150+ colour photographs • hardcover • $39.95

West Coast Identification Guides by Harbour Publishing

Wild Flowers of the Pacific Northwest Field Identification Guides
Lewis Clark, Edited by John G. Trelawny
Following the publication of his encyclopedic classic, *Wild Flowers of the Pacific Northwest*, the late Lewis Clark broke his massive masterwork down into six compact and affordable field guides organized by habitat. Collectively, they sold over 200,000 copies.
Thoroughly redesigned and updated, these Wild Flowers guides are essential reading for experienced botanists and afternoon strollers alike.
Wild Flowers of Field & Slope • 1-55017-255-7 • 5 1/2 x 8 1/2 • 80 pages • colour photos • paperback • $12.95

Wild Flowers of Forest & Woodland 1-55017-306-5 • 5 1/2 x 8 1/2 • 80 pages • colour photos • paperback • $12.95
Wild Flowers of the Mountains 1-55017-308-1 • 5 1/2 x 8 1/2 • 80 pages • colour photos • paperback • $12.95
Wild Flowers of the Sea Coast 1-55017-307-3 • 5 1/2 x 8 1/2 • 100 pages • colour photos • paperback • $12.95
Wild Flowers of the Pacific Northwest 1-55017-195-X • 8 1/2 x 11 • 604 pages • 550 colour photographs • hard-cover • $59.95

Wild Flowers of the Yukon, Alaska and Northwestern Canada
John G. Trelawny
John Trelawny's passion for northern landscapes is reflected in this guide. Hundreds of photographs are paired with informative descriptions that will assist both amateur naturalists and discriminating botanists.
1-55017-257-3 • 5 1/2 x 8 1/2 • 214 pages • 400 colour photos • paperback • $24.95

The Beachcomber's Guide to Seashore Life in the Pacific Northwest
J. Duane Sept
274 of the most common animals and plants found along the saltwater shores of the Pacific Northwest are described in this book. Illustrating each entry is a colour photo of the species in its natural habitat.
1-55017-204-2 • 5 1/2 x 8 1/2 • 240 pages • 500 colour photos • paperback • $24.95

Shells and Shellfish of the Pacific Northwest
Rick M. Harbo
This easy-to-follow, full-colour guide introduces more than 250 species of mollusks found along the beaches and shallow waters of the Pacific Northwest.
1-55017-146-1 • 5 1/2 x 8 1/2 • 272 pages • 350 colour photos • paperback • $25.95

Where to See Wildlife on Vancouver Island
Kim Goldberg
Packed with information and user-friendly, this guide introduces the 50 best wildlife viewing hot spots on Vancouver Island, from the busy Victoria waterfront to Nanaimo's Buttertubs Marsh to "Gator Gardens" in Alert Bay.
1-55017-160-7 • 5 1/2 x 8 1/2 • 174 pages • 100 colour photos • paperback • $20.95

Whales of the West Coast
David A.E. Spalding
Huge, powerful, intelligent and beautiful, whales have fascinated human beings for millennia. From the better-known orcas, greys and humpbacks to porpoises, blue whales and sperm whales.
1-55017-199-2 • 6 x 9 • 256 pages • 100 photos • paperback • $21.95

Books about British Columbia

Snowshoes and Spotted Dick
Chris Czajkowski
Chris Czajkowski chose to build her life and small ecotourism business on the shore of a high-altitude lake near the southern tip of Tweedsmuir Provincial Park. In these fascinating letters, Czajkowski details her often-solitary life in the wilderness and her challenges and triumphs as she tries to finish her cabin.
1-55017-279-4 • 6 1/2 x 8 • 304 pages • b&w photos and illustrations • paperback • $24.95

The Last Island: A Naturalist's Sojourn on Triangle Island
Alison Watt
Twenty-three year old Alison Watt spent an unforgettable summer studying puffin populations on a remote island north of Vancouver Island. Her award-winning memoir is filled with adventures and revelations and illustrated with delightful watercolour paintings. *The Last Island* is a beautifully written testament to the environment, friendship, and the endurance of the human spirit.
1-55017-296-4 • 6 1/2 x 9 1/2 • 192 pages • 40 colour illustrations • hardcover • $34.95